Unpacking Policy

Knowledge, Actors and Spaces in Poverty Reduction in Uganda and Nigeria

Editors

Karen Brock
Rosemary McGee
John Gaventa

Fountain Publishers

Fountain Publishers Ltd
P.O. Box 488
Kampala
E-mail: fountain@starcom.co.ug
Website: www.fountainpublishers.co.ug

ISBN 9970 02 428 0

Published by Fountain Publishers Ltd for the Institute of Development
Studies, University of Sussex, Brighton, UK

Contents

iii

Contributors

Oga Steve Abah is Professor of Theatre for Development at Ahmadu Bello University, Zaria, Nigeria, as well as Executive Director of the Theatre for Development Centre.

Karen Brock is a consultant, and was formerly researcher with the Participation Group at the Institute of Development Studies, University of Sussex, UK. With Rosemary McGee, she recently co-edited *Knowing Poverty: Critical reflections on participatory research and policy* (Earthscan, 2002).

John De Coninck is former Director of the Community Development Resources Network, a Ugandan NGO. As well as being a development practitioner, he has had a long career in research, with publications including *Evaluating the Impact of NGOs in rural Poverty Alleviation: The Case of Uganda* (Overseas Development Institute, 1992).

John Gaventa is a political sociologist who currently leads the Participation Group at the Institute of Development Studies, University of Sussex, UK. He is best known for *Power and Powerlessness: Quiesence and Rebellion in an Appalachian Valley* (University of Illinois Press/Clarendon Press, 1980); his more recent publications include *Global Citizen Action: Lessons and Challenges* (co-edited with Michael Edwards; Lynne Reiner/ Earthscan, 2001).

Yahaya Hashim works with the Development Research and Policy Centre in Kano, Nigeria. His previous work includes *Cross-border trade and the parallel currency market: Trade and finance in the context of structural adjustment,* (Scandinavian Institute of African Studies, 1999).

Rosemary McGee, a social development specialist with a background in anthropology, does research with the Participation

v

Group at the University of Sussex, UK. She is currently working with Christian Aid in Bogotá, Colombia.

Jenkeri Z. Okwori is a Senior Lecturer at Ahmadu Bello University, Zaria, Nigeria as well as being an NGO actor, specialising in Theatre for Development methodologies.

Peter Ozo-Eson is an economist, who at the time of this study worked for the Centre for Advanced Social Sciences in Port Harcourt, Nigeria. He currently works with the Nigeria Labour Congress.

F.O.N. Roberts has written widely on the dynamics of resource distribution in the Nigerian Delta and does research at the Nigerian Institute of Social and Economic Research, Ibadan, Nigeria.

Richard Ssewakiryanga currently works for the Uganda Participatory Poverty Assessment Programme in the Ministry of Finance, Planning and Economic Development, Kampala, Uganda. He is also a Research Associate of the Centre for Basic Research and has specialised in gender and development.

Olusade Taiwo is an economist who does research at the Nigerian Institute of Social and Economic Research, Ibadan, Nigeria as well as being Director of the Centre for Enterprise Development and Action Research, a Nigerian NGO.

Judith-Ann Walker works with the Development Resesach and Policy Centre in Kano, Nigeria, and her previous work includes research on civil society in Nigeria.

Acronyms

AD	Alliance for Democracy
BLP	Better Life Programme
BUGADEV	Buganda Cultural and Development Foundation
CAS	Country Assistance Strategy
CBO	Community Based Organisation
CBPRI	Community Based Poverty Reduction Initiative
CDA	Community Development Assistant
CDRN	Community Development Resources Network
CSO	Civil Society Organisation
CWIQ	Core Welfare Indicators Questionnaire
DENIVA	Development Network of Indigenous Voluntary Associations
DFID	Department for International Development
DFRRI	Department of Food, Roads and Rural Infrastructure
DPR	Department for Poverty Reduction
EPRC	Economic Policy Research Centre
ERP	Economic Recovery Programme
ESCOBRA	Ekiti State Community-Based Poverty Reduction Agency
ESRC	Economic and Social Researsch Council
ESRT	Ekiti State Reform Team
EU	European Union
FEAP	Family Economic Advancement Programme
FF	Farmers' Forum
GDP	Gross Domestic Product
HDR	Human Development Report
HIPC	Highly Indebted Poor Country
HTA	Home Town Association
IBRD	International Bank for Reconcstruction and Development
IDC	Ikere Development Council
IFI	International Financial Institution
IMF	International Monetary Fund

i-PRSP	Interim Poverty Reduction Strategy Paper
IYC	Ijaw Youth Council
JSPC	Jigawa State People's Congress
LC	Local Council
LGA	Local Government Area
LGDP	Local Government Decentralisation Programme
LRA	Lord's Resistance Army
MoFPED	Ministry of Finance, Planning and Economic Development
MoLG	Ministry of Local Government
NAPEC	National Poverty Eradication Council
NAPEP	National Poverty Eradication Programme
NAPRI	National Animal Production Institute
NASSI	National Association of Small Scale Industrialists
NCT	National Core Team
NDDC	Niger Delta Development Commission
NDE	National Directorate of Employment
NEPA	National Electric Power Authority
NGO	Non-governmental organisation
NINCOF	Nigerian Non-Governmental Organisation Consultative Forum
NLC	Nigerian Labour Congress
NPC	National Planning Commission
NRDCS	Natural Resources Development and Conservation Scheme
NRM	National Resistance Movement
NUSAF	Northern Uganda Social Action Fund
ODA	Overseas Development Administration
ODI	Overseas Developmet Institute
OMPADEC	Oil and Mineral Producing Areas Development Commission
OPS	Organised Private Sector
PAF	Poverty Action Fund
PAP	Poverty Alleviation Programme
PAPSCA	Programme for the Alleviation of Poverty and Social Costs of Adjustment

PDP	People's Democratic Party
PEAP	Poverty Eradication Action Plan
PIC	Project Implementation Committee
PMA	Plan for the Modernisation of Agriculture
PRA	Participatory Rural Appraisal
PRGF	Poverty Reduction Growth Facility
PRS	Poverty Reduction Strategy
PRSC	Poverty Reduction Support Credit
PRSP	Poverty Reduction Strategy Paper
RC	Resistance Council
RIDS	Rural Infrastructure Development Scheme
SAPRI	Structural Adjustment Participatory Review Initiative
SCC	Sub-county Chief
SDD	Social Development Department
Sida	Swedish International Development Co-operation Agency
SLGRP	State and Local Governance Reform Programme
SOWESS	Social Welfare Services Scheme
SPEC	State Poverty Eradication Council
SWAPs	Sector Wide Approaches
SWD	State Works Department
UBE	Universal Basic Education
UBoS	Ugandan Bureau of Statistics
UDC	Uganda Development Corporation
UDN	Uganda Debt Network
UNDP	United Nations Development Programme
UPDNet	Ugandan Participatory Development Network
UPE	Universal Primary Education
UPPAP	Uganda Participatory Poverty Assessment Programme
USAID	United States Agency for International Development
UWONET	Uganda Women's Organisations Network
WTO	World Trade Organisation
YES	Youth Employment Scheme

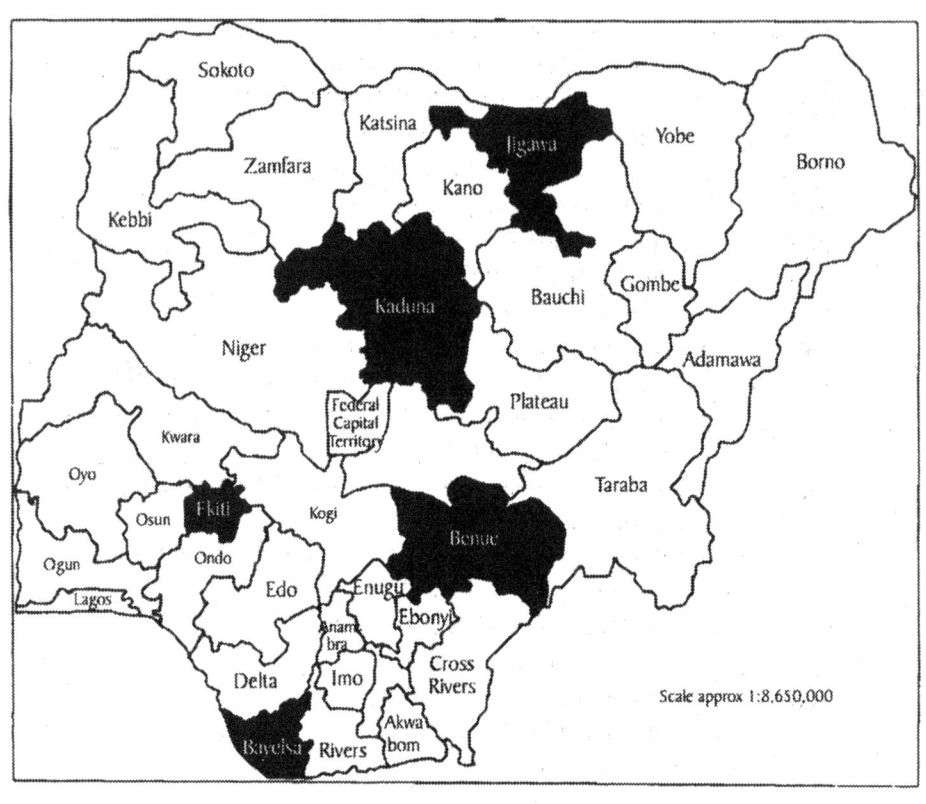

Map of Nigeria showing the Federal States

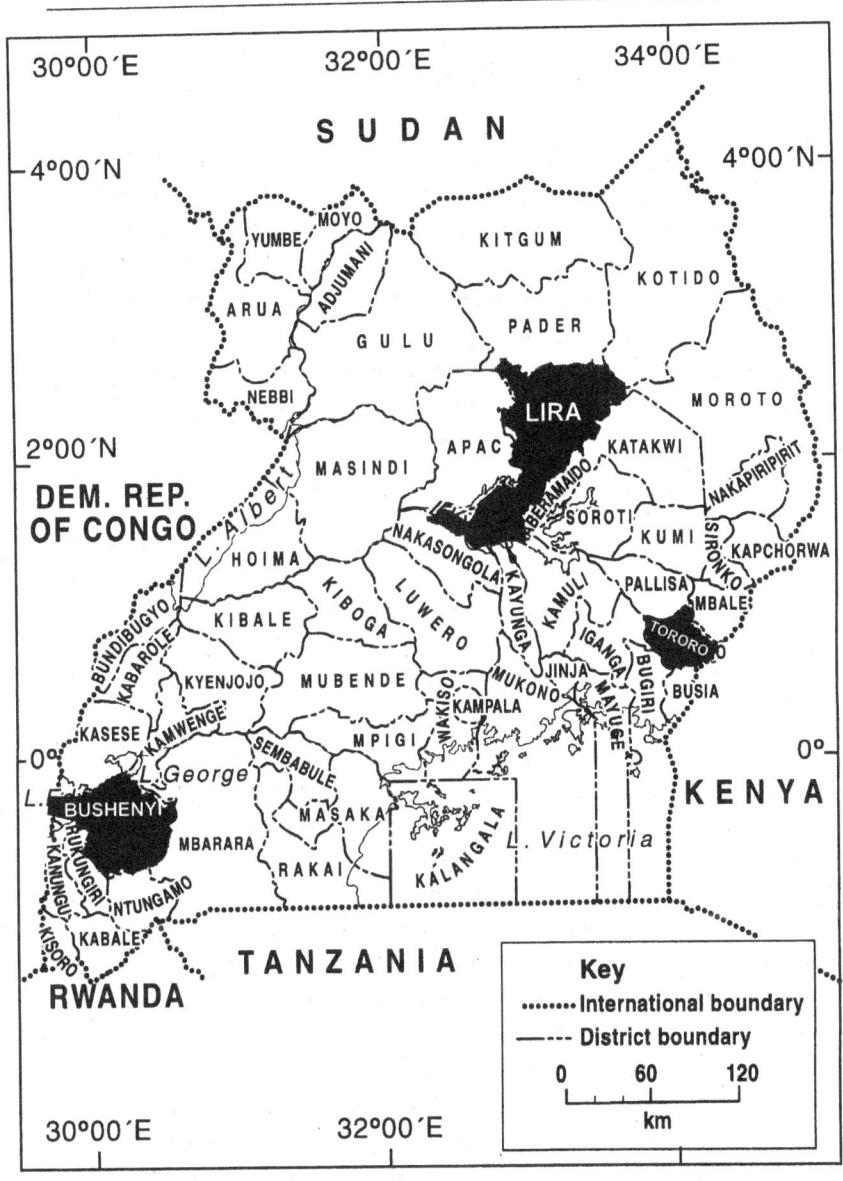

Map of Uganda showing the Districts

Preface

This book presents findings from a research project on 'Poverty Knowledge and Policy Processes', funded by the UK's Department for International Development. The research was carried out by a team of researchers based in the UK, Uganda and Nigeria.

At the time of the study, Karen Brock, Rosemary McGee and John Gaventa were all members of the Participation Group, Institute of Development Studies, University of Sussex UK. They were responsible for overall co-ordination of the research project, and the compilation and editing of this book.

In Uganda, the main partner organisation was the Community Development Resource Network (CDRN) in Kampala. Many CDRN staff took part in the research, principal amongst them John De Coninck, Rosemary Okech and Ssuuna Joseph. Richard Ssewakiryanga, of the Uganda Participatory Poverty Assessment Process, based in the Ministry of Finance, Planning and Economic Development was also part of the research team.

In Nigeria, team members were drawn from five organisations in different parts of the country. Peter Ozo-Eson was based at the Centre for Advanced Social Sciences, Port Harcourt at the time of the research. Yahaya Hashim and Judith-Ann Walker are with the Development Research and Projects Centre, Kano. F.O.N. Roberts and Sade Taiwo are at the Nigerian Institute for Social and Economic Research, Ibadan; and Sade Taiwo also works at the Centre for Development and Action Research, Ibadan. Oga Steve Abah and Jenks Okwori both come from the Theatre for Development Unit, Ahmadu Bello University, Zaria.

The conceptual framework for the research was developed during 2001 (see McGee, Chapter 1, this volume). Literature reviews, published as Brock, Cornwall and Gaventa (2001) and McGee and Brock (2001), informed the development of the framework. Fieldwork was undertaken from mid-2001 to mid-2002. The research aimed to be heavily empirical, remedying what we perceive to be a lack of detailed empirical study of what is actually going on under the name of poverty reduction initiatives and policy processes in Uganda and Nigeria.

Our approach was to take a 'vertical slice' through the policy process, from the interface of national governments with the international development community; to national governments themselves; to decentralised levels of local government; and to communities. Accordingly, fieldwork took place in 5 states of Nigeria (Bayelsa, Benue, Ekiti, Jigawa and Kaduna), focusing on two Local Government Areas within each state; and three districts of Uganda (Bushenyi, Lira and Tororo), focusing on two sub-counties within each district. In addition, fieldwork also took place in Abuja and Kampala.

In Nigeria the states were selected to include as many as possible of the six geo-political zones of the country. In Uganda, a range of selection criteria were used to choose districts, including regional location, livelihood, language and poverty level (for more detail see Brock *et al* 2003). One district, Bushenyi, was purposively selected as a 'better-off' district, and because it had been included in the earlier Uganda Participatory Poverty Assessment Process research.

Principal research methods were semi-structured interviews, focus group discussions and participant observation. The Kaduna and Benue team in Nigeria also used Theatre for Development methods. For the Uganda study, a Reference Group of policy actors was convened, who took an advisory role when they met periodically throughout the research to discuss preliminary findings. Some of the data analysis was carried out collectively in workshops by researchers and their advisors, and some relied on a qualitative data analysis software package.[1]

A range of written findings have been produced, and used in a very wide range of fora to disseminate the messages of the research. These fora – some of them policy spaces in their own right - included civil society workshops in Uganda, one in Kampala and one for CSOs working outside the capital; local-language radio shows, a poster campaign and an action planning workshop in the three Ugandan districts; a workshop for donor agency, academic and government staff in Abuja; a national meeting of the Nigerian Labour Congress;

and dissemination workshops in each of the Nigerian states. Of the latter, one included workshops with prospective election candidates, and used Theatre for Development methods to engage participants over issues of accountability and responsibility.

The structure of the book is as follows. Chapter 1 contextualises and introduces the conceptual and analytical framework used in the research, unpacking and exploring what we take to be the constituent elements of poverty reduction policy processes. Chapter 2 situates our research in the broader context of efforts to reduce poverty in African states, focusing on the disjuncture between external discourses of poverty reduction and domestic politics, with particular reference to Uganda and Nigeria.

Chapters 3 to 7 present findings from Uganda. In Chapter 3 John De Coninck gives a historical perspective on the context in which contemporary poverty reduction initiatives have emerged. Richard Ssewakiryanga picks up in Chapter 4 with an analysis of the drive for poverty reduction and the relationships between the state and the international donor community that underpin this. Another major group of actors, 'civil society', is the subject of Chapter 5, where Karen Brock sets out and challenges several fundamental narratives and assumptions about the role of civil society organisations in poverty reduction policy processes. Poverty knowledge in Uganda comes under scrutiny in Chapter 6, where Rosemary McGee reviews its current status and explores the implications of recent developments in this field for making policy processes more reflective of the poor's priorities. In Chapter 7, Karen Brock looks into policy spaces at the local level, using a micro-level empirical lens to shed light on their nature, dynamics and potential.

We then turn to Nigeria, starting at the Federal level. Karen Brock and John Gaventa examine in Chapter 8 the range of government, civil society and donor actors and how these are grouped around two distinct streams of poverty reduction policy. In Chapter 9 Karen Brock, John Gaventa and Sade Taiwo tell a story of Nigerian civil society and its engagements with the state and policy processes. We then move to State level. In Chapter 10, Peter Ozo-Eson and colleagues present a picture of contested control and complex power relations between key policy actors in oil-rich Bayelsa State. Sade Taiwo and F.O.N. Roberts explore the theme of knowledge and narratives on poverty in Ekiti State in Chapter 11. Moving northwards, in Chapter 12 Yahaya Hashim and Judith-Ann Walker look at the interplay of religion, politics and poverty reduction policies in Jigawa State. In Chapter 13 Steve Abah and Jenkeri Okwori recount people's perceptions of poverty and governance, gathered in Benue and Kaduna States.

Chapter 14 revisits the book's key themes of actors, knowledge and policy spaces in poverty reduction, bringing together some cross-cutting themes and illuminating contrasts from the case material presented in the foregoing chapters.In drawing conclusions and closing our book, it opens up to the broad community of poverty reduction policy actors the next set of challenges to be met in the quest for more inclusive and responsive poverty reduction policy.

We are grateful to the many people who contributed to this book, as well as to the Department for International Development, who funded the research.[2] We would like to express our gratitude first and foremost those who were interviewed in the course of the research, as well as all the members of the research teams. In Nigeria, particular thanks are due to Sade Taiwo who co-ordinated the whole process, as well as to Paul Spray, Kemi Williams, Foluso Okunmadewa and Sam Unom for their contributions. In Uganda, the members of the Reference Group were immensely helpful. In the UK, Andrea Cornwall made important contributions to formulation and early stages of the project. Paul Francis provided comments on the written outputs of the research. Laura Cornish gave administrative and logistical support throughout. We thank you all.

The Editors
IDS
April 2004

1. QSR Nud*ist 4.
2. Grant No. R7613, Committee for Social Science Research.

1

Unpacking Policy: Actors, Knowledge and Spaces

Rosemary McGee [1]

Setting the scene

Debates in the social sciences on political development, governance and globalisation were characterised in the 1990s by a growing body of challenges to conventional 'democracy'. Reformers have increasingly pointed out that representative democratic systems, for all their merits, have many flaws, among them that they tend not to be accountable to the poor (Abrahamsen 2000). To become so, the argument goes, the structures and the policy-making and implementing processes that take place within them need to be enhanced and complemented with consultative, deliberative or participatory aspects. Among the many ramifications of this is the opening-up and democratisation of the key tasks of government, and central among these tasks is the formulation and implementation of policy. It is this formulation and implementation, and the dynamics and patterns that surround it, that we call the policy process.

Meanwhile social science and policy circles have witnessed a growing trend, under the influence of the natural sciences, towards the idea of 'evidence-based policy' (Stone et al 2001). This notion has entered the development field relatively recently (Crewe and Young 2002), with several large scale research funding institutions and development agencies establishing research programmes aimed at bringing social science research nearer to the decision-making process, to strengthen the evidence base of policy formulation. What exactly does 'evidence-based' mean in the case of development policy? Germane as it is to ever more pressing questions about how far research influences development, and notwithstanding detailed analysis of the role of evidence and other factors in the very specific cases of science and environmental policy processes (Keeley and Scoones 1999), far more still needs to be known about the relationship between evidence and policy in the development sphere.

For poor southern countries, these simultaneous tendencies, promoted by the northern donor governments and other agencies on which they substantially depend, present them with a double challenge. On the one hand, their governments and policy processes are supposed to undergo profound overhauls in the interests of deepening democracy. On the other, the bases on which policy decisions rested are to come under scrutiny and be judged in terms of how far they constitute evidence. The twin challenges might be summed up as the democratisation both of knowledge and of involvement in policy processes.

Besides these broad tendencies in social science thought, a series of other trends were emerging in the discourses and practices of development donors and creditors, the implications of which were to be more direct and still more profound for relatively powerless southern countries. Whereas earlier models of development co-operation in the 50s, 60s and 70s were premised on the belief that the state should extend its control over development, the economy and society, subsequent models in the 80s and 90s propagated the opposite belief that the state's role should be minimal and that market forces should be allowed to operate unregulated and unfettered by state control. By 1997, according to the UK Department for International Development's White Paper on development policy, equilibrium between these views was emerging:

> There is now an opportunity to create a new synthesis which builds on the role of the state in facilitating economic growth and benefiting the poor. [...] We have learned that the virtuous state has a key role to play in supporting economic arrangements which encourage human development, stimulate enterprise and saving and create the environment necessary to mobilise domestic resources and attract foreign investment (DFID 1997: 12).

The state, then, was ushered back in; institutions sprang into focus; and since policies are their vehicles for change, policy reform became a vital means of influencing the orientation and performance of governments and the institutions that constitute them. A further publication of 1997, the World Bank's *World Development Report* (World Bank 1997), set out the likely direction of these influencing and reform processes: in the words of one commentator, the WDR addressed 'with absolute clarity the way in which the state should structure the relationship between macroeconomic discipline on the one hand, and decentralisation and participation on the other' (Cammack 2003: 8).

Further recent insights into the levers of pro-poor development are captured in the same 1997 White Paper. DFID commits the UK Government to 'work[ing] closely with other donors and development agencies to build partnerships with developing countries to strengthen the commitment to the elimination of poverty, and us[ing] our influence to help mobilise the political will to achieve the international development targets' (DFID 1997: 22). In doing so, it explicitly recognises that poor countries' decision-making processes relating to poverty reduction are dependent on political will; and implies that political will can be transformed into hard commitment through the channels of policy formulation and implementation, all in a way that is amenable to the influences of external actors such as donor and creditor agencies.

DFID's new focus on partnership and institutional and policy reform as a way of reducing poverty is a reflection of a wider shift in international development thinking towards a focus on developing consistent and effective policy frameworks at the macro and sectoral level, as a prerequisite for sustainable poverty reduction (Norton & Bird 1998: 1). This shift assumed new proportions in late 1999 with the launching of the Poverty Reduction Strategy Framework by the World Bank, International Monetary Fund and northern creditor governments. Behind it lies a rationale that draws on lessons learnt in the structural adjustment era of the 1980s and early 90s:

As [donor agencies' and IFIs'] poverty reduction goals have become more serious, they have come to recognise that external conditionality is not a very effective tool for persuading governments to adopt policies of which they are unconvinced.

The challenge now is to stimulate domestic policy-making towards the emergence of locally-generated strategies. What is at issue is not just the type or quality of policy that a government is willing to 'sign up' to but also the quality of its domestic political and bureaucratic processes. The underlying presumption is that an open and accountable process in which the poor have a voice and on which some sustainable coalition has been built, stands more chance of being sustainable than 'stroke of the pen' external conditions ..." (Healey et al 2000: 2).

The rationale of local ownership of poverty reduction initiatives and policy reforms has given rise to sweeping changes in language, nomenclature, and to some extent procedures (Groves and Hinton, 2003). What is less clear is whether powerful actors in the development field have absorbed the more profound implications of advocating and enabling local ownership, even when these contravene ideas and methods of the development 'partnership' held dear by donor and creditor agencies. In any case, within the broader logic of restoring the state and revising its developmental role, nationalisation and democratisation of poverty reduction initiatives in particular have brought national policy processes into still sharper focus for donor and creditor agencies that wield influence and give support.

Less subject to current trends and less doctrinal in nature, but nonetheless far-reaching, was a third tendency in development thinking: an increasing view of poor people as active participants in their own development – termed 'the actor perspective' (Long 1992; Arce & Long 2000). As Long (1992: 23-28) discusses, re-casting as actors the people long viewed as the beneficiaries of development illuminates the many emancipatory and empowering dimensions of human agency, both in conceptual terms and in its practical application. His discussion also highlights, however, ways in which the actor perspective has been deployed in the development process to justify a form of participation promoted by donor and creditor agencies in which the poor are enrolled, as protagonists, into projects, programmes and, in these days of deepening democracy, now policy processes, to share the workload and costs of these – rather than to exercise their rights as residents of the project area, members of interest or identity groups, or citizens of the state formulating the policy. In this manifestation, the actor-oriented perspective is clearly divested of much or all of its emancipatory and empowering potential; in fact it is likely to have quite the opposite effect.

Several assumptions underlie these shifts in focus by donors and creditors. In respect of the new interest in southern countries' poverty reduction policy processes, it is assumed, firstly, that the state is able and willing to make policy in a rational way, compatible with the rationale and objectives of donor 'pro-poor policy' thinking. Secondly, and reflecting the reservations that donors retain about this first assumption even while espousing it, it is assumed that non-state actors are able and willing to engage with the state in poverty reduction policy and, particularly, to act as checks and balances on state power and performance. A third assumption, deriving from the second, is that the southern country's polity is basically democratic and that there is a predisposition to enhance the structures and processes of representative democracy with initiatives in which citizens, including poor people, can play a role and express their opinions and wants in a more direct manner.

A further set of assumptions underpins the adoption of the quest for 'evidence-based policy' in the development sphere. At the most obvious level, to assume that evidence-based policy will be more effective at reducing poverty is also to assume that basing policy on 'evidence' is within the realms of possibility – an assumption that begs questions, given the realities of political dynamics and administrative and research capacity in most poor countries and, indeed, in many wealthy ones (Brock et al 2001, citing Lindblom 1959 and Weiss 1986). Moreover, to pursue evidence-based policy presupposes a consensus on what constitutes 'evidence': on what the criteria are for distinguishing what is valid, credible, useful evidence for policy purposes and what is not. It also risks obscuring important questions about the demand and supply of the knowledge on which policy is based: donors, the principal suppliers (directly or indirectly), tend also to be the only actors capable of exercising real, informed demand, so their current interests tend to dominate the field at any given time. At the level of interpretation, there has been a tendency by donors to conflate the quest for *evidence-based* poverty reduction policy with the production of *more* information about poverty and, in consequence, to generate a proliferation of poverty studies and profiles. Finally, pursuing evidence-based policy while at the same time espousing an actor perspective on the poor, has led donors to endorse and actively facilitate the entry of more actors, including poor people and organisations claiming to represent them, into the production of knowledge about poverty.

At the point where the actor perspective and the search for a more evidence-based model of policy meet, existing understandings of what constitutes evidence are challenged. One illustration of this concerns how to treat poor people's testimony: is it a valid basis on which to formulate and implement poverty reduction policy, or not? If not, what needs to be done to give more grounding and legitimacy to knowledge about poverty emanating from other, less first-hand, sources? And if so, what needs to be done with poor people's testimony to make it usable in framing policies?

The policy process: what is it?

The backdrop to the research on which this book is based, then, is the convergence of multiple strands of thinking and action which frame the policy process itself. Such convergence, however, cannot be taken as proof of a consensus about what the policy process is. On the contrary: inherent in the very projects of reforming and enhancing democratic governance, and of exploring more evidence-based forms of policy, is the need to explore and analyse – to 'unpack' policy itself and scrutinise its nature, components and dynamics.

So what is policy? The conceptual phase of the research on which this book is based included a review of recent literature on policy processes. In posing this question, we took as our starting point the 'linear model' of policy, dating from the 1950s. A simplified version of this is presented below (see also Grindle and Thomas 1990; Keeley and Scoones 1999; Sutton 1999; Hill 1993).

Formulation	**Implementation**
• A problem is identified by expert policy-makers. • Information is gathered about the problem by expert researchers. • A decision is taken about the solution.	• By 'implementers' who are usually seen as bureaucrats and technocrats.

According to this model, policy is a smooth, linear, top-down, essentially rational process, with two clearly distinct phases, formulation and implementation. In the first phase – formulation – expert policy-makers initiate the process by identifying a problem, on which expert researchers then gather and apply knowledge that is statistically representative, generalised, technical and quantified. The pivotal point between this and the next phase – implementation – is the all-important moment of the decision: problem identification and information-gathering all lead to and prepare for this moment. It is then that responsibility is handed over from the expert policy-makers and researchers to implementers whose task is to put the decision into effect.

The linear model may be old, but it remains popular (Turner and Hulme 1997), despite having been 'under attack for thirty [sic] years' (Crewe and Young 2000: 2). Although patently far removed from real life, it is surprisingly alive and well in policy, development and political circles, and even in many policy actors' own accounts of what kind of process they themselves are involved in. Our fieldwork confirmed this many times over, among many different kinds of actor and at every layer of the policy process. The great majority of people we interviewed, when asked, 'What is policy?' gave some version of this linear model. However, when they were asked about the processes that put policies into effect, their descriptions plainly contradicted the linear model. This suggests that the model lives on as a necessary fiction, held onto either consciously or subconsciously as a default option, or because few perceive any need to construct alternatives. One reason is that it assigns to policy actors simple, tangible, definable roles, relatively easily understood and narrated, whereas a model based more closely on real life would be characterised by indistinct roles, blurred boundaries and a high degree of insecurity among most policy actors about the part they play.

Constructing replacement models, however, could clarify how the new emphasis on involving poor people themselves in poverty reduction policy processes – and their benefits – could work in practice. What was required, in our view, was an alternative understanding of the policy process that threw into relief both the potential roles that could be played by poor people and those defending their interests, and the dynamics and relationships that would need to be negotiated to achieve that end.

Our conceptual framework for understanding policy reflected our *ex ante* rejection of the linear model, the 'necessary fiction'. In the first place, we put more emphasis on the range of levels spanned by 'policy', envisaging it as stretching from the uppermost levels of governance to the lowest. This takes it from the interface between national government actors and international agencies (for instance, the interface at which Ministry of Finance officials deal with the International Monetary Fund and World Bank); through national level (ministries, organisations with national reach), down through all the levels of local governance to the most local level of the village or community. We refer to this approach as taking a 'vertical slice' through the policy process. Secondly, we developed a conceptual framework that takes policy to be a dynamic process, key elements of which are actors – the people involved in framing and implementing the policy – and what we call the 'policy spaces' in which they interact, with all constituent elements in continuous dynamic flux.

We used this both as a descriptive framework, to organise our collection of data; and at the same time as an analytical framework, to analyse patterns emerging from the data. It is represented visually below.

The following sections explain what we mean by each of these terms, why we consider each useful for understanding the policy process, what meanings and usages are associated with it, and how we set out to use it in our research and in this book.

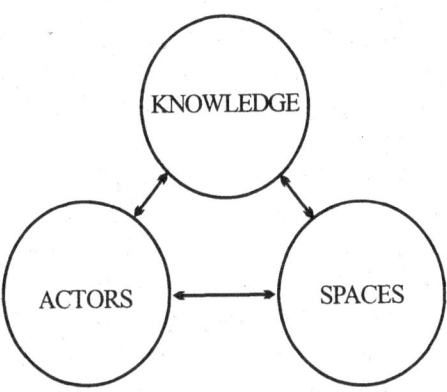

Actors

We count as actors all those located up and down the vertical slice, in government or outside of it, who have some role in policy processes. Thus the term includes local government officers (both elected representatives and technical staff, Lipsky's 'street level bureaucrats' (Lipsky 1980)); central government officials; a wide range of civil society organisations (non-governmental organisations, community based organisations, trade unions, pressure groups, academics, researchers and technical 'experts'); representatives of donor and creditor agencies both bilateral and multilateral, and others. More actors are coming into the policy process all the time, as part of the tendencies described above and in response to the donor agencies' presumptions about the superior prospects of success and sustainability in policy reform processes which involve poor people and the articulation of their interests.

Actors hold opinions and interests; they are embedded in institutional and political cultures; they exercise agency. [2] Each is a power-holder. The dynamism of the policy process inheres in each person's effective actions. Each belongs to one or more networks which cut across different spaces in the policy process. The labels we use (donors, CSOs, etc.) are themselves shorthand, disguising diverse interests and complex power dynamics. In particular, despite the convenience of collective labels such as 'civil society', these collectivities cannot in fact exercise agency as one unit, and should thus be recognised not as one collective actor but as many and diverse actors. (Long 1992: 23).

Several characteristics of actors contribute to the definition of their agency and their power. One is how long they have been engaged with policy processes – with the late 1990s acquiring special importance because it is since then that there has been a tendency to open the process up to more and diverse policy actors. Long-held conventional perceptions of the validity and credibility of actors and their contributions (probably set and perpetuated by longer-standing actors) are a significant factor, as are expectations of their behaviour and contributions. A further defining characteristic is the networks to which actors belong, and the constant and mutually-reinforcing dynamic between these networks and the narratives and discourses of poverty they promote and perpetuate, for:

> [...] agency (and power) depend crucially upon the emergence of a network of actors who become partially, though hardly ever completely, enrolled in the 'project' of some other person or persons. Effective agency then requires the strategic generation/ manipulation of a network of social relations and the channeling of specific items (such as claims, orders, goods, instruments and information) through certain 'nodal points' of interaction (Long 1992: 23).

Among the newer categories of actors in poverty reduction policy discourse are poor people, although in the policy process this is mainly through organisations that claim to represent them. The poor, suddenly moving to centre stage in development discourse, have all too often been cast not as full citizens of development processes or of their states, but as beneficiaries or consumers (Cornwall 2000). The risk inherent in the recent novelties in poverty reduction policy is that the poor will be brought into these policy processes not as citizens or political actors with rights to uphold and interests to defend, but as technical actors who can provide useful information. Even when they are cast as such, their actor status will be further compromised because the information they contribute will be subject to parameters of validity, credibility and policy-relevance set and upheld by other, longer-standing, better networked and more expert actors. But this takes us into the terrain of the second of our three key components of policy processes: knowledge.

Knowledge

For the purposes of our research, and in this book, we take a broad definition of knowledge, ranging from official knowledge constructed from national survey-based statistics, through poverty narratives woven and promoted by various actors, to popular knowledge based on people's own experience. The term 'poverty knowledge'[3] implies knowledge or information about poverty. However, poverty is so multidimensional, and the ways of addressing it so far-ranging, that knowledge about a myriad other things besides the income and consumption levels by which it is usually judged, is also relevant to poverty reduction policy. These dimensions bring into focus the importance of people's knowledge and experiences of citizenship, political and policy processes, and of the state and opportunities to engage with it. Thus, rather than 'poverty knowledge' we prefer to use the term 'knowledge in the poverty policy process'.

There are different ways of knowing, and hence different kinds of knowledge. One typology distinguishes between experiential, presentational, propositional and practical levels of knowledge (Heron 1996). The experiential tends to elude definition, because it is 'known' somewhere other than at the propositional level of language and theory (Hunt 2003: 3). The lived experience of poverty is very disconnected from the poverty policy process partly because those who make policy decisions tend not to have experienced poverty (McGee 2002a: 18). Experiental knowledge is somehow seen as less legitimate and does not lend itself as easily as the other types to being incorporated into policy processes. Writing about 'poverty knowledge' in the US, O'Connor (2001) echoes both this distinction and, implicitly, our differentiation of 'poverty knowledge' from knowledge in the poverty policy process:

> [...] contemporary poverty knowledge does not define itself as an inquiry into the political economy and culture of late twentieth-century capitalism; it is knowledge about the characteristics and behaviour and [...] welfare status of the poor. Nor does it countenance knowledge honed in direct action or everyday experience, whether generated from activism, programme implementation or, especially, from the living poor. Historically devalued as 'impressionistic', 'feminised' or 'ideological', this kind of knowledge simply does not translate into the measurable variables that are the common currency of 'objective', 'scientific' and hence authoritative poverty research (4).

Related to this technical, objective image, poverty knowledge thus defined '[...] rests on an ethos of political and ideological neutrality that has sustained it through a period of vast political change' (ibid: 4).

To return to the wider 'knowledge in the poverty policy process', we distinguish between two broad kinds. The first is knowledge that is specially *produced* by certain actors for certain kinds of users, for example household survey data to inform fiscal or health policy, and World Bank inter-country comparative data. These kinds of knowledge, which we call 'industrially produced knowledge' are O'Connor's 'knowledge about characteristics, behaviour and welfare status of the poor'. Most traditional poverty policy actors consider them to have the values of neutrality, impartiality, precision and general applicability for policy processes, but in fact they carry considerable quantities of ideological baggage (McGee and Brock 2001).

The second kind of knowledge is knowledge that is *constructed*, by a range of actors, through processes very different from the production of the first kind of data, and to different ends. Constructed knowledge is not always evident, visible or explicit. One example of constructed knowledge is experiential knowledge of poverty – O'Connor's 'knowledge honed in direct action or everyday experience' (op cit: 4) – which has tended to be largely invisible to policy processes. In principle, another example is participatory poverty research, where knowledge is co-constructed by poor people and outsider researchers for the purpose of programme design or policy. However, this approach has increasingly been applied in the form of national-level Participatory Poverty Assessments (PPAs) conducted under the auspices of the World Bank, international donors and national governments (see Brock 2002; Norton et al 2001). It has moved along the spectrum towards 'produced' knowledge and has increasingly been tested against similar values and criteria to household surveys.

Also constructed, but far from invisible, are discourses and narratives of development and poverty. Although not a focus in our work, these merit a mention as they are important forms of knowledge in the policy process. What *is* often invisible about them is the fact that they are constructed rather than being natural, given or self-evident.

Sutton defines development discourses as 'describ[ing] a way of thinking and looking, a system of values and priorities that marginalises other possible ways of thinking. A discourse is a configuration of ideas which provides the threads from which ideologies are woven' (1999: 6). Discourses are constructed and perpetuated through the selective use of knowledge, and also foster the production and construction of particular sorts of knowledge, in a logic of self-perpetuation and self-reinforcement.

Narratives are distinct from discourses: they are stories, 'having a beginning, a middle and an end, outlining a specific source of events which has gained the status of conventional wisdom within the development arena' (ibid: 7, citing Roe 1991). While discourses refer to a relatively wider set of values and ways of thinking, 'a narrative can be part of a discourse if it describes a specific "story" which is in line with the broader set of values and priorities of a discourse' (ibid: 7). Even when the validity of narratives is cast into doubt by evidence to the contrary, they persist because they offer convenient ways of simplifying complex processes and set out straightforward options for policy-makers (Roe 1991; Leach and Mearns 1996).

The importance of narratives and discourses in development, Abrahamsen reminds us, is that 'objects and subjects are constituted as such within discourse, [so] an understanding of the relevant discourses is a necessary part of any attempt to change prevailing conditions and relations of power' (2000: 14). More narrowly, in the process of constructing knowledge in the poverty policy process, narratives, discourses and interpretations of them matter because they help to establish what and whose participation in this process is legitimate, and to specify the boundaries for action in any policy space.

The degree to which one accepts the notion of 'construction' of knowledge depends on one's epistemological standpoint. A positivist paradigm, in which knowledge is held to be objective, absolute and based on a single truth, would eschew the idea, but in more postmodern and inductive paradigms which hold that there are many and diverse kinds of knowledge, construction and co-construction of knowledge by social actors is axiomatic. When actors come into contact, their interaction produces what Long refers to as a knowledge encounter: 'the struggle between actors who aim to enroll others in their "projects", getting them to accept particular frames of meaning, winning them over to their points of view. If they succeed then other parties "delegate" power to them' (1992: 27). The terrain of knowledge, then, must be seen as a battlefield, and knowledge in the policy process as an instrument of power, a political tool.

A crucial determinant of the outcomes of knowledge encounters is the degree of legitimacy attached to, or bestowed upon, different kinds of knowledge. Legitimacy is often ostensibly defined by technical criteria: what kind of knowledge can be generalised up to national scale? What kind can be validated, and its confidence intervals established, by conventional statistical means? Yet as well as the technical criteria for legitimacy, and often disguised under these, are political criteria: whose voice counts or has influence? The use of which poverty measure will provoke the least political backlash? Which explanation for regional poverty disparities is the most expedient? (McGee and Brock 2001; Brock et al 2002)

In the poverty policy process, legitimacy is won more easily by groups of actors presenting a unified discourse of poverty and poverty reduction, with actors 'talking the talk', reading the parts assigned to them in scripts written by government and international donor agencies, and aligning themselves comfortably with the dominant discourse, than by disparate voices presenting individual or group perspectives on their experience of poverty and its causes. It follows that through problematising and altering the framing, legitimacy and acceptability of knowledge in the poverty policy process, power dynamics in the process can be shifted and the process itself rendered more democratic. This approach to democratising the process stands in contrast to that which donor agencies have tended to adopt: the generation of more and more poverty studies, on occasion drawing in ever more multiple and diverse actors.

Actors, then, bring into a policy process their agendas and interests. They speak their narratives, rehearse their agendas, engage in discursive practices, and advocate for their own or other actors' interests. It is this process of application that alters the meanings of their agendas, interests and narratives, rendering them 'knowledge' in the policy process. In some cases, a range of agendas and interests might intertwine and interact to produce a single, coherent, convincing strand of knowledge. Conversely, they may amount to a confused mix of ideas and initiatives that appear, at least from below, to be largely disconnected from the realities of the poor. In this case, the resulting poverty discourse appears fragmented, because it is situated outside the realm of experiential knowledge, disconnected from the real experience of poverty. Given that the policy process involves complex interactions, knowledge encounters may occur at several different levels and moments of the process, with different outcomes. We turn now to look more closely at these levels and moments: the third element that, along with actors and knowledge, makes up the policy process.

Spaces

The concept of space provides a useful lens through which to view the everyday politics and practice of actors who are engaged in the policy process, and to examine how their power to act is enabled and constrained. It makes it possible to break down the policy process into observable, influenceable elements. It also raises questions about which actors gain access to which spaces, what they do there, what constrains or facilitates their actions, and what potential arises as a result of these.

The concept of 'space' and an assortment of spatial metaphors are now used widely in the literatures on political reform (Webster & Engberg 2002), policy change (Brock & McGee 2002), and citizen participation (Jones 2002), with usages that are distinct but overlapping within and between these various political and policy science literatures. It is perhaps easiest to understand how we use the term 'policy space' by laying out related usages of the same and similar terms and defining ours by reference to them.

'Political space' is the central analytical tool used by Webster & Engberg-Pedersen (2002) for exploring the role of the poor in poverty reduction. They define it as 'the types and range of possibilities present for pursuing poverty reduction by the poor or on behalf of the poor by local organisations' (ibid: 8), constituted by institutional channels through which policy processes can be accessed or controlled by the poor, political discourses focusing on poverty and poverty reduction, and social and political practices of the poor which serve to influence decision-making and policy or programme agendas (ibid: 8). The principal difference between their 'political space' and our policy spaces is that theirs denotes the existence of a single possibility within a given political and social context, whereas our spaces are multiple points in time or space in a policy process and, as well as sometimes signifying transformative potential, are actual observable opportunities, behaviours, actions and interactions.

The 'room for manoeuvre' of policy-makers, introduced by Clay and Schaffer in 1984 (see also Sutton 1999: 8 and Webster & Engberg-Pedersen 2002: 19), while drawn on both by Webster and Engberg-Pedersen (2002) and by ourselves in this research, is a more static and limited concept than either 'political space' or our usage of 'policy spaces'. It falls short of these in confining the analysis to the level of the individual policy-maker at a given point in time, and effectively excluding social and political forces and temporal dimensions that shape the institutions and practices within which he or she operates.

Recent literature that focuses specifically on the topic of spaces and places for citizen participation in development and in policy processes (Cornwall 2002a, 2002b; Jones 2001, 2002) includes detailed analysis of the genesis, use and implications of different kinds of space, what turns a space into a place, and spatial practices and dynamics. Our usage of 'policy spaces' is consistent with space as defined in this body of work, but by approaching the concept from the vantage-point of seeking to understand the policy process, rather than seeking to assess participation discourses and practices, we introduce a different emphasis. In this respect our usage is more in line with Cornwall's earlier discussion, in which spaces are 'sites in which different poverty discourses and policy actors interact, [...] permeated with power relations and bounded by forms of discourse used within and about them, raising questions about who participates, with which views of poverty, and to what effect' (Brock et al 2001: 7).

In a conceptual discussion of spaces for participation, Cornwall (2002b) conveys the pre-programmed nature of spaces: 'Etched into every space are the traces of its production, its "generative past" [...]; no newly created space can be entirely cleared of these assumptions and meanings' (p 7). The significance of these 'generative pasts' for policy spaces, in the sense in which we use the term, is driven home by Shore and Wright in their 'Anthropology of Policy':

> In one sense, the language of policy-making seems to endorse realism by presenting 'problems' as if they could be solved by filling knowledge gaps with new, objective data. But these gaps are not voids. They are crowded spaces already filled with moral values and preconceptions. They require prescriptive language which says what is *needed*, rather than desriptive accounts 'telling it as it *is*' (1997: 21).

The best-known use of the term 'policy spaces' is found in the influential work of Grindle and Thomas (1991), and it was their definition that we took as our starting-point. Policy spaces for them are '[...] moments in which interventions or events throw up new opportunities, reconfiguring relationships between actors or bringing in new ones, and opening up the possibilities of a shift in direction' (Brock et al 2001: 22, citing Grindle and Thomas 1991). We would reiterate the qualification made by McGee (2002b: 189, footnote 1) that 'moments' should not be taken to imply that policy spaces are in every case transient and fleeting, or necessarily temporal in nature; in our usage a policy space can be a sustained period of time, or an established social or behavioural institution or norm. A second qualification we would add is that the site where these things happen, as well as the happenings themselves, is part of what constitutes the policy space, although policy spaces are not exclusively, nor even mostly, physical spaces. What we share with Grindle and Thomas's definition is the sense that each policy process, and each governance system, is not itself one space but throws up many spaces. Both a policy process – let us say, for example, the formulation of a Poverty Reduction Strategy Paper – and the spaces that make it up are interesting units of analysis, but it is important not to lose sight of the fact that the policy process can be seen as a series of spaces, each with its own characteristics. Hence while one whole policy process might be referred to as an opportunity or an arena, we do not refer to it as a space, but view it as harbouring many different moments, opportunities, sites and events – spaces – all of which are inter-related parts of the process.

In assessing the potential for transformation of policy spaces, and indeed of each engagement by each actor in each space, the assumptions and meanings that shape each space are clearly decisive. This raises the broader question of what distinguishes one space from another, in terms of the scope for influencing policy and its import for poor people.

Through the course of our research a set of labels has emerged to distinguish particular kinds of space. We started off using loosely the terms *closed, invited* and *autonomous* or *autonomously created* space.

Closed spaces are where no participation is encouraged and powerful actors, belonging to the official, governmental sphere, operate on their own: the institutions of representative democracy, in the strictest and narrowest definition, are full of these. *Invited* spaces arise from our observation that endeavours to enhance these representative institutions with tentative experiments of more direct democracy opened up spaces for participation, into which the state *invited* other, non-state, participants. *Autonomous* spaces exist outside the ambit of official policy processes, and are spaces where a range of activities is established independently of the state, working in parallel, or sometimes in direct reaction to, official invited spaces.

The limitations of the 'invited' and 'autonomous' labels soon became clear. 'Invitations' can be issued by non-state actors into their spaces as well as by state actors into official spaces. One actor's 'autonomous' is another actor's 'co-opted'. Is any space ever in fact 'autonomous', or are they all just autonomous from one set of actors while being partially or fully controlled by another? (cf Shore and Wright 1997: 21, cited above). Limitations notwithstanding, all these adjectives are used in the text, as and when their use enlightens rather than obscures the kind of space being discussed.

Other possible labels, some of which are widely used elsewhere, we have avoided for reasons of precision: for instance, 'public/ private', because each of these terms is relative and contingent on whose perspective is adopted; and 'democratic space' because this is used rather indiscriminately, to refer to a range of things including the policy spaces that are built into the institutions of representative democracy; and particular behaviours or practices inspired by democratic values. We have also avoided any categorisation which associates particular kinds of space with particular levels of governance – central, district/provincial and local – because our research shows that this is not the most relevant category of analysis and that the full range of kinds and dimensions of spaces may be encountered at all levels.

For as well as there being different kinds of space, each space has a range of different dimensions. Through a process of refinement in the course of the research, and drawing on conceptual work by colleagues at the Institute of Development Studies (Cornwall 2002a; Jones 2002) and our own emerging research findings, we can now distinguish five dimensions that together constitute a policy space and define its potential: history, access, mechanics, dynamics and learning dimensions. Rather than being rigid and contained within tight boundaries, these overlap and co-evolve, in some cases considerably. We would argue that they are crucial factors for consideration by policy actors contemplating engagement or analysts attempting to understand what drives particular episodes or outcomes of policy processes.

The *history* of a space is how long it has existed, how and by whom it was created, and with impetus from where. Many policy spaces are created as a result of an impulse of some kind from the state at some level. Others are created by non-state actors, in reaction to, or with reference to, state-led processes. Whatever their origin, each space has certain rules of *access*: which actors come into it, what freedom of action they have within it, and what they can achieve there. Within a space, certain *mechanics* are readily observable: what actually happens there, who does what, against what backdrop, in what physical context. Mechanics may be fixed practices being rehearsed yet again by the same actors, new behaviours, or new actors' responses to old practices; they may emphasise deliberation for its own sake[4], or be strongly focused on decision-making. Underpinning the mechanics are the *dynamics* that affect the behaviour which occurs within the space, or changes which result from it. Dynamics encompass relationships, power relations, past histories, and the remembered experiences of participants in and convenors of the space. They both form part of the rules of the space, and are shaped by the rules that are carried within historic and access dimensions.

Finally, spaces offer scope for *learning* to occur. An actor's experience of engagement can – but does not necessarily – generate learning, and thus transform the actor, so that any subsequent engagements in this or other policy spaces will never start from quite the same point. Whether a given space offers a learning dimension or not, and whether the learning leads actors to future engagement or deters them from it, is contingent on all its other dimensions; but the critical condition for learning is that actors not only occupy and use the policy space, but also reflect on what has happened in it, how effective their engagement was, and how future action can best be informed by this. Many of the new spaces for participation that have been opened up in policy processes but have resulted in little sustained change in the nature and direction of those processes, have lacked this learning dimension.

All spaces can host both backstage and frontstage mechanics and dynamics, the key distinction being whether all actors engaging in that space are privy to these (frontstage) or not (backstage); the capacity of any actor(s) to operate backstage depends on their power – hidden or overt – vis-à-vis other actors in that space. In principle, any kind of space can be the site of consultation, formal decision-making or deliberative processes – and possibly of simultaneous combinations of these. For example, broad consultation on policy changes may be going on front stage while decisions on these are being taken backstage by a sub-set of actors.

Mechanics, dynamics and learning dimensions cannot be inferred from the basic characteristics of a space *per se*, but have to be observed and derived from analysis of what is observed, at the instant of the interaction and, in the case of the learning dimension, afterwards. History and access, on the other hand, can be understood without empirical observation. As we see it, replacing the labels of 'invited' and 'autonomous' with the recognition that every space has a history, is characterised by certain rules of access, and presents distinctive and observable mechanics, dynamics and possibly scope for learning, represents an analytical advance with respect to our earlier conceptual work, that has come principally from our fieldwork.

This more complex classificatory schema for spaces is not applied rigorously in the chapters that make up this book, because it has grown out of the very material included in – and indeed, some of that left out of – these chapters. Nor does the book apply it in an exhaustive, systematic and categorical analysis to all the real spaces we have described. We present it here because this research has highlighted the fact that power, of both transformative and conservative sorts, is vested – often hidden – in dimensions of spaces. For less powerful actors in poverty reduction policy processes, greater discernment about the nature, potential and power dynamics of the spaces available to them would enhance their scope to engage in these effectively and tranformatively.

Actors, knowledge and spaces in context

This description of the terms we are using brings us to the question of how the simple Actors-Knowledge-Spaces diagram above was fleshed out and enriched in the course of our research, and of what happens in the blank area surrounding the three constitutive elements. In our fieldwork, we engaged a series of poverty reduction policy actors, along the length of the 'vertical slice', in discussions about what policy is, how they view themselves and their roles in it, where their knowledge comes from, and what spaces they interact in. Their contributions confirmed for us the usefulness of our conceptual framework for understanding policy and investigating the potential for change. They also helped us to elaborate the framework further. Certain themes arose as central and all-pervading. The interplay of actors, knowledge and policy spaces is clearly dynamic and complex, and rather than three independent circles linked by arrows is probably better portrayed as three interlocking circles with the policy process at the intersection:

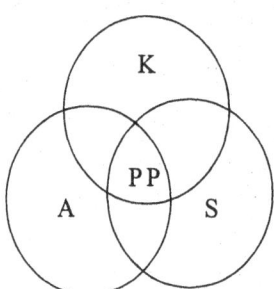

Moreover, their interaction does not take place in a vacuum. It happens in a context shot through with history, culture, political economy, politics and, above all, power relations which shape all aspects of the context, the policy spaces themselves and the way actors and knowledge interrelate in them:

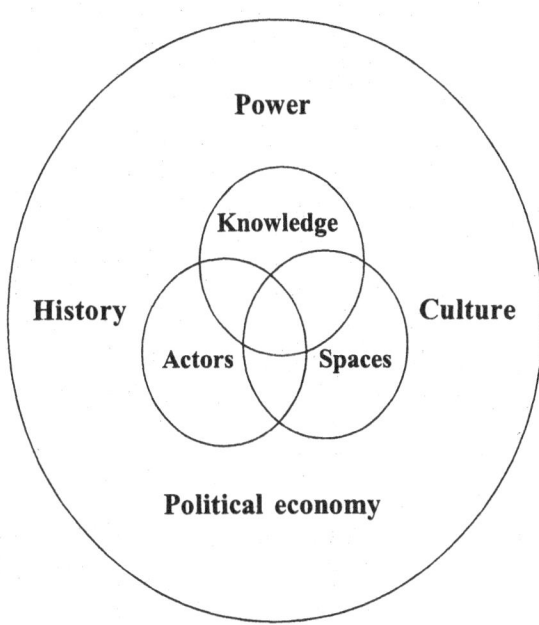

In examining this complex empirically, part of our purpose was to assess the scope for positive change for poor people to arise in this process through the interaction of actors and knowledge, in policy spaces, in the prevailing context of power dynamics, history, culture and political economy. Three cross-cutting themes emerged as key determinants of this scope for change:

1. Representation and accountability
2. Connections and disconnections between the different levels of the policy process up and down the vertical slice
3. The location and use of power.

The chapters that follow contain numerous examples of how weak or non-existent connections, lack of accountability, flawed representation or hidden power reveal how simplistic are notions such as a stable and benign equilibrium between an accountable state on the one hand, and civil society advocates representing the poor, on the other; or the enlightened and smooth transition from policy driven by 'politics' to policy informed by 'evidence'. The themes are picked up again in the concluding chapter. Here we dwell only on power, explaining how we use this slippery concept.

The very nature of spaces, and of action within them, is fundamentally determined by power. Power is 'a network of social boundaries that constrain and enable action for all actors' (Hayward 1998: 2, cited in Gaventa & Cornwall 2001: 72). It is 'not exerted by one individual or group over another, but is part of all social relations, dispersed through the network of normalising discourses and practices which construct boundaries of possibility around thought and action' (Jones 2001: 4). One effect of this dispersal is that 'discourses on poverty circumscribe the boundaries of action for "the poor" and for those who seek to intervene in their lives, by rendering "the poor" amenable to measurement, definition and intervention' (Brock et al 2001: 5-6). Discourses also render the poor less able than other actors to exercise a different kind of agency, not of measured subjects but of informed participants with citizen rights. The boundaries need to be acted on – what Hayward calls 'de-facing power' (1998: 12) – and re-shaped, to re-define what is possible (Gaventa & Cornwall 2001: 72, citing Hayward 1998).

The policy process, as we see it, is made of power dynamics and relationships. Building on the recognition by others that 'politics matters' (Booth 2004; Moore and Putzel 1999), we further assert that policy is, in fact, the enactment of politics. It is a form of politics that derives legitimacy from being portrayed as the technical implementation of a rational solution to a problem. Seeing it thus helps to explain why the necessary fiction of a linear, simple, rational policy process has been built and sustained. It also begs the question of whether policy should, and could, become more rational and evidence-based. When we look through new analytical lenses at the nature of policy, we face the prospect that replacing the current bases of policy with 'evidence' would undermine the very foundations of existing policy processes, and turn them into something else altogether. Of greater relevance than the truism that 'politics matter' could be an explicit acknowledgement that the dynamics of policy processes matter, and that some of their norms could be challenged and overturned through a critical awareness of these dynamics. Whatever the need for evidence-based policy, perhaps what is needed is an evidence-based *understanding* of the policy process, which takes far better account of political and social realities on the ground and, by identifying multiple entry points and pressure points in the policy process, offers ways for a range of actors and their diverse types of knowledge to explode the usual myths of legitimacy and rationalisation, and to counter and contest the usual enactments of politics.

To conclude by summing up the main propositions that informed this research: we adopt and advocate an understanding of the policy process that is radically different from the traditional linear model, one in which actors, knowledge and policy spaces interact in the making and doing of policy. We perceive the poor as actual or potential actors among many others in that process, including intermediary organisations which often purport to represent them. Furthermore we identify the poor as citizens who, as such, enjoy a set of rights and responsibilities in relation to policy processes that they can put into effect by self-organising or by taking up invitations extended by more powerful actors in the interests of 'deepening democracy', to participate in policy processes. If political systems and the policy processes through which they are enacted are to be democratised then, in our view, so should the knowledge base that feeds those policy processes. Democratising the knowledge base means working in an arena characterised by deliberative process rather than by all-determining moments of 'decision'; it means not just producing more poverty knowledge, nor just getting more actors involved, but also incorporating knowledge of more different kinds; it means differentiating more carefully between the respective roles and powers of discourses, narratives, experience and datasets; and reconstituting the prevailing cultures of 'legitimacy' and 'representation'.

Notes

1. This chapter has benefited greatly from the inputs of all the book contributors in synthesis workshops held in Uganda (2001), Nigeria (2002) and the UK (2003), as well as from the specific comments from co-editors Karen Brock and John Gaventa.
2. 'Agency' ... attributes to the individual actor the capacity to process social experience and to devise ways of coping with life, even under the most extreme forms of coercion ... Giddens points out that agency refers not to the intentions people have in doing things, but to their capability of doing those things in the first place. Long, 1989:223.
3. As used by DFID in the title of, and tender for, this research.
4. I use 'deliberation' in the sense in which it is used by Weeks (2000: 360) to define deliberative democracy: as about 'eliciting broad public participation in a process which provides citizens an opportunity to consider the issues, weigh alternatives, and express a judgement about which policy or candidate is preferred.'

2

Contextualising Poverty Reduction Policy: Dynamics of State and Society

Karen Brock

Poverty reduction policy can be viewed as a construct of development discourse. Like all discursive constructs, it can be understood only in the context of the balance of forces which gave rise to it. Chapter 1 has discussed part of this balance of forces by examining current meanings and assumptions about poverty reduction policy in the context of the international aid industry. This chapter examines efforts at making poverty reduction policy work in the broad context of African states, and the states of Uganda and Nigeria in particular. The everyday dynamics of a state and its relationship with society frame, interpret and give meaning to the constructs and ideologies imported from external discourses.

Policy is embedded in politics, firmly located in the realm of the social and the political. Despite this, development policy, which our research found to have an almost theatrical quality, has often been depoliticised, framed as a technical rather than a socio-political venture. Analyses of politics and institutions have become increasingly important in donor and creditor efforts to influence the policy directions taken by African countries; paradoxically, this focus has reinforced depoliticisation, rather than countered it. The institutionally-centred development discourse creates political and institutional characters with prescribed, idealised roles, names them 'state' and 'civil society,' and gives them a script to read from, called variously 'democratic good governance,' 'democratic decentralised governance' and 'pro-poor policy'. These discursive code-words are used to describe the political and social domains of African countries where politics and processes of development are enacted. Like many other such code-words employed in development, they are profoundly dislocated and separated from their historical origins.

This book discusses what happens when external discourses of poverty reduction policy meet domestic politics in Uganda and Nigeria. To extend the metaphor of poverty reduction policy as theatre, this means asking what is going on in the street outside the theatre, and who from the street is allowed in to the theatre, either to sit in the audience or to play out a role on the stage. The streets are the histories and politics of Uganda and Nigeria, located in turn within the broader patterns of social and political change in Africa. The role of this chapter is to situate our work in some of the broader debates about the nature of the state, the dynamics of democratisation, and the role of civil society in Africa.

The literature suggests several important themes which point to multiple dissonances between prescriptive external discourse and the dynamics of social and political change. These dissonances become particularly important in examining how and whether the needs and priorities of poor people can be served by poverty reduction policy.

The African state: a transformative agent for a democratised policy process?

While the prescribed role of the state in development shifted considerably over the last three decades of the twentieth century, it remains central to the act of making and implementing policy. The African state is currently assumed to be capable, or potentially capable, of moving towards pro-poor, evidence-based policy, implemented through the processes and structures of decentralised government (Chapter 1).This assumed capability is intimately linked to a normative model of development which considers a narrowly-defined democratic state to be the best political structure for economic liberalisation (Abrahamsen 2000).

The identity and structure of many African states, Nigeria and Uganda amongst them, have been shaped by lengthy experiences of war, inter-communal violence, repressive authoritarian rule, and a military firmly embedded in national politics. During the 80s and 90s however, there emerged across the continent a wave of new regimes which, to varying degrees, claimed the identity of democracy. The changes which heralded this wave were internally and externally catalysed, part of an interplay of forces which combined the failure of structural adjustment policies with a variety of internal demands for change (Abrahamsen 2000, Ferguson 1998, Petras and Veltmeyer, 2001). The impact of this wave of apparent democratisation on the state itself is in many ways the foundation of current attempts to break open the policy process, to increase the number and range of actors involved in decision-making, and so to move towards accountable policies and governance. It is critical, therefore, in examining the policy process, to understand some of the interpretations and meanings of 'democratisation' which are at play in African politics.

Central to processes of democratisation in Africa are the contextual continuities which shape political outcomes. Such continuities include the formal and informal rules of the political game, and the patterns of relationships between states and citizens. A great deal has been written about the crisis of the failing, neo-patrimonial African state, characterised as bifurcated between rural and urban (Mamdani 1996), existing in the absence of a social contract with society (Hickey 2003) – and existing only for itself and its own beneficiaries, a state without citizens (Ayoade 1998). Processes of democratisation, often heralded by the re-introduction of some form of a multiparty electoral political structure, have resulted in hybridised systems of governance that frequently graft the language and structures of democracy onto the existing foundations of the state. The key features of neo-patrimonialism – the personalisation of political power, the use of public office as a means of individual and communal gain, and the extension of power via patronage networks (Hickey 2003) – continue to shape bureaucracies and legislatures alike, at all levels of government (Hameso 2001), influenced but not transformed by the democratic identities of new regimes.

There is a strong definitional emphasis on elections and voting in contemporary claims to African democratisation. Thus the key single indicator of the existence of democracy is often presented as the holding of multiparty elections (Webster and Engberg-Pedersen 2002), an interpretation which places 'electoral competition [...] at the heart of the effort to globalise democracy' (Abrahamsen 2000:24).

It is also, however, an interpretation which underplays the instrumental meaning of elections in the African context. Chabal and Daloz note that in Africa 'the vote is not primarily a token of individual choice but part of a calculus of patrimonial reciprocity based on ties of solidarity' (1999:39). Such widely-held understandings of the nature and purpose of elections also encompass political parties, which are far more likely to function as machines of patronage than as machines of ideology (Harrison 2002).

The electoral focus also obscures the existence of other indicators of democracy – which include meaningful political competition, especially between parties, broad-based political participation and civil and political liberties, and attention to the claims and entitlements of citizenship – which are far less common features of African democratic systems and processes.[1] The challenge of deepening interpretations of democracy beyond the conduct of elections can be seen as a normative drive behind calls to open the policy process to a wider range of actors and sources and types of information – what we are calling *knowledges*. As McGee notes in the preceding chapter, existing state structures and the systems of social norms in which they are embedded shape the prospects for such a deepening.

Key amongst these factors is the patriarchal nature of the state. If altering the balance of gender relations is held to be an important factor in democratic political culture, continued male domination of the structures of the state may be seen as an enormous blockage to democratisation. The reasons that women may find it hard to actively participate in politics include lack of time, constraining husbands, and social norms about the conduct of women in public arenas (Ahikire *et al* 2002, Tripp 1998). While issues such as these are at the centre of many feminist agendas, they are seldom held up in mainstream political debate as areas that require meaningful interventions if democracy is to be deepened.

Like gender, ethnicity is a structural dimension of political systems which is underplayed by a focus on elections as proof of democratisation. Kasfir (1998) argues that 'public ethnic activity' is pervasive in Africa; the interweaving of ethnicity and politics is both a cause and an effect of neo-patrimonialism. Ethnic identity is a key variable in political outcomes in a wide variety of different situations, and shapes the agency and power of different political actors, as well as the structure of the state itself. Bayart's conceptualisation of a 'rhizome state' (1986), linked to society through a multiplicity of horizontal networks, provides one image of a state where ethnicity is a central concern and motivation of political actors, as well as a central part of their individual and collective identity. Salih (2001) links neo-patrimonial behaviour patterns with ethnicity and democracy when he observes that ethnic and religious groups in Nigeria have interpreted democracy, ethnicity and religion in the light of how much can be gained from each.

While recognition of ethnicity as one of the principle structural dynamics of African politics is reflected in the content of most studies of the African state, donor discourses of democratic governance, with their emphasis on accountability and the public good, are usually silent on the subject. Similarly understated in such discourses are the politics of class. A broadened notion of democratisation would at the very least take into account the conflict inherent in relationships between elites and the marginalised, and give rise to reflections about strategies for the representation of the marginalised beyond the ballot box. Even in those states where political structures have undergone a transition towards democracy, the elite nature of mainstream politics remains fundamentally unchallenged. Abrahamsen argues that this gives rise to 'exclusionary democracies, which allow for political competition but cannot incorporate or respond to the demands of the majority in any meaningful way.' (2000:xiv)

One explanation for this lack of responsiveness is the historical and contemporary position of many African elites, whose income and status is derived not only from their individual political identity, but from their relationship with the international system (Ferguson 1998). As such, political elites both inside and outside government have an interest in pleasing both domestic and external constituencies. Balancing the two in order to maximise individual and communal gain is a course of action which has contributed to a narrow interpretation of democracy.

The balance of variables like class, ethnicity and gender means that the 'wave of democratisation' contains within it a wide range of state forms and political outcomes. The current regimes in Uganda and Nigeria both claim 'democracy' as an important part of their ideological identity, but illustrate very different state forms. In each, a particular discourse of democracy has emerged in response to the historical experience of the post-colonial state. Both have in the past experienced to varying degrees civil war and military rule, bad governance, misuse of resources, self-serving and corrupt rulers, collusion between foreign and regional interests and regional and religious divides. As a result, the capabilities of each state to transform the process by which policy is made are very different, and imply different strategies for external actors.

The different state forms of Uganda and Nigeria give rise to contrasting potentials for transforming policy processes in a broad sense. When considering their potential to transform poverty reduction policy in particular, however, it is not only contrasts in state form and interpretation of democracy which are important. Any discussion of the political dynamics of state and society with reference to poverty reduction must at least briefly examine the context of geography, economy and poverty levels.

Poverty in Uganda and Nigeria: setting the context
Examining the available statistics concerning poverty in Uganda and Nigeria reveals very different profiles and experiences of the phenomenon of poverty. The table on page 34 shows key development indicators for the two countries, which outline some of the fundamental contrasts between the two. Clearly, size is a major difference, not only in terms of area and population, but also of economy and debt.

Despite levels of poverty which are broadly similar, one important contrast lies in the direction of income poverty trends. Household survey data suggest that whilst Uganda experienced an 11 percentage-point decrease in the proportion of the population experiencing income poverty between 1992 and 1998, and a further nine percentage-point decrease from 1998 to 2000, Nigeria experienced a 22% increase during the same period. In addition to rising levels of income poverty, income inequality in Nigeria has increased during the 1990s, illustrated by the rising Gini coefficient. These statistics present an image of one country where poverty is a story of scarce resources, and another where it is a story of the massively unequal distribution of more abundant resources.

Survey data for Nigeria suggest that education and literacy levels are poor and declining,[2] and levels of HIV/AIDS are rising. While the rural poor continue to outnumber the urban poor, urban income poverty is rising more quickly than rural income poverty (UNDP 1998). Lewis (1999) cites several sources of quantitative analysis which agree that, although income poverty decreased slightly in the late 1980s, it increased steadily throughout the 1990s. A national study carried out using participatory methods concurs: summaries of trend analyses carried out by residents of poor communities show the widespread perception that poverty has worsened in the last decade, and that economic strategies formerly thought of as coping mechanisms are now identified as livelihood strategies (Ayoola et al. 1999). Despite having the largest debt in Africa and rising poverty levels, Nigeria is not eligible for debt relief under HIPC, having been dropped from the original list of Highly Indebted Poor Countries on the grounds that it was eligible for non-concessional loans from the International Bank for Reconstruction and Development (IBRD). This was despite the fact that the Government of Nigeria had not taken a loan from IBRD since 1983. Some observers argue that the real reason behind Nigeria's removal from HIPC is that Nigeria's creditors deem it too costly to write off debts (Owusu 2001:18).

Survey data in Uganda suggest that the proportion of people living under the national poverty line decreased between 1992 and 2000; Gini coefficients from the same period suggest a small increase in inequality. Despite these favourable indications of economic growth and poverty reduction, human development indicators – particularly life expectancy and child and maternal mortality rates – remain very low, in part due to the impact of HIV/AIDS, which reached a peak in the mid-1990s when up to 30% of some sub-sections of the population were infected. A major study using participatory methods – the Uganda Participatory Poverty Assessment – suggested in 2000

	NIGERIA	UGANDA
Area[1]	923,770 km²	236,040 km²
Population estimate, 2002[2]	132.8 million	23.4 million
GDP, 2002[3]	US $ 43.5 billion	US $ 5.9 billion
Aid dependence: ODA/GNI, 2001[4]	0.5%	13.7%
Oil dependence: oil production/GDP, 2001[5]	20%	0%
Estimate of current debt, 2001[6]	US $ 32,130 m	US $ 3,107 m
Total debt service 2001 % of ex orts of oods and services	12.4%	7.0%

Income poverty - % of poor in total population according to national poverty line[8]		
		1992/93: 55.7
		1993/94: 51.2
	1985: 46.3%	1994/95: 50.2
	1992: 42.7%	1995/96: 49.1
	1996: 65.6%	1997/98: 44.4
		1999/00: 35.2

Gini coefficient[9]		
		1992/93: 0.364
		1993/94: 0.354
	1986: 0.370	1994/95: 0.365
	1993: 0.450	1995/96: 0.366
	1997: 0.506	1997/98: 0.347
		1999/00: 0.384

Average life expectancy, 2002[10]	45.3	43.1
Adult HIV prevalence at 2001[11]	5.8%	5.0%
Position in World Corruption Perceptions Index (out of 102 countries)[12]	101	93

Notes to table

[1] For Nigeria, World Bank 2003a; for Uganda, World Bank 2003b

[2] ibid.

[3] ibid.

[4] For Nigeria, OECD/DAC 2003a; for Uganda, OECD/DAC 2003b

[5] CIA 2003

[6] For Nigeria, World Bank 2003a; for Uganda, World Bank 2003b

[7] World Bank 2003c

[8] For Nigeria, Federal Office of Statistics 1999; for Uganda, Appleton 2001

[9] For Nigeria, UNU 2000; for Uganda, Appleton 2001

[10] For Nigeria, World Bank 2003a; for Uganda, World Bank 2003b

[11] For Nigeria, UNAIDS 2002a; for Uganda, UNAIDS 2002b

[12] Transparency International 2003

that many ordinary people see poverty increasing rather than declining[3] (MoFPED 2000). Since 2001, a slump in world coffee prices has begun to undermine Uganda's positive record of economic growth, and one outcome of this has been that the country's external debt, despite debt relief under the HIPC initiative, has once again reached unsustainable levels (Greenhill and Blackmore 2002).

As well as the very different profiles of poverty put forward through research and surveys, the two countries have very different public discourses around the causes and effects of poverty.

Nigeria is frequently presented as a paradox in terms of poverty: an oil producing country which is wealthy in human and natural capital, but where it is widely agreed that the incidence of multiple forms of poverty and deprivation is high. Widely held popular perceptions of poverty reveal a regional complexity which provides an important backdrop to understanding how policy might work in a multi-ethnic federation. In areas of the north, like Jigawa, poverty may be described in terms of lack of education; in the oil-rich areas, like Bayelsa, in terms of lack of access to benefits from mineral and oil wealth; in areas of the educated south west like Ekiti, as a failure to turn education into skills that can benefit others; and amongst minority ethnic groups all over the country, in terms of political marginalisation. Action on 'poverty policy' is mediated through such regional understandings of poverty as these, which arise from distinct social and economic phenomena.

In addition to a regional dimension to poverty, popular discourse on poverty in Nigeria is highly politicised and very diverse: the rhetoric of poverty reduction is used by a wide range of political actors, from the President to trades union leaders to anti-IMF demonstrators, from journalists to religious leaders. As such, poverty has become a word which occupies both the mainstream and the margins of domestic politics, charged with a different meaning in every space.

In contrast to this, public discourses of poverty reduction in Uganda are far more uniform, closely reflecting a remarkable convergence of agendas between the Government of Uganda and the international development community, with its large and highly visible presence in Kampala. The notion of poverty reduction as a principal goal of the development partnership between government, international development actors and civil society has been rehearsed over many years in the two national daily papers and through the structures of government and Movement.

While the distribution of poverty has a starkly regional dimension in Uganda, with the North considerably poorer in terms of income poverty and human development indicators, this situation has not led to the highly politicised public debate we see in Nigeria. The political debate about the continued war in northern Uganda is not framed by government discourse as a poverty reduction issue, but rather a question of 'national security'. This is despite local opinion in the North which firmly frames war and insecurity as the principal causes of poverty in the region.

Discourses about poverty and the nature and dynamics of the phenomenon itself both describe the challenges of poverty reduction which face the Ugandan and Nigerian governments. In the next section, we examine further the question of those challenges faced by two states with different forms and different democratic identities, and the implications of this for poverty reduction policy.

The state in Uganda and Nigeria: three points of contrast

Three points of contrast between Uganda and Nigeria stand out as being particularly relevant in making sense of how African states claiming a democratic identity interface with the challenges of poverty reduction. These are: their different positions in the international political economy of globalisation and development; the historic and contemporary relationships between the state and its citizens; and the status and meaning of decentralisation. The tensions and balances between these three overlapping areas, and the way that they have been managed by the Nigerian and Ugandan governments, illuminate not only the evolution of democratic identities in each country, but begin to explain the way that processes of making policy for poverty reduction have emerged, and the form that they have taken.

A complex configuration of factors dictates the position of a southern state in relation to the international system. Nigeria's negotiating power, as an oil-exporting economy with a wealth of human resources, is very different from that of Uganda, a small state whose economic production is dominated by subsistence agriculture. While both economies are deeply indebted, the Nigerian government's relationship with the IFIs is largely about implementing reforms which will ensure an economic seal of approval for foreign private investment. Uganda, on the other hand, received debt relief under the HIPC II agreement, but the government relies on external assistance to fund almost half of its public expenditure, and the IFIs and donors have a strong, direct influence over domestic political processes, particularly decentralisation. Although it may be an oversimplification, we can say that the wealth of Nigeria's economy buys a degree of independence with respect to powerful international actors which is unavailable to Uganda.

Clearly, the situation is far more subtle than this simplified image implies, not least because of Uganda's almost unique position amongst sub-Saharan African countries in the 1990s of achieving a degree of economic growth, and an apparent fall in income poverty. This phenomenon of growth is interpreted, contested and explained in a variety of different ways, but the 'success of Uganda's poverty reduction' has become a policy narrative frequently drawn on, particularly by the World Bank, to show that structural adjustment can result in poverty reduction. The role of providing such a 'showcase', affirmative narrative has afforded the Ugandan government a certain amount of room for manoeuvre in introducing and incrementally reforming a political system which, while initially offering a transformation to democracy without multi-party elections, presents a significant variation on the normalising external discourse of democratic good governance.

Every sub-Saharan African government is obliged to walk the tightrope of relationships with donors and creditors. The agency of southern governments to define policy is influenced as much by the status of their economy as it is by the perceived democratic complexion of their regime, as much by considerations of pleasing their development partners as by the claims and counter-claims of domestic politics. External and internal forces are inextricably linked. The tension between them shapes what happens when externally initiated efforts are made to influence the way that policy gets made.

The second point of contrast between Ugandan and Nigerian states concerns the nature of the relationship between state and citizens, which underpins any effort to make effective policy. State legitimacy in colonial and post-colonial Africa has evolved according to a diverse set of reference points, not least those labelled 'patronage, nepotism, corruption...which knit the fabric of an instrumental legitimacy for the state by substituting patron-client links for its lack of moral foundations.' (Englebert, 2000:5). In many cases, African understandings of citizenship are defined according to the identities – regional, ethnic, religious or familial – which define the position of an individual within systems of patronage, rather than in terms of nation or state (Abah and Okwori 2002).

Uganda and Nigeria present two very different patterns of relationship between the state and citizens. In Uganda, we find a rare example of a regime with its historical roots in a resistance movement, which forged a social contract with citizens through the process of a bush war (de Waal 1996), and has subsequently maintained both power and a degree of popularity. While the regime uses the language of democracy, and is a civilian not a military government, it is only now, in 2004, creating the multiparty electoral system often deemed necessary for democratisation.[4] In power since 1986, Yoweri Museveni has undoubtedly presided over a trajectory of political transformation, in which an early popular mandate for change was followed by a period of regime consolidation, and the gradual implementation of political and fiscal decentralisation. The resulting state, characterised by a pyramidal structure of local councils and a complex system of direct and indirect elections, is centred around the National Resistance Movement, framed as an all-embracing representative political entity to which everyone belongs, in an attempt to avoid the violent fragmentation which resulted from historic attempts at multiparty democracy.[5]

Hickey (2003) notes that the most enduring elements of the NRM's social contract have been a commitment to political stability, a decentralised form of rule which makes provision for marginal groups, and commitment to securing development for local people. He also observes, however, that the logic of patrimonialism continues to infuse the bureaucratic system, and that many of the common indicators of a neo-patrimonial state are increasing rather than decreasing. The findings of the Uganda Participatory Poverty Assessments (MoFPED 2000 and MoFPED 2002) confirm that corruption and lack of accountability are everyday characteristics of decentralised governance, part of the experiential knowledge of poverty which is the domain of the majority of Uganda's citizens.

In Nigeria, by contrast, there is a fragile attempt at transition to multiparty democracy which is set in the historical context of a crisis of state ownership, (Osaghae 2001) and its attendant social and political conflict. Osaghae argues that the crisis of ownership has its roots in the disjuncture between the state and society that emerged during the colonial era; many saw that the colonial state, being owned by 'others' and serving their interests, rather than those of the colonised peoples, was undeserving of loyalty and support. Such understandings have endured and in many ways been strengthened by the experience of the post-colonial state, characterised by four decades of military rule interspersed with brief, fragile periods of civilian rule. The command character of military rule, which dominated the post-colonial experience of government – as it did for some time in Uganda – stifled the development of democratic values, accountability and transparency amongst political elites (Ayam 2000), while experience of civilian rule barely penetrated the political culture of the state. Further, following the discovery of oil, the rentier nature of the state exacerbated the crisis of ownership, giving rise to regimes characterised as arbitrary and kleptocratic.

One response to this state has been the 'exit' of millions of citizens into alternative sites of self-help and governance (Hirschman 1970, Osaghae 2001). Relationships between the Nigerian state and its citizens take place within a culture of entitlement in which even those who no longer feel a relationship with the state continue to perceive it principally in terms of largesse which may be exploited through patron-client relationships. The entitlements of citizenship are thus defined in terms of patronage. A popular image is put forward by Osaghae, that of 'a state sharing the proverbial National Cake in a manner that is theoretically equitable but in practice discriminates among individuals and communities on the basis of proximity to power holders and levels of loyalty and support.' (2001:14)

Nigeria's current regime represents the country's most enduring attempt at multiparty democracy: in 2003 Obasanjo became the first of Nigeria's civilian presidents to be re-elected. Despite this successful transition, the state remains dislocated from society, suffers considerable internal disjunctures between the federal, state and local government levels, is disabled by the historic continuities of bureaucratic and political behaviour, and governs in a context of increasing levels of violence and inter-regional and ethnic tension. Osaghae's crisis of ownership has endured despite the shift to a multiparty democratic electoral system.

The contrasting patterns of citizen-state relations in Uganda and Nigeria give very different backdrops to the adoption of models of policy which place an emphasis on the accountability of states to citizens, and the ability of citizens and their allies to claim the entitlements of citizenship. Unsurprisingly, newer, more consultative approaches to poverty reduction policy are more commonly encountered in Uganda – best exemplified by the Poverty Eradication

Action Plan (PEAP, see Glossary) – where the state enjoys a degree of support amongst the majority of citizens, and where the rhetoric of participatory or direct democracy is far from unknown. In Nigeria, a conventional, top-down, paternalistic and fragmented approach to government poverty reduction policy endures – exemplified by the National Poverty Eradication Programme (NAPEP, see Glossary) – despite being popularly viewed as corrupt and politicised; and a parallel attempt to elaborate a Poverty Reduction Strategy Paper (PRSP, see Glossary), catalysed by donors, has become mired in inter-governmental politics and wrangling. While Uganda perhaps represents more fruitful ground in terms of growing a culture of state accountability in the context of a dominant political culture, when one comes to examine the dynamics at play at the lower levels of the representative system, it becomes clear that the 'business as usual' of the state – corruption, the politics of blame, personal enrichment, and the continued marginalisation of excluded groups – continues regardless of what is going on at the centre.

This brings us to a third point of contrast between the two states, namely their contrasting experiences of decentralisation. Osaghae (2001) notes that decentralisation remains the most popular and practicable means of linking the state with society, because it is held to promote accountability and responsiveness. Research into a range of experiences of decentralisation suggests a series of conditions which might be necessary for decentralisation to meet these goals. These include downward accountability and reliable local taxation revenue (Crook and Manor 1998, Moore and Putzel 1999), which are of critical importance in both Uganda and Nigeria. Further, a willingness of central government to challenge local elites may be necessary to ensure policy implementation in decentralised systems (Crook and Sverrison 2001).

At the risk of further oversimplification, Nigeria's efforts at decentralisation may be broadly characterised as top-down (Osaghae 1989), whereas Uganda's efforts may be seen as having something of a 'bottom-up' identity, due principally to the origins of the current decentralised structure of the state in the Resistance Councils established by the National Resistance Army during the bush war in the early 1980s. The RCs were a pyramidal structure of local committees from village to district levels, later re-named local councils (LCs).[6]

In Nigeria, decentralisation has been instigated and managed by the federal government, which gives it a particular political complexion within national politics, where state and federal governments are often in conflict. While the principle that local matters are best left to local government (Gboyega 1987) has guided the rhetoric of Nigerian decentralisation, some have contended that Local Government Councils were created by federal government to serve as distribution outlets for state largesse (Osaghae 2001). It has been argued that this considerably reduces their potential as spaces for autonomous or accountable action. While the number of Local Government Areas (LGAs) has steadily increased throughout the 1990s,[7] the expected benefits of decentralisation have failed to materialise. This is due not least to severely stretched LGA budgets; allocations from the federal account are relatively small, some revenue is deducted at source, and constitutionally-mandated staffing levels in the LGA are high. Many LGAs have no revenue available to spend on development activities (Francis and Nweze 2003).[8]

Most LGAs are crippled by the dual burden of a lack of local revenue and a lack of control over revenue from the federal government, and most remain profoundly dislocated from the people whose needs they are intended to serve. Osaghae notes that 'although the over-centralising tendencies bequeathed by prolonged military rule is largely blamed for this, the top-down approach is congruent with the Father Christmas image of the state, and is also partly attributable to the totalising strategies of legitimacy by which hegemony-seeking state power holders hope to curtail the space for opposition ... the Nigerian case followed perhaps the worst trajectory of decentralisation, despite the ample room the country's federal system afforded, at least in theory, for local self-determination and self-government' (2001:16). While the Obasanjo regime, on coming to power in 1999, was under a great deal of pressure to deliver 'democracy dividends' to its citizens, it did not see this challenge in terms of attempting to transform the mechanisms of local government in the direction of service delivery or accountability; rather, LGAs were used as they often had been under previous regimes, as channels for delivering some material benefits to selected beneficiaries.

By contrast, the process by which the Ugandan government has created and pursued decentralisation owes a great deal to the NRM's need to find new mechanisms for the articulation of state and society to replace those which had failed so disastrously in the post-colonial era (Karlström 1999), resulting in state terror and an absence of rational government under the rule of Amin (1971-1979) and Obote (1980-1986). A local council system existed before the Resistance Councils were formed under the NRM but these were very much extensions of central government. Under the NRM, members of the local councils (LCs) are elected, while administration is a civil service responsibility. The process of spreading the LC system across the whole country and investing it with meaning has been lengthy and complex. Constitutional change, a Local Government Act, fiscal decentralisation and latterly a World Bank/UNDP-funded Local Government Development Programme are some of the overlapping stages in Uganda's trajectory of decentralisation.

Francis and James (2003) have examined the dynamics of decentralisation at the lower tiers of the LC system, looking at the prospects for accountability. They put forward an idealised view of accountable decentralisation, where the community makes demands upwards, and enfranchisement and better services flow downwards; this is contrasted with an 'informal reality' where loyalty and local revenue flow upwards, and patronage and control flow downwards. They build on this understanding to suggest that there are two 'complexes' at play in decentralised governance in Uganda – one related to the centre, the source of conditional grants and donor poverty reduction priorities; and one related to local processes, where local actors work with resources from unconditional grants and locally generated revenue. They argue that the dual-complex system allows central control to exist alongside a simulation of popular democracy and that, given the direction and flow of accountability and the nature of resources to which local governments have access, moving beyond this simulation is not currently a possibility. Thus, while it is undoubtedly the case that decentralisation in Uganda is at a more advanced stage than decentralisation in Nigeria, the obstacles encountered in creating accountability at the lower tiers persist. The pathologies of the neo-patrimonial state continue to echo through all its levels, despite structural reforms and alterations to democratic identity.

The three points of contrast between the Ugandan and Nigerian transitions to democracy put forward here only begin to illustrate the complexity of the context in which efforts to make accountable policy for poverty reduction might be taken forward by the state. The contrasts between the 'no-party' and the multiparty systems, bottom-up and top-down decentralisation, the unitary and the federal state, the aid-dependent and the oil-dependent economy, obligatory inclusion and pragmatic exit, are only some of the lines of difference which demarcate the way that democracy is interpreted, and its meanings applied to the process of making policy.

The contextual differences which have shaped the Ugandan and Nigerian states mean that their governments have made very different sense of the prescribed models of poverty reduction policy suggested by international development discourses. Uganda's Poverty Eradication Action Plan, often framed as a model poverty reduction policy, owes as much to the emergent shape of the NRM state, and the mechanisms through which it maintains its legitimacy, as it does to the PRSP model which has emerged from Washington. Nigeria's two streams of poverty reduction policy, the NAPEP and the interim-PRSP (i-PRSP, see Glossary), reflect a bifurcation of internally and externally generated approaches to policy, further influenced by the existence of state-led poverty reduction initiatives in some parts of the country. The outcomes of each of these patterns of policy are dictated not only by the forms, structures and practices of the state, but by the wider social systems in which the state is located. In the final sections of this chapter, we examine some of these broader contextual dynamics, looking beyond the state towards the contested and much-analysed realms of civil society.

Civil society in poverty reduction policy: challenging binaries and boundaries

Civil society is a phrase, open to multiple interpretations, which entered the lexicon of development with force in the late 1980s. It provided a convenient shorthand for those examining the shortcomings of state-led development, seeking a distinct realm in which to locate alternative routes towards economic growth and poverty reduction.

Common usage in development discourse assumes the state and civil society to be distinct, and possessed of different attributes. The state-civil society binary[8] forms an integral part of mainstream definitions and narratives of good governance. The implication is that the existence of state and civil society as distinct entities creates realms of action with boundaries, which provide the contextual background against which actors play out their different identities.

Civil society is a term has been comprehensively analysed with reference to its relevance to the African context. A common critique is that the separation of state and civil society is a false division, which does not reflect the complex realities of many African countries, where the boundary between the two is sometimes blurred and sometimes non-existent. Many of the factors discussed above as influences on the democratising state – class, gender, ethnicity, religion – apply also to the dynamics of civil society; most of them are similarly silenced in mainstream development discourse. The lines of patronage, the dynamics of patriarchal society, the importance of ethnic and religious identity in determining social behaviour: these variables influence all social and political activities, not only the activities of government.

Perhaps ironically, challenges to the state-civil society binary have often been framed with reference to its inability to adequately encompass or explain other opposing pairs of variables which define social actors and domains, such as private and public (Tripp 1989) and rural and urban (Osaghae 2001). Similarly, Osaghae's development of Ekeh's (1975) work on civil and and what they term 'primordial publics' illuminates some of the key difficulties with applying the state-civil society binary to Nigeria, with useful implications for other African countries.[10]

Ekeh argued that two publics or societies, rather than one, exist in most parts of Africa: the civic and the primordial. Osaghae suggests that the dividing line between them is best captured by the distinction made in the language of the Igbo between *olu oyibo* (white man's business, which captures the essence of Ekeh's civic public) and *olu obodo* (community's business, which approximates to the primordial public). The *olu oyibo*, which is coterminous with the state, is seen as undeserving of individual and corporate support (e.g. payment of taxes), lacking accountability and can therefore be plundered to feather private nests (Joseph 1987). By contrast, the *olu obodo*, which consists mainly of voluntary community associations, traditional guilds and local co-operatives, and what Ekeh (1983) calls emergent social formations (ethnic and hometown development associations) belongs to the community and is claimed by most ordinary people as their own. Thus members of the *olu obodo* feel obliged to it and are fiercely protective of its interests, and conduct within this realm is governed by traditions of self-help, self-government and a high degree of accountability.

These two publics could be seen as analogous to the state-civil society binary, especially since the *olu obodo* in Nigeria is marked by the fact that vast segments of ordinary people feel no relationship for – have in effect exited from – the state. Osaghae observes that:

> Taken to its logical conclusion, the notion of two publics can be objected to on the grounds of reification, and because it undermines the fact that the same sets of people actually operate in the two publics. But that is precisely the problem, namely, the fact that the two publics generate contradictory pulls, and operate according to different rules and norms.

This analysis can be applied to the state-civil society binary in two ways. Firstly, it draws our attention to the mutability of identity. A single actor can not only engage in multiple spaces (labelled state, or civil society) or publics (labelled civic, or primordial) but can also adopt a subtly different identity in each. Secondly, it draws our attention to contradiction and conflict. Dynamic and mutable actor identities are intertwined with the diverse rules and norms of the spaces an actor operates in.

Without doubt, deeply complex and sometimes conflicting motivations influence the role that different actors might play with regard to society, the state, and policy; and this complexity cannot be adequately captured by a simple binary like 'state-civil society'. But the use of the binary in the language of development discourse does not solely or even principally set out to describe a reality: rather, it carries with it ideological baggage. As Abrahamsen points out, 'development discourse has produced and constructed certain subjects and put them in a hierarchical and unequal relationship to each other' (2002:2). In constructing state and civil society and placing them in an unequal relationship to each other, a particular approach to development, governance and poverty reduction is normalised, and begins to be enacted. 'Civil society actor' is no longer simply an identity with foreign origins: it has been internalised through its adoption by a huge swathe of individuals and organisations that now identify themselves as part of civil society; and thus the meaning of the term and the construction of role have co-evolved.[11] The result is that these civil society actors, in line with their constructed role and identity – whether to demand an accountable state, to claim to represent the poor, to engage in the provision of services – have been increasingly involved in the processes by which policy gets made.

The adoption and interpretation of the notion of civil society in Uganda and Nigeria has validated certain types of actor as legitimate participants in the policy process. The contrasting power of donors, as well as the very different legacies of non-state social forms, result in very different balances between those civil society actors who are invited to participate in the government-donor project of 'poverty reduction', and those who are not.

The multi-layered decentralised Movement state in Uganda has in many ways effectively diverted, and perhaps politically neutralised, social organisations that might normally be held to be part of civil society in rural and peripheral areas, leading some to characterise civil society as weak, despite the recent and increasing proliferation of community-based organisations. At the centre, by contrast, the congruence of donor and government agendas has resulted in a wave of consultative policy initiatives, which issue invitations to participate to formally constituted NGOs with a service delivery or advocacy agenda. Thus a small but specialised sub-division of civil society has emerged, often closely linked to international NGOs and increasingly capable of meeting the demands of invited consultation, to greater or lesser effect. The focus is on negotiated consensus rather than ideological conflict, and episodes of consultation have a technical rather than a political flavour.

Although donors in Nigeria have similarly focused on a sub-section of civil society with which to engage, the intense historic mistrust of government and the dislocation of state and society mean that the phenomenon of invited consultation is relatively minor. This is especially so if those civil society organisations (CSOs) which do engage in consultative initiatives are seen in context as urban-based, elite NGOs, which exist at several removes from the rich associational life of many rural communities, which operate through an enormous range of institutional forms. Federal government seems only superficially convinced of the need to engage with civil society actors; donor influence in this regard can be seen in some areas, but initiatives to engage are limited in number. For many in civil society, political opposition to the excesses of the state is a powerful historic template. While there is some continuity between historic struggles for civil and political rights and the rights-based approaches put forward by some contemporary donors, this convergence has yet to be effectively applied to a poverty reduction agenda.

These glimpses at two different landscapes of civil society begin to describe some of the dissonances between the prescribed identities and actual behaviours of civil society actors; subsequent chapters discuss these in far greater detail. The dissonances imply that making sense of what happens when external policy models are applied requires an acceptance that civil society exists in two distinct ways. Firstly, it is the constructed and hybridised identity of a legitimised group of participants in processes of governance. Secondly, it is a limited term that fails to describe a complex reality. We should also bear in mind Ferguson's warning that :

> The current (often ahistorical and uncritical) use of the concept of civil society in the study of African politics obscures more than it reveals, and [...] it often serves to help legitimate a profoundly anti-democratic transnational politics (1998:47).

Continued critical analysis of development terms and their usage, and how such terms relate to different versions of reality, is central to understanding the prospects for poverty reduction policies to reach and positively influence the lives of those they purport to serve.

Notes

1. Perhaps the most extreme recent example of this interpretation of 'democracy' is the 2002 Zimbabwean elections, which were conducted in the almost complete absence of any indicators of democracy apart from the existence of political parties and a poll, and against a backdrop of state terror. The 2003 Nigerian elections, while lacking the endemic violence of the Zimbabwean case, were also characterised by bribery, thuggery, threats and electoral returns that were tampered with. In both cases, the international community seemed placated by the mere fact that an election was held.
2. There are strong differences in literacy rates between the North, where rates are very low, and the SW and SE, where they are higher
3. See McGee 2000 for a discussion of apparently conflicting research findings on poverty trends in Uganda.
4. Multiparty elections are expected to be held in 2006.
5. The National Resistance Movement, though refusing to call itself a political party, is now transforming itself into an Organisation in preparation for the multiparty elections.
6. See Annexe One for description of the contemporary structure and responsibilities of the local council system.
7. 453 in 1989, 589 in 1991 and 774 in 1996
8. See Annexe for explanation of the role and responsibilities of different levels of government in Nigeria).
9. In policy discourse, binaries are contrasting or opposing features. Apthorpe (1986) outlines their importance – corrupt and honest,

planned economy and market economy – and suggests that policy messages are often strengthened or weakened according to a good-bad binary.

10. The next two paragraphs draw heavily on Osaghae, 2001.

11. Co-evolution: a term borrowed from ecology, and introduced by Richard Norgaard in development analysis to refer to human or environmental conditions as the product of complex processes of interaction in which mutual influence is exercised, thus denying the existence of one-way lines of causality (Pelling 2003).

3

The State, Civil Society and Development Policy in Uganda: Where are We coming from?

John De Coninck

In recent years Uganda has been held up as a leading example of poverty reduction policy bearing fruit in sub-Saharan Africa. Government, we are often told, working hand in hand with a committed international community, can be credited with a measurable reduction in the number of poor people in the country, against many odds. To what extent and why has this been possible? The premise of this chapter is that a historical perspective on the context in which this success has emerged offers insights into the nature and limitations of that success, as well as throwing into relief the technocratic and usually imported discourse in which poverty reduction statements and analysis are often couched.

When we attempt to trace the origins of the current development policy environment and of some of the assumptions that guide it, there indeed appears to be much continuity between what we see today and the events and thoughts that have characterised the Uganda polity in colonial times and throughout the first decades of its post-colonial existence. We start by looking at some of the key events and institutional actors that shaped this recent history and policy arena.

The roots of a hegemonic state and an emerging civil society: 1920-1986

It is often recalled that, at the time of independence in 1962, Uganda was viewed as one of the more promising emerging states in sub-Saharan Africa. This optimism was informed by the country's natural resources endowment, the way these resources had been harnessed during the colonial era and, most especially, how these had allowed for the existence of relatively well-developed and efficient services provided and managed by an omnipresent state.[1]

Uganda's mode of insertion into the international economy had been determined by the 1920s and has remained a constant for most of the subsequent period. Decisions made by the colonial authorities eighty years ago continue to shape the country's socio-economic landscape. This mode of insertion informed a development policy essentially framed to service the needs of an export-oriented economy based on peasant agriculture, as opposed to the settler or plantation economies of Kenya or Zimbabwe. The focus was thus the construction of the necessary regulatory framework, which was also demarcated along racial lines.[2] It included control over labour supply, through tax measures and the promotion of cash crop growing in selected parts of the country, as well as a land policy guided by the creation of a private land market, from which foreigners were excluded. It also comprised the regulation of trade and marketing through minimum pricing mechanisms, marketing boards and licensing regulations, and control over business enterprises (initially export crop processing).[3] The basis of a smallholder peasant economy had thus been firmly established well before World War Two.

While the state was seen as the main provider of services needed to make this possible, a measured development of what were much later to be described as 'civil society organisations'[4] had been encouraged by the colonial authorities. The state however extended its regulatory arm into this arena as well, forging a symbiotic relationship with civil society, whose characteristics are still much in evidence today. Of the institutions making up civil society in the colonial era, perhaps the most important were the co-operatives of export crop growers, initially established by the Buganda middle peasantry in the 1930s. While officially sanctioned, these were placed under statutory authority immediately after World War Two. Similarly, trade unions came under state control, with nationwide unions banned in 1952 and others placed under the tutelage of a new Labour Department.

Civil society additionally comprised mission-established hospitals and educational establishments – the first actors to engage in social service delivery – as well as other charitable institutions, such as the Uganda Red Cross and Asian-inspired philanthropic organisations.

While the colonial state welcomed the former into public service delivery roles, the products of these institutions threatened its current form. Mission secondary schools, for instance, bred young men and a few young women who questioned the legitimacy of the colonial order. More broadly, this highly regulated and racially-divided environment did not go unchallenged. Emergent trade associations and militant co-operatives increasingly engaged in political activism, while trade unions were amongst the first organised groupings to openly confront the economic edifice, and thus the basis of colonial rule (Mamdani 1976: 181).

The colonial authorities responded by guardedly opening certain doors and shaping the environment that Uganda inherited at independence. Co-operatives, for instance, were assisted to acquire cotton ginneries, until then the preserve of Asian and European businesses. A parastatal, the Uganda Development Corporation (UDC), was established to make selective investments in the industrial sector and African participation in trade was promoted.

In an attempt to ensure the development of a middle class with a stake in the system, a delicate relationship was thus created with civil society institutions, some of which were later to give rise to pre-Independence political parties. This provided the backbone for Uganda's transition towards an independent state, with the Buganda monarch as its first head, uneasily co-existing with an elected prime minister, Milton Obote.

At the outset of independence, little changed. Fundamental policy shifts were precluded by the unstable balance within the political structures of the country, which a ruling bureaucratic elite only managed to alter in 1966.[5] The state became increasingly militarised and re-affirmed its central position in Uganda's political economy. Colonial development policy was initially maintained in the form of five-year development plans, whose main planks were the expansion of export production, import substitution and infrastructural development – a true mirror of dominant development discourses outside Uganda. The state continued to service an export-oriented economy based on smallholders, encouraged to become 'progressive farmers' with secure land rights.[6]

But development policy in the 1960s also emphasised the direct promotion of the private sector, mainly through partnerships between UDC and Indian capital, as well as the promotion of indigenous business interests.[7] This reflected an all-important 'Africanisation' drive, a conscious effort by the state to displace the dominant Asian interests, notably through monopolistic marketing boards. Despite accelerating towards the end of the decade, this drive ultimately failed, and its failure heralded Amin's coup in 1971. The late 1960s were marked by lower export prices, growing capital outflows and increased reliance on IMF loans. Time was bought to avert crisis. The ascendancy of a bureaucratic elite was further advanced by state involvement in new areas, concretised by Obote's Move to the Left and Common Man's Charter (1969), reminiscent of Ujamaa and the Arusha Declaration in neighbouring Tanzania. Much of the manufacturing sector was henceforth monopolised by the state, and parastatal corporations proliferated.

Simultaneously, the co-operative movement – the largest segment of organised civil society – was further expanded and bureaucratised,[8] with the distinctions between civil society and business and between civil society and state both becoming more blurred. The second largest organised segment within civil society remained the trade unions. These were also increasingly controlled; reflecting the government strategy of 'African Socialism', all unions now came under the direct supervision of the Department of Labour, while import substitution, though reflected in growing industrial GDP, resulted in fewer people being employed in manufacturing. The emasculation of trade unions culminated in the expulsion of the more militant workers of Kenyan origin, and the banning of strike action, also in the name of 'socialism', in 1970.

The growing role of the state challenged civil society in other ways, too (Bayart 1986: 112). Political parties were eventually banned, mission schools were integrated within the state system under the 1970 Education Act; and other forms of political dissent, often associated with the traditional kingdoms, were severely controlled. Civil society was confined to operating in more traditional fields ('charity', health delivery) and was sustained in this by the early interventions of charity-oriented international NGOs, with Save the Children-UK from 1956 and Oxfam a few years later.

The parlous state of the economy, marked by high inflation and scarcities, the growing international and internal isolation of the regime, its failure to co-opt the Buganda elite, and the continuous dominance of Asians in trade, all contributed to Amin's military take-over in 1971. On paper, development policy continued to be generated as before. Uganda's last 5-year Development Plan, while signed by Amin, was a legacy of the previous regime. A growing gap between policy on paper and real policy was, however, soon to be become evident. In 1972, the President declared an 'Economic War' and the Asian community was forcefully evicted. Over the ensuing years, as public resources were plundered in an increasingly ad hoc and unregulated fashion, and further contracted as a result of the Asian expulsion, contradictions deepened. The state apparatus itself – so central until then – was reduced to its repressive form. Its ability to offer services to the population considerably diminished and, while any form of dissent that could be orchestrated by civil society was banned, the churches and church-linked organisations played an increasing role in filling widening gaps in the provision of social services. [9]

Further isolated by the terror it unleashed and largely dependent on a mercenary army, Amin's regime saw its economic base shrink as its mainstay, the small peasants, retreated further and further into subsistence agriculture or engaged in production for export on a thriving black market. By 1980, real GDP per capita was only 62% of that in 1971, and the collapse of the industrial sector and the end of crop subsidies further eroded the influence of two historic pillars of civil society, the trade unions and the co-operatives (Livingstone 1998: 38). The heightened use of repression eventually led to the regime's downfall. After 500,000 deaths, Milton Obote returned to power in 1980 and with him the semblance of a democratic order.[10]

The arrival of two new entrants signalled Uganda's brief return to international respectability and confidence. International NGOs started large-scale relief operations, with their most high-profile intervention in famine-stricken Karamoja in the early 1980s.

International donor agencies also made their presence felt in Uganda for the first time, in the guise that is now familiar, with IMF and WB-led Stabilisation and Structural Adjustment Programmes. Experiments with these characterised development policy in the period 1981-1985, foisted upon a government constantly struggling for survival. Superficially, there were initial successes: inflation was brought under control, exports resumed, admittedly from a very low base, and credits started flowing into the country.

Obote had inherited a state whose survival was initially only possible thanks to the presence of foreign (Tanzanian) troops. In February 1981, Yoweri Museveni, contesting the validity of the 1980 general elections widely regarded as fraudulent, launched a guerrilla war that captured increasing amounts of the government's attention. Economic policy acquired a surreal quality. As the recently arrived IMF and World Bank advisors barricaded themselves indoors during nights of widespread gunfire in the capital, the black market and currency speculation flourished, and the army, under-resourced, deeply divided and undisciplined, ultimately proved unable to sustain the regime.

A circuitous journey: the NRM era (1986 to date)

In spite of this turmoil and isolation, Uganda's policy trajectory had followed a pattern not unlike that witnessed in other sub-Saharan countries, from an all-encompassing state at the helm of the economy, to a repositioning of its role through structural adjustment. In the initial post-independence period, the policy process was firmly in the hands of a semi-autonomous state bureaucracy. This directly benefited from its involvement in the economy, through the multiplication of parastatal entities, the imposition of taxes on export production, and the co-option of the co-operative movement.

Some aspects of this trajectory were, however, specific to Uganda. From the mid-1970s, the state had withered to a condition of near collapse, with very limited capacity to implement any kind of government policy, whether of a structural adjustment or any other nature. Further, chaos only allowed a truncated form of civil society to emerge, much weaker than in other parts of East Africa at the time. Young, cowed, and used to close state supervision, it emerged either politicised (the churches), moribund (the trade unions), banned (the traditional kingdoms) or complacent with its cosy, non-confrontational relationship with the state (development organisations, mostly expatriate-managed and dominated by high-profile international relief NGOs).

When Yoweri Museveni came to power in 1986, re-establishing the ascendancy of the state was imperative (see Collier and Pradhan 1998: 20). This was first to be achieved through the extension of the Resistance Council (RC) structure – originally put in place in areas of the country liberated by Museveni's guerrilla army – to all parts of the national territory and in firm reaction to the autocratic practices of the earlier regimes.[11] 'Grassroots democracy' through RCs took the form of resolution of disputes, provision of security and the all-important distribution of sugar and other essential commodities to local residents.

Secondly, a political system was put in place that was meant to be inclusive of all factions that had made up Uganda's political landscape in the previous decades, under the umbrella of the National Resistance Movement. As an NRM-linked author notes:

The concept 'movement' most fully conveys what was needed and what happened. (...) A society which was oppressed by the state, but which also lacked 'motion' because of centuries-old stagnation needed a cataclysmic push, a national coalition of democratic, political and social forces to spark the process of revolutionary change (Kabwegyere 2000: 102).

And thirdly, the state re-asserted its presence in the economic sphere. For a while, there was a complete break with the earlier economic orthodoxy: barter trade was, for instance, initiated to exchange primary products for road construction and technical assistance, the national currency was revalued, and marketing of scarce commodities was organised by the state through the RCs.

This period of reconstruction provided space for the emergence of indigenous civil society organisations, symbolised by the creation of an umbrella organisation, The Development Network of Indigenous Voluntary Associations (DENIVA).[11] With social service delivery still beyond the capacity of government and with donor funding to NGOs in Uganda no longer compromised by political instability, a laissez-faire attitude by government towards NGOs characterised the late 1980s and early 1990s, so long as they had no political agenda.[12] Simultaneously, the relative peace that prevailed in many parts of the country after 1986 encouraged people to build their own local community-based organisations, including many types of voluntary associations, self-help farmers' groups, and parent-teacher associations.

This era of growth for civil society organisations, with most engaged in service delivery, accelerated as the World Bank and other donors forced fiscal orthodoxy upon government. Seen as ideologically preferable to state delivery, CSOs were considered 'less corrupt and closer to the people' (Clayton 1998: 11).[13] This was the heyday of NGOs. Generously funded, they could act with impunity and without reference to government policies. Government functionaries viewed the resources flowing to these stalwarts with a good measure of envy and even cynicism.[14] This era also established two important dimensions of civil society in Uganda: firstly, the lasting association – even equation – of 'civil society' with NGOs, while its other components, trade unions and co-operatives, were being undermined by structural adjustment, liberalisation and retrenchment; and secondly, the tendency for NGO growth to be driven by the availability of donor funding rather than the need to provide a direct answer to specific locally rooted social or political imperatives.

The failure of its initial experiments with a command economy had led the government to revert to the policy context that had been pioneered during the Obote II regime. Structural adjustment, privatisation, and liberalisation again became the order of the day. This was concretised in the 1987 Economic Recovery Programme (ERP). Aimed at macro-economic stability and infrastructure rehabilitation, with extensive external financing, the ERP entailed a substantial review of the role of the state in the economic sphere. A pro-poor agenda appeared for the first time, and with it an explicit role for civil society: 'A distinctive feature of the policy [was] its heavy reliance on NGOs and community-based rural organisations (the resistance councils) which are well placed to supplement the government's capacity to implement projects directed at the poor' (Twaddle & Hansen 1998: 9).

Nevertheless, as the state reasserted itself, the democratic flourishing of the early years was slowly supplanted by a more exclusive vision of its role. Resistance Councils were turned into bureaucratised and salaried local councils and were complemented by various other local structures.[15] The long arm of the state could be felt in all the country's villages through councils that increasingly acted as transmission belts for the policies and edicts originating in Kampala. Further, a new constitution, deferring the re-introduction of party politics and entrenching the 'Movement system', was adopted by parliament in 1995 and crowned by presidential and parliamentary elections the following year, stamping the NRM imprimatur for another five years. The presidential and parliamentary elections in 2001 extended Museveni's and the Movement's governing position until 2006, when multiparty elections are expected to be held.

The 1990s saw a number of policy undertakings, some of a pioneering nature on the continent. In 1990, a Programme for the Alleviation of Poverty and Social Costs of Adjustment (PAPSCA) was launched which was among the first World Bank Social Funds and pioneered direct funding through NGOs. The government started a micro-credit scheme in 1995 and universal primary education (UPE)was announced a year later. In 1997, a wide-ranging Decentralisation Act was passed, entailing the devolution of responsibility for political, financial and administrative affairs, to districts and sub-counties, with locally elected representatives and extension staff responsible towards directly elected district councils. This was made possible in part by a regular increase in international assistance provided to the government[16] and by a decentralisation process that allowed donors to target their assistance through the adoption of particular districts.

It was also during this period that the role of the state was revisited by international opinion. The 1997 World Development Report (World Bank 1997) and the DFID White Paper 'Eliminating World Poverty' (DFID 1997), for instance, questioned the minimalist view that had so far prevailed. Donor influence and familiarity, the nascent decentralisation context and growing concerns with poverty reduction continued to make Uganda fertile ground on which to test new approaches. The focus was now on an expanding local government apparatus and on the central authorities' attempt to eradicate poverty through a new policy initiative, the Poverty Eradication Action Plan (MoFPED 1997b).

Within civil society, the bonanza years for NGOs were over. The latitude for their involvement in service delivery was narrowing while donors were reconsidering the funding of such activities through NGOs. The larger NGOs, with their burgeoning bureaucracies, were confronted by the new and difficult challenge of downsizing and the need to explore new funding mechanisms, especially sub-contracting or, less frequently, state grants. At the political level, the emergence of a relatively well-resourced corporatist state also led to the redefinition of the political space that civil society would be allowed to occupy. A new NGO Bill was drafted, placing civil society organisations under strict supervision by the Ministry of Internal Affairs.[17]

But this new vision has not gone unchallenged. The NRM has been in uninterrupted power since 1986. While the vested interests of an entrenched elite have deepened, protected by the increasing militarisation of public life, resistance is assuming a number of different forms. On the one hand, although relatively inexperienced and poorly organised, some elements in civil society have been increasingly vocal in their questioning of government policy. The churches have denounced the perpetuation of violence in the North, the Uganda Debt Network (UDN) has taken an active stance against corruption in public life, the Uganda Joint Christian Council has denounced electoral irregularities, the *Monitor* newspaper has taken an independent political stance on many issues. Secondly, the electorate increasingly uses its power at local levels to express frustrations by recalling local council officials, or at least needs to be cowed into voting 'wisely'. Thirdly, donors have more frequently and more openly expressed disquiet at the 'slow nature of progress towards democratic governance'.[18] And finally, armed opposition continued in several parts of the country, in part reflecting local feelings of exclusion from mainstream political processes and their accompanying rewards. At the beginning of 2004, the northern 'rebels', the Lord's Resistance Army (LRA) were still causing havoc but without a clear political agenda. Thousands of internally displaced persons were living in camps. Civil society took on a new, militaristic role as local people joined government sanctioned militias to defend their communities.

Where are we now? The persistence of poverty and the new wisdom

From 1988, Uganda complied with World Bank prescriptions, the acceptability of the regime grew, and positive indicators provided succour and legitimacy to the international recipe for development. The experiment had been shown to succeed. Uganda came to epitomise success, the showcase of orthodox development practice on the continent.

As the 1990s proceeded, this vision proved increasingly problematic. The figures were not so glowing after all. If the percentage of the population under the poverty line had indeed declined,[19] this was not the case in the northern part of the country and persistent critics, including some in the tripartite government-donor-NGO partnership UPPAP (see Chapter 5), were questioning the validity of the data. GDP growth was showing signs of slowing down and, in the all-important agriculture sector, was barely keeping pace with the rapid population growth. State revenues were stagnant,[20] military expenditure was growing, as conflict in the north persisted, as was the external stock of debt. The high dependence on donors showed every sign of persisting and local savings rates were failing to grow. Further, earnings from the main export crop, coffee, declined by 70% in dollar terms between 1998/9 and 2001/22.[21]

Independent Uganda inherited a foreign-inspired notion of a state that, while symbolising the new nation, from 1966 in reality quickly proved unable to discharge even its most basic responsibility of territorial integrity. As elsewhere in Africa, the state had preceded the nation.[22] Further, after the first few post-independence years, much of the post-colonial period was marked by a contraction of the state's responsibilities and the increased use of violence to ensure compliance by the local population.

With the advent of the NRM, supported by keen donors, Uganda has seen the introduction and consolidation of a pervasive local council structure, decentralised governance and the re-affirmation of the role of the state in service provision, albeit using resources mostly provided by development partners. Far from the state withering away, the reverse has occurred, sometimes surreptitiously, and the numbers of people depending on the state's continued existence has grown rapidly.

Nevertheless, the contemporary Ugandan state remains fragile. Its assertion of power is not unchallenged country-wide, and still depends on a well-resourced repressive apparatus and access to foreign resources. The current reintroduction of multipartyism renews old rivalries and a debate on the desirability of a federal versus a unitary state continues. Its prominence on the institutional landscape, as the 'weak Leviathan' (Bratton 1989: 410), reflects the relative weakness of other actors, rather than its inherent strength.

This relative weakness has prompted donors and others to foist upon civil society (mainly, as noted above, NGOs) a new role, that of holding government accountable. From cheap and honest service deliverers, NGOs are now to become agents for democratisation. This expectation emerges in a context where civil society, by playing this accountability role, could lend legitimacy to the regime – a potentially useful function now that donors have become more vocal in demanding progress towards multi-party democratic forms of governance. Tarsis Kabwegyere notes:

> The multiplicity of diverse civil society organisations and their growing participation and assertiveness clearly proves that no-party democracy is by no means a negation of pluralism. As civil society gains influence to shape public policy, political leaders

will be compelled to be more accountable and transparent (Kabwegyere 2000: 107-8).

If civil society is given the opportunity to play the role of political parties, whether ascribed by government or by donors, can it take up the challenge? This may not be easy, given its immaturity, its limited self-awareness, its fragmented and apolitical nature and, more specifically, its development in an environment where its existence has been seen as supportive to the ruling order. While civil society organisations played an important role in the independence struggle, we have seen that they were swiftly co-opted by the state and, from 1986, concentrated on the uncontroversial provision of social services. In any case, from long before independence, civil society has been closely enmeshed with the state. The demarcation between civil society and government thus remains blurred: individuals, for instance, move seemingly effortlessly from one to the other, as indeed they move from state to donor employment. Further, working for a recognised NGO, often 'middle-class' and 'urban' in its cultural orientation especially where an international NGO is concerned, remains a prized social achievement, accompanied by what many consider a luxurious lifestyle.

Many CSOs, as we shall see later, appear to be preoccupied with accountability to their donors and their own self-perpetuation, rather than with accountability to their would-be constituencies. The sector is increasingly pervaded by the business ethics that characterise sub-contracting.[23] Further, the persistence of peasant agriculture and of an atomised social life makes bridging the gap between NGOs and their would-be local constituencies problematic, while the many community-based organisations also operate in a heavily regulated environment.

The foregoing helps us appreciate the absence of conflict between state and civil society. According to a recent study on the relationship between CSOs and local governments (CDRN 2001), CSO representatives sought to collaborate more closely with government, in the form of co-operation on specific projects, rather than to develop an independent stance on, say, local planning mechanisms, or the political rather than technical dimensions of project implementation. Further, competition for funds and contracts among NGOs fosters atomisation, disunity and a greater distance from common social agendas. Civil society, therefore, does not seriously threaten the space currently occupied by the political elite: quite the contrary, it can be seen to provide it with the legitimacy that allows its perpetuation. [24]

This might explain why civil society organisations have such difficulty in meeting donors' expectations with regard to holding government to account. While exceptions do exist, as with UDN, they mostly occur at central level, where the local contradictions, such as with the demands of sub-contracting, are least intense. Nevertheless, as the daily *Monitor* noted:

> There is a lot of irony (…). Most independent human rights groups (…) have shunned the activist role which directly campaigns against violations and chosen show activities, like seminars and workshops (…) They fudge or claim they are 'working quietly behind the scenes' (cited in Bazaara 2000: 43).

International NGOs, meanwhile, have also had to adapt. The resources at their disposal made this process easier than for many local NGOs, but they have had to contend with a donor environment that increasingly questioned their operational role in the country, often said to have created 'islands of excellence'. Many have re-invented themselves as capacity-builders for local NGOs and local government and/or focused on an advocacy agenda.

But international NGOs are also donors in their own right. Many of the challenges faced by CSOs reflect the growing influence of donors since the late 1980s. One illustration of this lies in the adoption of messages that, given government's and NGOs' dependence on foreign funding, have quickly become akin to conditionality and have resulted in a de facto donor monopoly on ideas underpinning development policy-making.

Donor funding in Uganda has, for instance, coincided with an increased acceptance of the need for participation in the development process. This has manifested itself, in the first instance, in the need for consultations whenever development policy has to be defined. Many development actors are consulted, including prominent NGOs. A recent study indicates that these selective invitations are in turn used by government and donors to stamp a seal of approval on particular partners (Lister and Nyamugasira 2003) and that such consultations are sometimes seen to provide a legitimisation of what is often considered a screen for cosmetic change (UPDNet 2002; Porter and Olaa 1999).

Secondly, participation has been extolled in development field practice. Here again, Uganda has provided a conducive experimentation ground, with an explosion in the early 1990s in the use of Participatory Rapid Appraisal (PRA) and related approaches in a wide range of situations. Villagers have been known to ask the (often white) development worker: 'Which type of map would you like us to draw? A resource map? A social map?' PRA has found its way into community development work, official government guidelines for local councils (Ministry of Local Government 2002) and the development-speak of any self-respecting government functionary in Kampala and in the districts. As PRA has become an explicit condition for funding, one-day PRA courses can easily be organised by the burgeoning consultancy companies in the capital. So long as a certificate is issued, practice matters little.

'Poverty reduction' is another illustration. As we have noted, tackling poverty did not immediately appear as a stated goal of government policy. However, from about 1992, when government finally succeeded in stabilising the economy, poverty reduction provided an increasingly important rationale for the regime's existence, with solid prompting from the donor community. The elaboration of such policy was initially seen as the sole prerogative of the state and its development partners, the donors, drawing on their own information and without recourse to CSOs (see Chapter 6). Donors have since become the key actors in attaching legitimacy to subsequent policy initiatives for poverty reduction. First amongst these initiatives has been the Poverty Eradication Action Plan (PEAP), the local equivalent of the Poverty Reduction Strategy Paper (PRSP). Intended as a broadly owned policy initiative, the PEAP nonetheless appears to have mainly provided a medium for negotiations between donors and government, rather than a collective, national initiative to focus efforts for national development. Secondly, the much-hailed Uganda Participatory Poverty Assessment Process (see Chapter 6), while promoting the 'voices of the poor' as part of the now-accepted consensus around poverty as a multifaceted phenomenon, has been largely centralised among selected ministries, donors and a few CSOs in Kampala.[25]

For different reasons, the discourse of 'gender' also found a fertile environment. The new regime, having antecedents as a guerrilla organisation with women soldiers and women representatives on its clandestine Resistance Councils, had provided space for women's voices to be heard. Building on this opportunity, after 1986 a small, educated elite fostered affirmative action for women in a number of fora, including women representatives at all local government levels and in parliament. Simultaneously, however, 'gender' became the catchword of many donor-inspired interventions. Gender officers proliferated in development agencies, and the elaboration of a 'gender policy' became another hurdle to be overcome by whichever local organisation was seeking donor funding, to accompany the strategic plan or log frame.

'Advocacy', 'governance' and 'accountability' have also been much bandied about. The accountability agenda has been most visible within debates on decentralisation, 'grassroots democracy' and the role of CSOs. Donors have been enthusiastic supporters of the decentralisation process, in part perhaps because decentralisation has afforded them a technical blueprint solution and a legitimisation of their support to a regime which might appear less than democratic to their home public. The government has not been slow to recognise this, as decentralisation provided it with internal justification, too. Kabwegyere notes:

> The involvement of millions of people directly or through their representatives in discussing public affairs at all levels of the LC system has certainly done a lot more to enhance the process of democratisation than was ever achieved under multiparty politics (Kabwegyere 2000: 103).

As subsequent chapters show, the reality is somewhat different. The decentralisation drive has done much to reinforce local power-holders. We have also seen that the decentralisation process has allowed the state to re-legitimise itself and reaffirm its primary role in service delivery, with considerable resources now being channelled to the local level. Central government has recognised some of the risks involved: developing accountability in the districts remains a priority and the Ministry of Local Government continues to play a key supervisory role.

This accountability channel currently appears to be much more important than any played by CSOs, although, as noted, donors have placed much emphasis on the necessity of civil society developing its voice in this respect. As Chabal noted some years ago:

In situations where formal institutions of political representation – elections, political parties, legislatures – have been emasculated by executive monopoly, accountability comes to 'depend almost entirely on the ability of civil society to curb the hegemony of the state'. (Chabal, cited by Bratton 1989: 416).

Development in the local context

While Uganda's development experience is often hailed as the epitome of 'participatory development', as subsequent chapters in this volume show, the poor still feel disenfranchised. How does this relate to the context described above?

We must first recall the pervasive and long-standing autocratic environment in which the attempts at participatory development are situated. In the period under review, for instance, it is only in the last few years that people have had the opportunity to have their voices heard. Arguably, for some, the last genuine elections were held in 1962. Since then, it is mainly the LC structure (rather than civil society organisations) that has provided this channel to the population. But this is not a straightforward channel. Belonging to this structure is, in the first instance, mandatory for every citizen and exclusive of other options. 'Participation' must therefore be exercised within a single and all-encompassing political perimeter. With the years, as noted, this structure has been increasingly used by the state for its own purpose: the population has been pressed into its age-old cultural mould of 'the chief commands', nurtured in school establishments where the teacher is always right. The LC structures are therefore increasingly rarely used other than as transmission belts for central decision-making, while often providing convenient spaces for the powerful to dictate at local level. LCs have been assimilated into a local culture in which accountability must defer to seniority and power, and in spaces where clientelism is the accepted mechanism for resource allocation.

The application of an array of participatory methodologies mentioned above seems to have made relatively limited impact on the power relationships shaping these structures. While bottom-up planning is everywhere the order of the day, much of the planning has been stripped of its intent as a methodology for facilitating social change and reduced to a set of slavishly applied steps and methods. Here also, a set of participatory techniques has been appropriated within a cultural context and political practice where participation and representation often remain elusive.[26]

Linked to the above is the painfully slow progress towards an 'accountable state', to use an imported phrase. In spite of the presence of the multitude of local councils listed above, situated moreover in a highly decentralised context, local power-holders continually seem to 'get away with it'. Corruption has become an accepted way of life and is reminiscent of earlier regimes. Suspect deals and semi-legitimate activities proliferate, in spite of high profile inquiries. Although corruption is widely deplored – and publicised – it is often accepted as an inevitable fact of life. It is no wonder, therefore, that international league tables continue to place Uganda amongst the most corrupt countries. At a more general level, the state, by clearly indicating which topics are open for discussion and which are not (defence expenditure, for instance), has also set boundaries beyond which participation is not applicable and, in so doing, has reinforced what local communities have learnt from their history, the history of a non-accountable colonial and post-colonial state. Participation thus co-exists with highly restricted forms of accountability and its rhetoric is used to legitimise various situations and systems.[27]

Limited accountability is not the sole prerogative of government and local councils, however. As we have mentioned, civil society organisations have also found it difficult to develop their own mechanisms to be answerable to those they profess to serve. Even where membership organisations are concerned, members are often resigned to seeing their leadership amass power, resources or other privileges with impunity. Further, many civil society organisations uneasily combine philanthropic objectives, for donor consumption, with economic advancement objectives for their membership and leadership. Must not donors' liberal expectations of CSOs acting as standard bearers for accountability therefore be re-evaluated?

The paradox described above highlights the deepening legitimacy gap which the NRM regime currently has to confront. Inclusiveness and grassroots democracy increasingly seem to lack substance, while demands for 'opening up' the political system proliferate in different quarters: the urban population, elements of the press, sections of the intelligentsia and, importantly, donors who find justifying their on-going support to their respective public opinions ever more difficult.[28] It is too early to tell whether the proposed new multiparty politics will lead to greater grassroots democracy.

Within this context, the poverty reduction agenda assumes a new urgency. Faced with growing disillusionment, the regime is under increasing pressure to demonstrate that the Movement system delivers. While advances are undeniable and while many, particularly in the rural areas, acknowledge the gains made by government in providing desperately needed social and physical infrastructure, many of these gains are being eroded by high population growth and rapid environmental destruction. Regional disparity is also persisting, with large areas of the north, still wracked by brutal rebel activity, lagging way behind the rest of the country. This regional imbalance reflects the antecedents of the Ugandan state, a creation, as noted above, of colonial convenience. The Movement, in spite of its inclusive character, is still struggling with overcoming the fractious nature of this state. While national unity remains a costly[29] and time-consuming effort, ethnicity has persisted as a commonly held explanation for patterns of resource allocation at macro and micro levels. The state is widely perceived to be dominated by one group, whose interests it primarily serves, at the expense of others.

By the time Yoweri Museveni's band of guerrillas captured the state, a persuasive rhetoric of self-reliant development had become established (National Resistance Movement 1986). The early years of the new regime created a climate favourable to the discourse on participatory development and saw active steps being taken to put this into practice. With time, a deepening chasm appears to have developed between rhetoric and reality. Both local and international influences account for this. Within Uganda, we have noted how the regime has successfully adopted a discourse of 'bottom-up development' not only to promote local governance, but also to cloak its sustained grip on power. This has been possible thanks to the conjunction of institutions with relatively poor accountability mechanisms: local councils and other state institutions; dependent civil society organisations and donors with a stake in the success of their Uganda enterprise.

Simultaneously, the international agenda has stressed the privatisation of development and its technocratic nature. Here again, Uganda has provided fertile soil. Beginning as a social movement, 'development' has become epitomised by successful private endeavour. This has been applied to the development industry itself: consultants and NGOs (themselves increasingly turned into commercial enterprises), promote business plans and a vision of development that rests on the ability of the individual Ugandan to surmount, essentially alone, the considerable challenges she or he faces.

It is against this historical backdrop that the research on which this book is based explores how policy processes take place at local and national levels, who the key actors are and how knowledge about poverty is constructed.

Notes

1. Thus from 1963 to 1970,economic growth averaged 6% p.a. and Uganda had the fourth highest GDP per capita in sub-Saharan Africa; gross primary school enrolment was 67% (De Coninck, 1992). This central position of the state had nevertheless allowed for the development of a business sector, based on a few plantations as well as a few industries, in part controlled by a community of Asian origin.

2. Ugandans were initially excluded from business and trade, to the benefit of an Asian commercial community of small traders and export processors.

3. At the same time, the 1929 Colonial Development Act established an aid fund, the precursor of DFID. In Uganda's case, initiatives eligible for assistance included agricultural research and extension, transport and communications, water supplies and public health among others.

4. Loosely described here as autonomous or semi-autonomous non-government organisations of citizens, beyond the family, situated outside the state, but not necessarily in confrontation with it (See Bayart, 1986:111).

5. The power of the Buganda kingdom (and of chiefs and middle peasants associated with it) was swept away that year when Obote's armed forces, led by Gen. Idi Amin, invaded the palace and forced its king into exile. The post-independence federal constitution was replaced by a unitary one in 1967.

6. The parallels with the current Programme for Modernisation of Agriculture (PMA) and the Land Act are striking. A central (and extremely expensive) element of this policy was a tractor hire scheme launched in the early 1950s but greatly expanded in the mid-1960s.

7. The World Bank, in one its first activities in Uganda, for instance, supported an entity called African Business Promotion Ltd with, amongst others, training schemes and credit guarantees for small traders. Other efforts included the establishment of a Management Training Centre (a joint project by Government and the ILO) and extension services. For a discussion of these various initiatives, see De Coninck, 1980. Here again, the parallel with contemporary policy is striking: the equivalents of ABP Ltd, currently consist of various donor-funded private sector promotion schemes.

8. See Brett (1970).

9. The Churches also played an increasingly important behind-the-scenes political role, leading to state repression, symbolised by the murder of

the Anglican archbishop Janani Luwum in 1977. Similarly, the leadership of the co-operative movement was decimated and all non-governmental media outlawed. Asian-founded charities did not survive the community's physical removal.

10. Uganda was invaded by Tanzanian forces in 1979. After three short-lived transition governments, Obote returned to power in December 1980, after general elections, widely regarded as fraudulent and the first to be held since 1962.

11. The Development Network of Indigenous Voluntary Associations, established in 1988, immediately after a group of NGO workers and academics attended a conference in Sudan.

12. This also arose out of pragmatic considerations. While the 1989 NGO Registration Act, administered by the Ministry of Internal Affairs, called for close supervision of NGOs, the capacity to do so has been absent (De Coninck, 2000: 15).

13. From 160 registered NGOs in 1986, their number grew to over 600 in 1990 and 3500 in 2000 (De Coninck, 1992; Tulya-Muhika, 2002).

14. In 1992-3, for instance, expenditure by NGOs in Uganda was estimated at US$ 125 million, almost equivalent to the World Bank's contribution to the Rehabilitation and Development Plan that year (Dicklitch 1998: 148). The term 'briefcase NGO' also emerged at the time to characterise shady undertakings masquerading as NGOs.

15. Movement committees, youth councils, women's councils, organisations of people with disabilities. Local councillors at certain levels became eligible for stipends.

16. Donor aid has continued to increase – from 9.1% of GDP, for instance, in 1998/9 to 13% in 2001/2. Uganda was also the first country worldwide to benefit (from 1997 onwards) from the HIPC initiative. This has not prevented Uganda's debt stock from continuing to rise from 62% of GDP in 1998/9 to 70% in 2001/2 (Ministry of Finance, 2003).

17. At the time of writing, this Bill has been withdrawn from the parliamentary timetable to allow for further consultations with civil society organisations and other parties.

18. See, for instance, NGO Forum, 2001.

19. From 56% in 1992 to 35% in 2000 (MoFPED 2003b:164)

20. The fiscal deficit widened from 6.7 % of GDP in 1997-8 to 12.7% in 2001-2 (MoFPED 2003a).

21. MoFPED 2003b.

22. Chabal, quoted in Clayton 1998: 9.

23. See CDRN (2003). Similarly, the engagement of CSOs in national development programmes has been mainly scrutinised from a technocratic perspective (UPDNet: 2002).
24. Where such conflict develops, the state intervenes with vigour. An apex organisation for NGOs, the NGO Forum, was refused registration in 1998 when first created, much as in colonial times nation-wide trade unions were banned. Police were called to disband its meetings in 1999. *The Monitor* newspaper was banned for a week in 2002 for 'publishing false news' – a charge now ruled by the court of appeal as too restrictive of freedom of speech. NGOs are thus allowed as 'facilitators of NRM objectives, not alternative sources of power', just as political parties were until 2004 allowed to exist, not to act (Dicklitch, 1998: 152).
25. As described by other contributors to this volume, the PEAP and UPPAP have also been instrumental in providing the two windows of opportunity that heralded participation of civil society in the national policy process with regard to poverty reduction.
26. As Midgley noted elsewhere: 'The state supports community participation for ulterior motives, for purposes of political and social control (...) to reduce the costs of programmes (and) to neutralise spontaneous participatory activities' (quoted in Dicklich, 1998:152)
27. Thus, whatever its original intent, UPPAP was not conducted with a view to rendering accountability to the local poor (see Chapter 6).
28. See NGO Forum: 2001.
29. Thus in 2002/3, several ministries found their budgets cut overnight to accommodate additional defence spending, the latter exceeding its budgetary allocation by 16% three quarters of the way through the financial year.

4

The corporatist State, the parallel State and Prospects for representative and accountable Policy

Richard Ssewakiryanga

Within the international development discourse on poverty reduction, the post-1986 Ugandan state has been characterised by the increased participation of a range of policy actors in the poverty eradication arena. These actors include central government, local governments, civil society organisations, donors and poor people themselves. This chapter submits that this expanded participation must be seen firstly in the context of the broader historical patterns of state formation which characterise the Ugandan state. After setting this context, it explores some of the changing patterns of the participation of different actors in the policy process at several critical interfaces: between government and international actors, between central and local government, and between bureaucrats and politicians.

The post-1986 government in Uganda grew out of a history of struggle against state violence. These regimes of violence forced a broad alliance of actors to work together in the name of ending tyranny over the Ugandan population. The coalition of actors brought together in the National Resistance Movement went on to form the institutions of the new state. Although this coming together of various actors permitted the triumph of people's power over oppressive regimes, the NRM coalition encountered difficulty in translating the inclusiveness of the resistance movement into institutions that could uphold the principles of accountable and representative policy.

This chapter asks how the identities of government and donor actors are played out through poverty eradication policy processes, in a country where efforts to decentralise are comparatively advanced, and where donors are significant players. In order to make sense of the ways in which poverty policy is implemented, it is necessary to look first at the evolution of the post-1986 Ugandan state, locating the poverty reduction policy process within it. Next, the chapter looks at how this evolution impacts on the current pro-poor policy actors'practices and actions, particularly with regard to some defining features of the relationship between donors and central government. Finally, the chapter examines some of the dynamics which influence the implementation of poverty reduction policies, particularly those between central and local government actors.

The changing state in Uganda

In order to understand how the post-1986 Ugandan state has evolved, it is useful to start with theoretical formulations about the historical factors that have led to the emergence of the state in Africa. The way that states are organised has a lot to do with how policies are delivered, especially if the policy process is viewed as dynamic, and embedded in political interests (Keeley and Scoones 1999).

As discussed in Chapter 2, Ekeh (1975, 1994) argues that colonialism in Africa left two kinds of publics – a civic public and a primordial public – with individuals upholding the virtues of the civic public whilst simultaneously remaining loyal to their primordial public. This clash of norms and interests generates some negative tendencies that have come to be known as tribalism and corruption.

Ekeh submits that in Africa there is no formulation of the notion of the individual as a worthy citizen, partly because of the way foreign intrusions of slave trade and colonialism contributed to the alienation of the African state from its citizens. Individual citizens therefore lack both the power and the tradition to interact directly with the state (1994:235). Ekeh's arguments can be linked to the school of patrimonialism, which argues that the legitimacy of any politician depends on the ability to deliver goods to their constituency, which in this case is located within the realm of ethnicity, religion and tradition (Hyden 1983). There is a clear indication both in the patrimonialism school and in Ekeh's work that the distinction between the private and public spheres is blurred. Indeed, as Jarvis and Paolini (1995) argue, the state is at once a problematic concept, and simultaneously one which binds our lives in an interaction with a whole series of markers and signifiers: nation, ethnicity, culture and identity.

Arguments about the two publics and the patrimonial nature of the state in Africa are further developed by Mamdani (1996) who, as quoted in Chapter 2, argues that colonialism in Africa institutionalised a form of 'bifurcated state' with dichotomous types of organisations of state structures and modes of power. The urban areas, he argues, were governed by civil law and the rural areas by customary law. Elements of this bifurcation of the state with both customary and civil rules governing the policy process remain evident across a range of policy spaces.

The conceptual linkage which these commentaries brings to light is that social differentiation between state actors is a critical component in defining how the state works. During the resistance war, the NRM was very inclusive, a resistance movement based in a primordial public. Scaling up to take control of the country was hard, partly because the inherited state was rooted in a civic public. The evolution of the state has revealed the vagaries of a somewhat unstable marriage between peasant empowerment and, amongst others, the interests of urban civil society, opposition political parties and trade unions. The NRM version of broad-based governance has tried to unite a diversity of actors by including them within the boundaries of a singular political grouping, the Movement itself. The inclusion of socially-differentiated actors in an all-embracing, corporatist-style state, while not always comfortable, provided foundations for the subsequent trend towards increased participation in the policy process.

As Mbembe (2001:77) has written on the post-colonial state:

...African states may well follow different itineraries. Fragmentation, break-up, concentration of power to the benefit of a small number of regional powers, reproduction of lineage or chieftaincy logics within the state, or accentuation of practices reflecting dual power are within the range of the possible. But whatever the diversity of trajectories that local societies take, the future of the state will be settled, as has happened previously in the world, at the point where the three factors of war, coercion, and capital meet.

In the case of the Ugandan state, the meeting point of war (represented by the 1980s bush war), coercion (represented by contemporary state power) and capital (represented by donor money) can be located in the poverty reduction policy arena, as will be illustrated in the sections that follow.

Donors: Citizens in a parallel state?

The end of the 1980s bush war, the return to peace and the political promise of participatory democracy, meant that the need to rehabilitate and reconstruct the Ugandan state and economy were priority issues both for Ugandan liberators and the international community. The international development actors, the donors, intervened in the Ugandan economy for various reasons. First was the need to continue the structural adjustment programmes which, as part of the global neo-liberal development agenda had been initiated during the Obote II regime, but which did not initially have the support of the new Museveni regime. Second was the need to fund the rehabilitation of the sectors of the economy destroyed during the bush war. Starting with projects on poverty that were mostly delivered through international non-governmental organisations,[1] the interventions of donors have now grown to become a very sizeable proportion of the Uganda Government budget.[2] The growth in funding has been accompanied by an increased need for donors to monitor how their money is used, and also to participate in designing programmes for poverty eradication.

Donor influence in the making and framing of Ugandan poverty reduction policy is therefore no small matter. The international community has had to find innovative ways of 'assisting' Uganda's policy makers towards models of poverty reduction policy which are congruent with donor agendas. But they also have to report back to their own citizens how their support is improving the lives of the poor. What emerges from this configuration can be characterised as a scenario of 'donor citizens' participating in the management of a donor-driven country through processes where they use the power of their finances to create knowledge, to open and close spaces for the making and shaping of poverty policy. Taken to its extreme, this scenario may be seen as the emergence of a parallel state[3] in which donors and selected central government policy actors claim their entitlements to define Uganda's route to development. Donors-as-citizens in this parallel state purchase their entitlements, rather than claiming them by right; in doing so, they frequently have more influence on the way the Ugandan state functions than do its domestic citizens. The scenario is characterised by the interlocking of actors, which has made the distinction between donors and central government actors at the central level as blurred as the distinction between Ekeh's two publics (Allen 2002).

As discussed in Chapter 1, the traditional linear policy paradigms delineate different roles for actors in the policy community and do not reflect the complex realities of the policy process, where power relations – hidden, visible and invisible – are as important as ascribed roles in determining what actors actually do, and where boundaries between actors are blurred rather than clear.

In the Ugandan context, donors have been very influential in working with selected government actors in shaping various policies. They participate in a range of spaces, and in a range of ways. A DFID respondent who has some misgivings about the power of donor participation in review meetings notes:

> ...I attended a review meeting of the Poverty Reduction Support Credit but sitting there and making decisions about allocations to different sectors that will affect the whole Ugandan population made me feel like I was in cabinet deciding the country's future...

Like it or not, the future of Uganda partly depends on the outcomes of and the negotiations that go on in these review meetings. While they are spaces in which key policy decisions are made, they are not static, but affected by contextual dynamics. One government actor noted that:

...it is to do with confidence – their confidence in us, and what we are doing. We also are a lot more informed. Ten years ago, we were hiding everything, going to cabinet with secret decisions – but now we start our processes with the donors, they are involved from the start. But the same sort of changes have happened with them too – ten years ago I would have spit on them!

Indeed, the relationship between donors and central government actors is now a very intimate one, to the extent that sometimes a distinction between donor and government positions on a policy become indistinguishable. Although there are many instances where this works well, there are also a number of areas where donors or government actors feel uneasy in this cosy and supposedly egalitarian relationship. Differences are perhaps most marked around questions of accountability for funding.

Donor annual review meetings for different sectors have become a very important space, not only for negotiating positions, but also for deciding the future direction of development funding in the country. These negotiations take place between actors with different power positions who use their knowledge, the power they hold and opportunities that are available to negotiate certain positions. As one donor representative says:

... We have a lot of discretion as donors and we have had a lot of activities and now we try and work on the financial management, audit and control systems. If you cannot control poverty money it will go only to the elite...

It is apparent that donors are aware of the power they hold but also that they surround it with narratives that legitimise certain power positions[4] in the name of the poor. Power positions here refer to the various influential opinions and actions that an actor can hold or use within the policy process. What needs to be said at this point is that the power that is exhibited in the review meeting is only one part of the process of policy making and the review meeting is only one space in the policy process. It is often not possible to pinpoint a clear cut moment when decisions are made; instead, we see more 'small acts' that set limits in the policy world; sometimes it is only in retrospect that we know that policy has been made (Brock et al, 2001). As Keeley and Scoones (1999) have mentioned, a single moment of decision-making is a fiction in the context of the multitude of overlapping processes that constitute policy-making. A vivid example of this concerns the decision to convert Uganda's existing Poverty Eradication Action Plan (PEAP) into the Poverty Reduction Strategy Paper (PRSP) which the World Bank was demanding from the government of Uganda, narrated by a participant in a critical meeting at the Ministry of Finance, Planning and Economic Development:

> When the Bank and IMF delegation came early 2000 they sat at the top table. The PEAP revision process was ongoing. They introduced the idea of the PRSP and Keith Muhakanizi [Director Economic Affairs, MoFPED] spoke up and said 'This [the PEAP] is the PRSP, because it is Uganda's poverty eradication action plan'. And slowly it spread around the room, with everyone saying, 'The PEAP is the PRSP'. So the Ministry staff cut through the narrative of the PRSP, and told the Bank and IMF that what they should be doing is working with the sector working groups [sectorally-focused bodies which had already been put in place, charged with producing a revised, updated version of the PEAP].

This quotation raises two key issues. One is that 'cutting through the narrative', while an important decision point, is not the only moment of decision, because the work that goes on in other spaces, such as the sector working groups, is important in outlining the detailed knowledge that ends up forming the content of the policy. Further, if power is the ability to frame the boundaries of policy spaces, to dominate the discussion with a particular kind of knowledge, to aggregate the knowledge, to frame the discourse itself, to present knowledge and use it (Hayward 1998), then this quotation is a good illustration of the way power relations are played out in discrete spaces in the policy process.

There are many kinds of legitimate power at play in the policy process. According to some authors (Lukes 1974; Gaventa 1999; VeneKlasen and Miller 2003), power has three critical dimensions. One is visible power, for example the power invested in a president by a constitution, the 'definable aspects of political power' (VeneKlasen and Miller, 2003: 47). There is also hidden power, which manifests itself in backstage spaces and informal relationships, where 'powerful people and institutions maintain their influence by controlling who gets to the decision-making table and what gets on the agenda' (*op. cit.*) Then there is invisible power, the power related to the fact that actors may subconsciously accept conditions as they are. Invisible power may function to inhibit the agency of those actors and make them less powerful.

In the discussions about the PEAP as the PRSP, there is the visible power of the donors and the top government officials, but there is also the hidden power which informs the discussions that come before or after the kind of meeting described. This further elaborates the point that how policy gets shaped in various spaces depends on what kind of power is mobilised in favour of one position against another; and that some of that mobilisation takes place outside the spatial boundaries represented by a particular meeting or event.

Another illustration of power dynamics at play in the making of PEAP/PRSP comes from a Ugandan government consultant:

> ... then the Bank came with the 'crazy idea' of the PRSP. They were demanding more consultations – they had given some funding to the CSO taskforce [on the PEAP]. But the consultations we had already done allowed them to agree on the PEAP as PRSP. 15 guys came from Washington and told us that the PRSP must have five goals, but we said, 'no, we have four, what is missing?' – these guys couldn't convince us. They changed their mind on the spot in a meeting at MoFPED.

The two quotations taken together illustrate that the transformation of the PEAP into the PRSP involved negotiation, bargaining and the invoking of different kinds of power in order to make the positions of different actors acceptable. What is clear is that there is no straight progression of power from one end to another but a 'science of muddling through'[5] several layers of bureaucratic politics.

Despite this muddling through, and the lack of linear progressions of power, donors in Uganda have increasingly tried to act in a co-ordinated way. Donor co-ordination is certainly an important item on the poverty reduction agenda, and one which has multiple meanings. It gives many donors the space to operate in ways that can allow for more inter-donor discussion, and to increase their bargaining power, especially with reference to specific policy areas. But the same co-ordination mechanism sometimes acts as a way of shutting some donors out of specific policy discussions. For example, non-English speaking donors may find it difficult to get their points of view across to other donors. The language factor is important because in fields of specialised knowledge, language is a strong constituent of power, providing space for inclusion or exclusion. Language therefore has implications both on how non-English speaking donors are able to contribute to policy debates where several actors are involved, and on which kind of strategies they adopt to pursue their interests. It also reminds us that within the donor community itself there are more and less powerful actors, with major international donors being supported by numerous sub-groups with different roles.

Notwithstanding the invisible variable of language, donor sub-groups are important spaces where the 'donor stamp' that publicly authenticates the policy processes is delivered. Donor sub-groups are used by donors to strategise about their priorities, and also to launch into more closed dialogue with government actors. In some cases, this happens through inviting top level government actors like permanent secretaries and directors to participate in the donor sub-groups, or by government inviting donors into their own official spaces. The latter is illustrated in a case described by a UNDP representative:

We recently received a letter from the PS-Finance asking us to indicate which sector working groups for the budget were we interested in joining. Some of the donors felt that they need to just go into the groups and listen and not to interfere a lot. Other members felt that we need to go in there but also be able to make modest comments on the issues being discussed. The consensus was that we should not overload the working groups with donor presence but try as much as possible to have at least two people in each of the groups.

Donors on the Ugandan policy scene are therefore not just funders but actors who contribute to various policy processes and are also very aware of the power that they wield in shaping policy. Although the existence of donor sub-groups as policy spaces gives donors a chance to contribute to different policy debates, they also give donors the chance to discuss with central government actors behind closed doors. In the end, donors use sub-groups to have their way with government; but at the same time, government has a chance to read donor positions before policies become crystallised. This helps to ensure less conflict and fewer visible power struggles in subsequent discussions and the production of consensus-laden policy discourses that are then presented as 'official government policy'.

Basket and project funding: keeping our eyes on the 'dollar on the ground'

As already mentioned, donors in Uganda are influential players in the policy process because they finance most of the poverty reduction initiatives of the state. But do the contemporary mechanisms for disbursement of donor funds move us closer to realising effective pro-poor policy through accountable processes?

The debate about financing of projects is whether to move from project support to budget support. The debate is informed by the experiences of various evaluations of the conditionality measures of structural adjustment programmes. The key arguments made against project support included the high transaction costs of delivering aid through projects, and the ability of donors to force their priorities upon governments and to tie procurement to their own country contractors, leading to inefficient spending. The unpredictability in funding levels due to different funding conditions, the continuing undermining of the effectiveness of government systems and, finally, donor-specific mechanisms of accountability were all seen to be corroding the structures of domestic democratic accountability. [6]

As part of the ongoing process of searching for a solution to project funding, in 1998 the World Bank released a publication entitled *Assessing Aid: What Works, What Doesn't and Why*. This publication became the master narrative for advancing the case for moving away from supporting individual projects to what have been defined as Sector Wide Approaches[7](SWAps). General budget support, the narrative goes, reduces transaction costs, increases the efficiency of allocating funds in public spending, creates greater predictability of aid flows, increases the effectiveness of the state and public administration and creates stronger domestic accountability. [8] One of the key arguments in favour of budget support is that it will increase government's accountability to its own citizens rather than to the donors. It will be important in the sections that follow to reflect on the point of how budget support has reduced conditionalities and enhanced accountability.

For Uganda, the budget support discourse has been put into practice through processes like the HIPC agreement and budget support from the World Bank and others.[9] Although this seems to indicate a broad trend of movement towards budget support, different donors continue to make different interpretations of budget support.

The donor respondents quoted below show that there are various angles in debate about the manner of funding. They illustrate the different ways in which actors use their power to negotiate positions in the policy process. Some kind of consensus is evolving about how funding should be brought to central government level, and of the diverse ways that different actors align to the policy discourse. However, there is also some selective application of the consensus, depending on whose interests are at stake.

Sida has decided to participate in the SWAps approach to funding. But it has still got some projects. The experience of working with project support has shown that most of them have worked very successfully but immediately the project ends then everything ends there with the investments deteriorating and even collapsing. We also do not want to just have parallel structures being created outside the institutions mandated to do service delivery. We have realised that transaction costs were very high for the recipient countries.

Here, the Sida representative narrates the position of his agency in a way that is very well aligned to the dominant discourse on the advantages of budget support. However, it is interesting to read this in juxtaposition with a perspective from the World Bank in which the respondent says:

It [budget support] is more an issue of bureaucratic convenience – the government likes it, because it means less conditionality, but it makes our job very difficult. Until the system is accountable – and it isn't – we just don't know where the money goes. There are costs and benefits to budget support – the benefits are that we can help the MoFPED to finance its programmes properly; the costs are loss of flexibility, and having to trust the system. But – we are still engaged in sectors, through Technical Assistance, and we can monitor the MoFPED, but this is very limited.

In spite of this scepticism, the World Bank does not fund solely by budget support. An interesting twist in the World Bank's selection of which support strategy to adopt is its continuation of project funding. Perhaps the best example of this is the Northern Uganda Social Action Fund (NUSAF). The World Bank claims that it was government who asked for funding to be in the form of a project, to which the World Bank agreed. A government respondent quoted below, however, claims that the World Bank was first asked for funding under budget support but refused, preferring to have it as a project under the office of the prime minister.

I asked the Bank to put it (NUSAF) under the budget, but they would not. What is important, however, is not this, but that recent research by the Poverty Monitoring and Analysis Unit shows that in terms of resource allocation, the north remains underfunded in a normative sense, and that we should be putting money there. So it is good. Our weakness however is politics – and that's what the location of the NUSAF is all about; politics in the Bank, politics in government. But if I am going forward ten steps and back two, then I don't really care.

The World Bank official, when asked if they were not supposed to be moving away from project to budget, noted that:

> The government is saying that the North needs special attention – it is very clear in this year's (2001) budget speech – it needs to be mainstreamed ... then it will be able to absorb more from budget support.

Budget support is therefore selectively applied according to different criteria articulated by different actors. According to the World Bank, project support is justified for marginalised parts of the country as a step towards the full coverage given by budget support. The question of when and where project support will continue, and who decides, remains unresolved in the debates of the policy community.

From the government side, the major argument for budget support is that it will reduce transaction costs, reduce disproportionate donor flows to those districts that are directly funded by donors and that the Ministry of Finance, Planning and Economic Development (MoFPED) can retain control over the overall allocation of resources in the Medium Term Economic Framework (MTEF) in line with set priorities.[10] One important complication of budget support is that it strengthens the arm of central government over local governments. Budget support presumably takes away some of the visible power that donors enjoyed in the days when structural adjustment policies were the norm, but it also transfers conditionality from one actor to another. If in the past it was central government who had to tussle it out with donors on conditionalities, now local governments have to tussle it out with central government. This therefore leads us into an analysis of the bifurcated state by moving out of the donor/central government arena and into the realm of central government/local government.

There are governments and there are governments ...

Up to this point this discussion has concentrated on the connections between the ways different players, particularly donors, have intervened in the policy processes of central government. This section examines the dynamics surrounding the relationships between central and local government actors, particularly in the implementation of poverty reduction policy. The discussion starts with a look at the different ways in which the process of decentralisation has evolved. This will be followed with a key example of a programme that brings together central, local and donor actors in the policy-making process as they negotiate for and control power positions in the delivery of pro-poor policy.

In Uganda, decentralisation has given rise to fundamental changes in the relationship between central and local governments. In 1995 the new constitution set out explicitly a number of national objectives, including one on the active participation of all citizens in governance.[11] Two years later the Local Government Act was drafted as a document that forms the basis for good governance policies. The cumulative effect of the legislative reforms encompassed by the LGA has been to change the basic responsibilities of the central government and the relationships between the centre and local governments. Responsibility for service delivery has been decentralised to local governments; however, ministries are required to inspect, monitor, offer technical advice, support supervision and training within their respective sectors to ensure the effective implementation of national policies and standards by local governments.

This formulation of the roles for the central government follows the supposedly logical linear sequence of policy-making from formulation, to implementation and evaluation. However, what seems clear from research at the district level is that there are a series of disconnections between the various government actors both within and across different levels of decentralised government. There are many differences between how government actors see themselves and how they are viewed by others within government, often caused by political positionings which remove actors from the idealised roles put forward by official policy models.

One key programme that was designed by the government and donors to support decentralisation is the $80.9 million Local Government Development Programme (LGDP). Examining some of the dynamics at play in the implemention of the LGDP illustrates well some of the disconnections that exist between central and local governments. This programme is supposed to be an innovation in devolving the development budget to the local governments. LGDP aims to:

Improve LGs' performance of their statutory service obligations through the delivery of effective, efficient and participatory local government planning, budgeting and resource allocation procedures, and enhance the capacities of the Ministry of Local Government, the Local Government Finance Commission Secretariat and the LGs to better deliver on their mandate and consequently contribute towards the national development goal of economic growth and reduction of poverty. [12]

This programme penalises and rewards local governments, according to technical criteria. If a local government fails to meet certain set criteria, one of them being the inclusion of poverty analysis in the district development plan, then it is penalised. If it meets the criteria, which essentially translates into narrating the central government discourses, including poverty analysis, then it gets a reward.[14] As this central government actor notes:

The principle that guides the LGDP is that those who have performed well are rewarded and those who have not performed well are not rewarded. We also organise feedback meetings where the different local governments are presented with their results. We call in the district leaders, heads of departments, sub-county representatives and tell them how the district has performed on each of the different issues they were assessed on. We find that some of the issues are affected by political leadership. For example, in Mbale, some of the sub-counties used the LGDP money for mobile phones and they had not rolled their development plans – and the Chairman was giving money to schools just like that. So we decided to withhold their whole year's budget.

What this suggests is the existence of considerable agency among central bureaucratic players in the process of decentralised government. Different parts of bureaucracies are engaged in complex re-workings of decentralised governance. Central government actors, the bureaucrats, become assessors of local governments. They view local government actors as subjects who are taught the art of good governance, with central government as the ones who offer the 'right ways' and knowledge to use for good governance. For example, the concept of 'rolling development plans' that the respondent refers to is one where the local government is expected to come up with new priorities in which they want to invest, through institutional techniques of bottom-up planning. Such bottom-up planning processes are, however, marked by numerous disconnections, one of which is the separation of planning from evidence. Despite the rhetoric, the analysis of development plans does not show a genuine commitment to consulting with the poor but rather a process that political actors use to demonstrate their claims to legitimacy as representatives of the people, and bureaucratic actors use to align local community issues with those priorities that fall within the guidelines from the centre (Brock et al, 2003).

The LGDP can therefore be seen as a policy that is used by central and local government actors in the pursuit of different objectives. For the central government actors one can see a tailoring of the process so that outcomes point to the necessity of intervention in the local government policy process. As the quote from a Ministry of Local Government (MoLG) respondent shows:

The threat to decentralisation is not from politicians, but from the bureaucracy – it's their power you would be giving way. I've never been an LCV Chair but I have controlled a budget – and now I would be told that all I have to do is monitor and receive money?... This would take away my resources, my influence, my patronage. So it does require political will, but on the part of bureaucrats, not politicians. But currently, political decentralisation is leading the rest of the process.

'Taking power back to the people' may be a useful marketing catchword for politicians, but the bureaucrat at the central or even local government level will always read it differently. As in central government, local government is divided into political policy makers (elected) and an administrative structure under the civil service. There is also a resident district commissioner appointed by the president to oversee the implementation of projects in the district. Front line bureaucrats are themselves prime movers in the ways policies are shaped through implementation. In a situation like this it is evident that if decentralisation is to deliver pro-poor policies, the principal obstacles and considerations are not only the politics of elected politicians, but also the politics of bureaucracy. For central government bureaucrats, this is the need to control budget expenditure by local government; for district government bureaucrats, it is controlling budgets to sub-counties. Bureaucratic politics of this nature imply that shaping pro-poor policies in a situation where the bulk of funding for local government is from central government grants, which in turn originate with donors, may serve more to entrench top-down policies than to encourage bottom-up planning.

The story of bureaucratic politics is further elaborated by the quote below:

The challenges of co-ordination are not so much at the level of ministerial consultation but in how we relate to Local Governments. One finds [the Ministry of] Health going with its programme and also different conditions and guidelines, the same goes for [the Ministry of] Education and Agriculture and all the rest. This brings problems of co-ordination and we are now talking with [the

Ministry of] Finance to try and find a way of making sure that we have one unified reporting format that is shared with all the Ministries. This debate is ongoing and is being discussed under the broad framework of fiscal decentralisation.

Although our respondent casts the discussion as one of reporting formats, this quote tells us more than meets the eye. Even if the challenges were simply about reporting formats, what the ministry would be encouraging is not accountability to local communities where services are delivered, but paper accountability to central government actors where the money comes from. These paper accountabilities are then dressed up very nicely as progress reports that make a grand entrance into the joint donor-government annual review meetings and more money is disbursed in the name of poverty reduction.

Unfortunately, this is not only a story of patrimonialism by central government actors. It continues – in fact is replayed – if one looks at the relationships that are developing between the local government and the sub-county which are the only two corporate bodies in Uganda's decentralised system. As the Secretary for the Works Committee of Tororo District Council narrates:

Local Governments are supposed to be implementers – but we need flexibility. Funding comes with very definite instructions – but this leaves us no flexibility, about whether to spend the funds in a labour intensive way and get it done slowly or, in a capital intensive way to get it done quickly. So we have to do it the way we are told, even when there are times that it really doesn't make sense[...] Donor money must be utilised for the job it has been given for – the World Bank is saying this. They talk, talk and talk but they never come to us. If there was regular dialogue at district level ... [...] They think the local governments are mediocre. But here all the members of the Executive Committee are graduates. They must address us to get to the sub-county, the 'unit of development' – we know the strengths and weaknesses of our own chiefs –how can they know that? When the World Bank does come they just talk to a few people in Finance [at the district level], no one else.

This actor throws up a number of very interesting disconnections. First, the respondent shows how the local government has internalised the invisible power of the central government to the extent that they are now seeing themselves only as implementers and not policy makers. Secondly, the respondent points out the constraining power that the central government actors impose on local governments. The third disconnection relates to the rhetoric of accountability that accompanies financing from the central level government, but which is not followed up with any monitoring by the central government.

Conclusion

The overall arguments of this chapter are threefold. One is that the post-1986 state in Uganda grew out of a history of regimes of violence in Uganda. These regimes of violence enabled several actors for a political cause to come together in the name of ending tyranny. The same coalition of political forces was also used to create the institutions of the post-1986 Uganda state, as we know it today. In spite of initially uniting different actors, the corporate state has not been able to adequately translate these old 'all-inclusive' institutions into institutions that can uphold the notions of accountable policy. This is not least because of the role of donors in Uganda.

Secondly, the post-conflict state in Uganda was instrumental in rallying donor support for the country. This has brought much-needed money to provide essential services, but it has also brought increased powers to donors. Donor power has grown to the extent that one can actually start seeing a parallel donor-state with donor citizens, within a corporatist state. What this emerging identity of donors does to the attainment of the objectives of pro-poor policy is more complicated than meets the eye, especially when it is seen in connection with the processes of power.

Thirdly, the question arises of how government actors in a fairly decentralised corporatist state deliver pro-poor policy. What is clear is that bureaucratic politics are alive and kicking, and that they influence how policies are delivered. Bureaucratic actors in the realm of policy making are not just neutral executors but are active agents in the remaking and unmaking of policy. It is therefore important to emphasise that in order to move to more accountable and representative pro-poor policies there is a need to act with more awareness of the ways in which power influences and shapes poverty reduction policies.

Notes

1. See discussions in Chapter 3.
2. Lister and Nyamugasira (2003) note that 52% of the development expenditure budget is supported by donor funds
3. The metaphor of a parallel state is used to connote the power of donors in shaping policy, but also to show how the Ugandan state operates and functions especially in relation to the programmes they fund. The notion of a parallel state suggests two prevailing systems of governance which influence each other, in which access to rights is acquired in different ways.
4. Poverty Reduction Support Credit (PRSC): World Bank programme loan availability to countries in support of a Poverty Reduction Strategy Paper (PRSP).
5. Lindblom (1959) quoted in Keeley and Scoones (1999:5)
6. For a detailed discussion see Overseas Development Institute/Oxford Policy Management (2002).
7. SWAps have been defined as a sustained partnership, led by national government, involving different arms of government, groups in civil society and one or more funding agencies with the goal of contributing to national human development objectives in the context of a coherent sector, defined by an appropriate institutional structure and national financing programme through a collaborative programme of work. See Cassels, 1997.
8. ibid: iv
9. Foster and Mijumbi, 2002
10. Of the Ministry of Finance, Planning and Economic Development
11. Foster and Mijumbi (2002:25)
12. See The Republic of Uganda (1995) Constitution of the Republic of Uganda, National Objectives and Directive Principles of state policy, II (i)
13. See World Bank (1999).
14. The key planning document produced and used at the district level.
15. From interview with Ministry of Local Government official.

5

Ugandan Civil Society in the Policy Process: Challenging orthodox Narratives

Karen Brock

The rise of civil society in development narrative and practice is an indicator of broader shifts in the way that development finance is disbursed, administered and evaluated. Current orthodoxy constructs civil society organisations as crucial actors in poverty reduction and policy, transmitting the voices of ordinary people to decision-makers, creating a constituency to ensure efficient, demand-driven service delivery, and holding governments accountable for their actions. Evidence of civil society participation has become a marker of legitimacy for poverty reduction policy processes, particularly since the advent of Poverty Reduction Strategy Papers (PRSP).

Many African scholars, examining both theory and practice, have concluded that there is a severe disconnection between narratives of civil society originating in the North, and the complex histories and realities of states and societies in Africa (Mamdani, 1995; Oloka-Onyango and Barya, 1997; Chabal and Daloz, 1999; Lewis 2002). As Oloka-Onyango and Barya observe, 'accompanying conceptual confusion is the fact that the historical legacy of the notion of civil society in Africa is suspiciously like other alien imports, of both convoluted pedigree and questionable validity' (1997:115).

These two threads of experience, the imported narratives of the role and position of civil society, and the local histories and realities in which civil society is embedded, are essential background to an examination of how civil society actors participate in the poverty reduction policy process in Uganda. The broad contradictions between the two are made more acute by the particularities of Ugandan history and development, and by the unusual uniformity of donor understandings of the role of civil society organisations which is articulated in the Ugandan context.

The violent closure of associational space that took place under

Amin and Obote's second regime, and during the civil war, meant that civil society, as well as the state itself and the formal economy, were barely functioning when Museveni gained power in 1986 (Himbara and Sultan 1995, Kabwegyere 2000). The Movement system of government, with its rhetorical and structural focus on inclusion and decentralisation, has subsequently shaped a political landscape where the dividing line between state and non-state actors is blurred (Allen 2002, Lister and Nyamugasira, 2003).

Into this landscape have come the international financial and development institutions, who have wielded extraordinary power in the Ugandan economy and policy process since the early 1990s.[1] The varied, but nonetheless similar, development narratives of institutions like the World Bank, the UNDP and DFID have eased the passage of 'civil society' into common parlance amongst local development actors, partly replacing the collective 'NGOs' which were the focus of the late 80s and early 90s.

Beyond this shift in words, external actors have also catalysed opportunities for the participation of civil society actors in the policy process, often by encouraging government to create invited spaces for participation. The resultant expansion of spaces for participation was contiguous with a sharp growth in the number of civil society organisations since the late 1980s, and has resulted in a dramatic increase in the range and variety of actors who participate in the policy process. The quality and effect of this participation, however, is shaped not only by the preferences of international development actors, but by the historically situated dynamics of politics and power, which mediate the role of state and civil society actors from the centre to the peripheries of Ugandan politics.

This chapter critically examines the participation of civil society organisations as actors in the poverty reduction policy process, at both the centre and the district levels. It begins by discussing some of the broad assumptions and contradictions implicit in the application of external narratives about civil society to Uganda. It continues by examining different perspectives about the role of civil society in the policy process. It then discusses the dynamics of the wide range of spaces in the policy process which are occupied by civil society actors. In conclusion, some areas of challenge for a more accountable, responsive policy process are presented.

Definitions, assumptions and contradictions

In Uganda, largely due to the nature of the state, the arena of civil society is somewhat narrower than in many other African countries. Some civil society organisations, such as trades unions and co-operatives, have either been systematically weakened by or absorbed into the state itself. This has led some to characterise Ugandan civil society as 'weak' or 'underdeveloped' (Okuku 2002). Nonetheless there is a diverse range of organisations which operate in the arena of civil society, encompassing a wide variety of institutional forms and agendas for action. Notwithstanding such diversity, the written statements put forward by a range of policy actors reveal a common set of assumptions about what civil society consists of, and its role vis-à-vis development, poverty reduction and the state:

> Attempts to engage 'civil society' in the partnership process present a formidable challenge [...] but citizens need to be empowered and the 'voiceless' need to be heard in setting development priorities. (Poverty Eradication Action Plan Volume I Government of Uganda: Ministry of Finance Planning and Economic Development, July 2000:13)

> Civil society, including NGOs, has roles both in service-delivery and in contributing to public debate about poverty-reduction. Government cannot control the activities of NGOs. (Poverty Eradication Action Plan Volume III Government of Uganda Ministry of Finance Planning and Economic Development, December 2001:25)

> Civil society in Uganda is starting to play a more prominent role in raising awareness of rights, undertaking advocacy on behalf of disadvantaged groups and generally holding the Government to account. (DFID Country Strategy Paper, January 1999:6)

Civil society organisations are [...] important in the analysis and articulation of the critical needs of society [...] as well as addressing poverty, inequity and marginalisation. (ActionAid Uganda Country Strategy Paper 2001:7)

Implicit across this range of statements are several key assumptions, the most basic of which is that civil society has, in some sense, an identity with clear boundaries, with CSOs having similar identities and purposes.[2] On the contrary, however, in addition to diversity of form and function, we encountered marked differences in CSO identities between Kampala and the districts.

CSOs in the capital, heavily shaped by direct engagement with international development actors and latterly with the government, conform quite closely to the image of modern, formally constituted institutions and structures – capable of advocacy, service delivery and contributions to public debates – which emerges from the narratives. CSOs at the district level and below, however, while including formally-constituted NGOs, also include local, small-scale self-help organisations, often based on structures of clan and lineage. These structures, usually informal, are frequently vital in local people's efforts to sustain their livelihoods in the absence of services. Many members of such groups stated that there was little point in their attempting to engage a governmental system which they perceived as seldom acting in their interests.

A second fundamental assumption implicit in the documents cited is that civil society is a separate entity from the state. Interviews with civil society actors at the district level and below suggest that this is far from the case, with many actors in local processes of planning and politics having more than one identity, being simultaneously active in government, in civil society, as well as in their geographic and social constituencies. Examples range from the 'Councillor-led CSOs' of Tororo District, where elected officials have founded NGOs to take advantage of contracts arising from the service provision activities of local government,[3] to a women's NGO in Bushenyi, founded and headed by a local MP. Allen labels this phenomenon as part of a broader process of 'enmeshment' of state and civil society, which arises partly from the tentacular structure of the Movement state, and notes that there is a tendency amongst development planners who come from outside to assume 'that the state and civil society are, or at least should be, distinct.' (2002:50)

Many of the functions ascribed to CSOs – particularly that of holding government accountable for its actions – rest on the idea that civil society has a separate identity from the state. The act of holding government accountable also relies on there being adequate political freedom for dissent and criticism of government. The assertion made by the Ministry of Finance in the Poverty Eradication Action Plan, that 'government cannot control the activities of NGOs,' contributes to the assumption that there is not only a separate identity for civil society actors, but that there exists adequate civil society autonomy for accountability to be exercised. The government's use of its NGO Registration Statute, however, suggests otherwise; as the co-ordinator of a national women's organisation commented, 'they often remind us of our registration, which requires us to be non-political, non-partisan, non-everything. So whenever there is a controversy, they tell us we are violating our statute' (Human Rights Watch 1999:8).

Similarly, the visions of civil society as 'addressing poverty', 'undertaking advocacy on behalf of disadvantaged groups,' and providing 'voice' for 'empowered citizens' obscure the political realities of the composition of CSOs, positioning them squarely as representatives of the less powerful. This belies the class identity of CSOs; at both centre and periphery, the leaders and staff of CSOs usually come from a contextually-defined elite. At local levels, elite status is closely related to educational profile, as well to the position of an individual in social and family networks. Similarly, those engaged in CSOs at the centre are also likely to be highly educated, and to be urban-based.

As the observations of the leader of Kampala-based women's CSO observes, elite identities have implications for representation:

Some of the men criticise us that our arguments are from elitist women, but we answer back that 'it is only elitist women who discuss with elitist men'... For example during our land advocacy campaign, we brought some women from the rural areas and they spoke for themselves. Some of them were breaking down in tears as they narrated their stories. But we were criticised for bringing in emotions and the Vice-President said that this was stage-managed.

An important, if underlying, component of elite politics, certainly at the centre, is ethnicity. Many of the leaders of CSOs who have successfully participated in the policy process are from Western Uganda, the ethno-geographic power base of the current regime.[4] As one research respondent observed, 'many of these persons may argue that they do not benefit from their ethnicity ... but the silence about ethnicity in Uganda does say a lot about the noise it makes in shaping the local political terrain.' Such considerations contest the assertion of a simple, representative relationship between 'civil society' and a constituency of unrepresented, unempowered citizens.

Challenging some of the broad assumptions that underpin publicly-stated perspectives on civil society participation thus reveals a disconnetion between rhetorical public statements and political realities. This is no surprise; the frequent use in policy of terms with multiple meanings allows room for competing interpretations to emerge (Brock et al, 2001:11). Examining in more detail the dissonance between policy narratives and their interpretation in practice by a range of differently positioned actors creates an opportunity to examine the prospects for an improved quality of civil society participation in the policy process.

Occupying the middle ground between government and external actors?

Central government to local government is a tug of war, with each protecting their own turf. Maybe civil society can be a middle ground – getting central and local government to declare their processes. Ugandan NGOs used to rely on their larger brothers the international NGOs, but if they are to do advocacy, then we want their considered opinion to provide horizontal accountability. They would be more independent advocates, beyond service delivery, if they had central government as their larger brother. (Interview with Government Official, Ministry of Decentralisation)

Much of the space opened up here [for civil society participation] has been opened because of what the donors say. How far would it have opened up if the donors didn't think it was the best way to do things? What happens if donors stop pressing the government of Uganda to take on participation? What is the likelihood that the government will continue creating the spaces necessary for NGOs to participate? (Interview with Ugandan NGO Director)

The extent to which civil society participation is both positioned between and 'manufactured'[5] by government and international development actors, is an important feature of invited spaces and the power dynamics that surround them. Such a positioning results in civil society actors being largely reactive, responsive to resources offered for a particular range of activities and functions. This in turn limits their capacity to develop autonomous agendas and raises questions about where their accountability lies. Simultaneously, however, it does create opportunities for participation which civil society actors can use to articulate their own agendas and pursue actions congruent with them.

The role of international development actors in opening spaces for civil society actors is unquestionable, and has undoubtedly had positive impacts in terms of a more diverse range of actors gaining access to some parts of the policy process. Interviews with a range of international development actors in Kampala show that all of them consider their principal development partner to be the government; this is well illustrated by a broad movement in the system of aid disbursement towards sector wide approaches and budget support (Lister and Nyamugasira, 2003). With such a governmental focus, their relationship with civil society organisations is often framed by the influence that CSOs might have on the state; almost all respondents mentioned that they use some resources to strengthen civil society in order to hold government accountable. Three extracts from interviews with staff of bilateral and multilateral agencies point to some of the constraints to civil society participation implied by this:

> Government has to do its job and the CSOs have also to control the government, both at the district and at the sub-county level. At the centre we have enough good CSOs.

> Donors spot NGOs and think they are very politically correct to support; and they drown them with project funds, but not with funds for recurrent costs – this leads to corruption scandals.

> We have tried to bring in effective and meaningful CSOs – before it was just the Farmers Union [...] The Plan for the Modernisation of Agriculture[6] is open to interpretation – one wants a good critique, but wants to make it constructive, without cramping the space of either the government or of civil society. (Interviews with staff of international development agencies, Kampala)

These views suggest that the boundaries of invited spaces for civil society participation are drawn partly by the opinions of external actors concerning what is 'good', 'constructive,' 'effective', 'meaningful' or 'politically correct'. While this has clearly strengthened some CSOs, it excludes others. At the centre there may be 'enough' CSOs, but the autonomy they require to 'control' the government is constrained by necessary compliance with external agendas. This results in an over-emphasis on the politics of consensus, as opposed to an acknowledgement of a range of interests which may challenge or conflict with these external agendas; this in turn reinforces the tendency, noted earlier, of the interlocking of government and non-governmental actors.

At district level and below, international development actors have less of a visible presence, and formally constituted CSOs are less numerous or vocal than they are at the centre. The response of one Chief Administrative Officer, asked about the role of NGOs in the policy process, is instructive about the relative power of different actors at the district level:

In principle, CSOs are vocal and speak out, they write papers which can then be discussed. Their views can somehow influence change – but here it is not very significant. The group which is significant is the donors. It is very influential because it has the money. We say it's not fair, because sometimes they don't conceptualise the real issues behind the problems. Sometimes the policies behind their money are very hurting.

Similar comments from a range of respondents in all three districts reiterate this point: it is access to resources which buys the influence necessary for participation in the policy process to have an impact. Donors, in many senses 'invisible' at the district level because of the current emphasis away from projects and towards budget support, in fact wield considerable power as policy actors at this level, sometimes to the detriment of the CSOs they profess to support.

These findings imply that the progression from 'strengthening civil society' to 'holding the government to account' contains several assumptions which do not necessarily stand up to rigorous inspection. The idea of a civil society with an autonomous identity and self-defined agendas at either central or district level is questionable, given the resilience of linkages with donors and the lack of alternative sources of funding. This is shown to some extent by the difficulty many CSO respondents described in occupying positions which oppose or criticise dominant narratives of poverty reduction. It is also shown by a lack of critical reflection within civil society, noted by some CSO actors themselves, about its own role and motives.

The lack of an autonomous identity is also, however, inextricably linked to government. While the direct interface between donors and CSOs is principally situated in Kampala, the multiple interfaces between CSOs and government stretch from Kampala to the most isolated rural village, thanks to the LC system. The mechanisms that link CSOs and government are far more diverse and complex than those that link them to international development actors, partly due to the interlinking noted above.

At the centre there is a greater separation of identity between government and civil society actors than at the lower levels. The principal visible mechanism of interaction between central government and CSOs in the policy process is invitation. Since the first revision of the Poverty Eradication Action Plan, government has increasingly issued invitations to civil society to take part in different stages of the policy process. As an interview at the NRM Secretariat testifies, by issuing such invitations, the government enhances its claims that the NRM provides a participatory and consultative political system for Ugandan citizens. When asked about poverty alleviation policy, an NRM respondent went to find a copy of the UPPAP report[7] and said 'Have you seen this? There were meetings at the sub-county, at the parish, giving views on how things ought to be done. The PMA is the same – it made wide consultations – even the very constitution itself. People come and they are encouraged to speak.'

While this phenomenon of invitation to CSOs is relatively new, it is already the dominant mechanism for their participation in the policy process at the centre, whether in a task force, a budget conference or a sector working group. Only one CSO respondent identified a process of civil society participation instigated from outside government, the case of the Land Act. One outcome of this invitation culture is a separation between the dynamics involved in getting a seat at the policy table, and those involved in acting on behalf of poor people once this seat has been taken. Getting a place at the table requires tactics of accommodation and amicability, while acting on behalf of poor people may require more adversarial approaches; it cannot be assumed that the former will lead automatically and seamlessly to the latter.

Many CSOs in Kampala seem to be at the level of actively pursuing the single goal of getting their people onto seats in meetings or committees; and reactively responding to any invitation issued to take part in any public forum which might afford profile to the organisation or the issue on which it works. These activities are pursued with apparently little analysis of the impact that they might have: an all-consuming fixation with what might be termed 'the politics of presence' rather than the politics of influence.[8] Some of those more experienced in advocacy use the 'politics of presence' consciously, as one strand of a broader strategy which embraces a range of approaches to representing issues of concern. Oxfam GB/ Uganda, for instance, pursues its lobbying work on internal displacement partly by bringing internally displaced people into the same room as decision-makers. A national NGO claims that if it ceased to seek and secure a presence at every table 'people would ask, "Where are the women?"', an indication that the 'politics of presence' tactic meets – but fails to challenge – strongly held expectations and understandings that representative democracy amounts to merely getting people of all kinds onto seats.

What are the implications of the invitation culture and the politics of presence? The research found that whether an invitation for civil society participation is delivered depends on the issue at stake. While government is currently inviting participation on many issues that are clearly framed as poverty reduction, other subject areas, some of which lie outside the frame, but have critical influence on the prospects for poverty reduction, do not produce the same invitations. With civil society actors so intensively engaged with government in poverty-framed debates, these issues – which include the impact of the current round of the WTO, and the negotiations surrounding the Poverty Reduction Strategy Credit (PRSC, see Glossary) and the Poverty Reduction Growth Facility (PRGF, see Glossary) – are therefore being subjected to much less public debate than is desirable. (Nyamugasira and Rowden, 2002)

Much of this section has discussed government and international development actors as dominant, 'intrusive' and 'dominating' in relation to civil society. While their power undoubtedly has a part in shaping the spaces in which policy is made, it is not the only influence. Civil society organisations themselves, while their agency may be limited as well as facilitated by other actors with greater access to financial and political resources, make their voices heard and exercise influence through their invited participation. It is to the challenges which arise in exercising opportunities for participation that we now turn.

Along a vertical slice: spatial dynamics of civil society participation

The diversity of CSO activities and identities means that CSOs can occupy a range of spaces in the policy process. The activities that take place in those spaces, and the nature of the spaces themselves, differ between the centre and the district.

At the centre, these activities are frequently labelled 'advocacy', and are often undertaken by one or two individuals, either acting to represent a single CSO with an interest in the policy issue being discussed, or to represent an issue-based CSO network. Members of these networks in turn represent wider constituencies. Some of these constituencies – those of international NGOs – lie in part outside Uganda, others are membership-based, and some have started at the centre and are trying to build decentralised structures at the district level to support their campaigning activities.

At the district level, the activities which take place when CSOs occupy spaces in the policy process are much more likely to be labelled as 'participation in decentralised planning'. Although some CSO actors did report experience of participating in formal political spaces such as the district council, most, if they engage directly with government processes in any capacity, are much more familiar with the arenas in which service delivery is planned and implemented. While the number of invited spaces for engagement in planning and implementation has increased, especially as the decentralised structures of the Poverty Action Fund (PAF) and the Plan for the Modernisation of Agriculture (PMA) have been rolled out, there is a sense of doubt amongst CSOs concerning the impact that their participation might have.

Given the range of spaces on offer for civil society participation in the policy process, it is important to understand what is necessary for the effective occupation of different kinds of space. The nature of spaces is dynamic, and is shaped by the expectations of those who occupy them about what participation consists of, and can or should achieve (Brock, Cornwall and Gaventa, 2001).

Some civil society actors at the centre see participation as a right; one commented that 'there are constitutional powers given to civil society to participate in governance, so civil society derives its power from the Constitution itself.' Making this right real takes the form both of invoking rights to create new spaces, and of enlarging or subverting existing ones. Another civil society actor commented that 'someone who creates it can say the space starts and ends here'. The opportunities for pushing the boundaries of or further enlarging an existing space depend in part on the power of those who initially created it, and in changing their expectations of what it exists for.

Many note that increased civil society participation has resulted in changing attitudes amongst government actors, which can be exploited to expand space. The opportunity presented to CSOs to participate more actively in setting the agenda for the 2001 Consultative Group meeting was cited as evidence of a change in expectations: 'increasingly, as well as asking CS to contribute to analyses of what is the problem, government is asking for contributions towards the solutions.' Another respondent cited the importance of the government's ownership of the UPPAP process in 'converting government people to civil society views'. In recognising this, both actors noted that they now felt empowered to take issue with government concerning the limits to current invited spaces for participation, in one case feeling able to challenge the Ministry of Finance concerning the timing and nature of the current PEAP revision, which had previously been driven by the timetables of the international financial institutions.

This process of challenging expectations and taking advantage of changing attitudes in order to widen invited spaces may, however, involve expressions of dissent which mean CSOs moving towards the margins of what is deemed legitimate behaviour. One respondent noted:

> ... when you push too far you get an oppressive response from state. This comes in various forms, some very personalised – the Permanent Secretary rings our Director and tells him to stop saying what he is saying. Relations between government and civil society are maybe only cordial because we aren't challenging government, we are being yes-people. We need the skills to know how to proceed when push comes to shove.

This account also alerts us to the importance of 'backstage' spaces in the politics of invited participation. It is in these spaces at all levels that decisions are made and political relationships are enacted. They shape what goes on in the invited spaces. In the case of the Plan for the Modernisation of Agriculture, which makes claims to have been elaborated in a consultative way, one international development actor noted that 'there is some resentment – CSOs were not at the PMA tea parties. The PMA was done and dusted before it was presented to a workshop.' The 'tea parties', exclusive gatherings of the more powerful and their allies, are in this case the spaces in the policy process where the basic decisions about policy direction and structure are made; and civil society actors in this case were not part of that conversation.

CSOs themselves use informal spaces as part of their activities, placing a premium on changing the attitudes of powerful individuals within their own arenas, and their allies. Ugandan Joint Council of Churches, for example, does a great deal of work around the parliamentary process, lobbying and alliance-building. A member of UJCC noted that its effectiveness in this regard is in part due to its being regarded as 'a very respectable CSO', and in part due to the skills and capabilities of the organisation. Others noted that it is essential to access these backstage spaces where possible, as it is often the only way to access the 'few people who are not accessible' on whom a 'final output' depends. These people seldom enter invited spaces for participation, sending junior staff in their place.

In the districts, the dynamics of effectively participating in invited spaces are very different from the strategies of occupying backstage spaces or taking advantage of shifting attitudes that are found at the centre. This is in large part because of the relative lack of formal invitation, and of the principal functions of CSOs at this level, which are social provision and mutual self-help. Many CSO respondents argued that it is far easier to influence what is in front of you than to undertake the more abstract work of creating broader changes to a 'policy' which is not always clearly articulated. Further, and perhaps most importantly, they pointed out that there is a need for CSOs to follow resources: being sub-contracted to provide services is a crucial source of income.

Engaging in service delivery, however, is much more than a default choice for some CSOs. Several respondents were keen to emphasise that their strength is to have a positive influence on development through good practice in service delivery. One respondent in Lira gave the example of a credit programme which was failing because of the inflexible terms of government management. When it was handed over to an NGO experienced in managing credit programmes, the repayment rate recovered, and the NGO was able to attract additional funding to expand the programme. The respondent saw this as an example of positive change to policy through the action of better practice in implementation.

Further, while several CSOs emphasised that service delivery for them was a positive opportunity, many saw it as a preferable option to engaging in the policy process, which was seen as both corrupt and corrupting. Beyond the fears of what would happen if engagement were to take place, there are also uncertainties derived from 'the habit of non-consultation', which have made CSOs feel sidelined from the policy process. Many are now unsure if they are actually invited to engage, and if so, under what terms and in which spaces. The comments of one CSO worker in Lira illustrate the thoughts of many: 'District council meetings are theoretically open to all comers, but CSOs don't even know that their attendance is invited ... If planning meetings take place and other people are sent invitation letters, how can you attend if you have not received a letter? This creates fear in us.'

The arena of civil society exists beyond NGOs engaged in service delivery. Looking past the district level to the dynamics of communkity based organisations (CBOs) pushes orthodox understandings of civil society to its limits, yet it is instructive to those who consider that poor people, as citizens, have a right to be represented in decisions that are made about their lives. Howell and Pearce note that 'donors have defined civil society as an arena of formal and modern associations, distinct not only from a venal, inefficient state but also from an amorphous array of informal and primordial associations.' (2001:17). The civil society organisations of Ugandan villages, however, are firmly rooted within this amorphous array, tending to be informal, unregistered and arising out of the existing social configurations of kinship and clan. If the challenge of 'representing the grassroots' in the policy process is to be met, learning from the spatial dynamics of this level becomes critical. As Howell concludes, excluding this domain from a discussion of 'civil society' overlooks the fact that 'family, tribe and clan-based associations might also be the locus of social and political change' (*ibid.*) While there is variance and flexibility in the way that different donors approach this domain of local civil society, the tendency to overlook it in favour of CSOs with formal and modern structures remains strong.

CBO formation is frequently linked to a local understanding of poverty – women's credit unions as a solution to income poverty, or digging groups as a response to loss of cattle through cattle raiding. A member of a village women's credit group, asked why the group had formed, replied 'Enough is enough – we can't go on depending on men, even reaching to the extent of having to ask them for money to buy salt and soap for home use. Women want to be able to sustain their families and themselves. We women have to take charge and without money we can't do that.' A sense of 'taking charge' of a situation which is normally beyond control is an important feature of the formation of many CBOs.

One district-based NGO staff member argued that most CBOs rely on their own collective efforts, discussing their own ideas and initiatives for development; it is on the basis of their collective initiative that others come in and support them. This is not, however, the whole story. External stimulus, often in the form of the provision of resources, is commonly a trigger to group formation, as well as a source of support after formation. One CBO in Bushenyi, headed by an educated woman resident in a town, was created specifically in response to an advertisement placed by the Ministry of Health, looking for CBOs to raise awareness about AIDS prevention. As the head of the CBO candidly stated, 'It was more for business reasons.'

Also in Bushenyi, a representative of the District Farmers' Association pointed out that they actively encourage the formation of 'interest groups' at the parish level – centred around the production of a particular crop – so that farmers can be directed towards a market for their harvest. Such externally-stimulated agriculture-based CBOs are proliferating as the Plan for the Modernisation of Agriculture is more fully implemented, creating Farmers' Fora (FF) at the sub-county level which decide three priorities for crop or livestock production systems which will receive agricultural extension services.[9]

Some CBOs are formed in response to a perceived promise of external resources and are subsequently disappointed. This was particularly common in Tororo, where a women's councillor commented, 'Some are from the district, some are from NGOs, some are from the centre – but they are all saying that groups should be formed. But groups have formed and they have got nothing from these people who told them to form groups.' This process had resulted in groups becoming demoralised, and was seen by some to represent a culture of dependency which severely reduced the potential for collective action.

While it is difficult to generalise, the most stable and effective CBOs encountered in the course of the study were those which were either the result of indigenous collective action, or based on a culturally-embedded institutional pattern which is adaptable to current circumstances. Perhaps the best example of the latter is the proliferation of neighbourhood digging groups in Lira District. These allow farming households to maximise their labour while they are forced to practise unmechanised agriculture because they have lost most of their cattle to cattle raiders. In this way, a traditional Lango[10] lineage-based institution has been adapted to a contemporary political reality – Karimojong[11] cattle raiding – in a direct attempt to prevent whole communities falling further into poverty and food insecurity. The contrast with the 'empty promise CBOs' of Tororo could not be greater.

Despite these differences between the form and function of CBOs, one thing that most of them hold in common is a feeling that they are disconnected from the activities of the lower local councils (LCs) and that 'poverty reduction' activities, of the kind which they actually practise but do not necessarily label as such, are disconnected from the services and programmes of government. As such, they exist in a space somewhat removed from the LC system, but are nonetheless embedded in local politics and society.[12]

Notably, however, no CBO we encountered was formed to allow ordinary people to pursue from government the entitlements which are their rights as citizens.[13] Early experience with the implementation of the PMA has meant that the local landscape of civil society has become more densely populated with hybrid institutions formed to create privatised, 'demand-driven' service delivery, mandated by central government policy. These could provide different mechanisms through which claims for entitlements could be made by the poor; or they could allow local elites to co-opt the resources for themselves.

Occupying newly-opened spaces on the basis that participation in decisions that affect one's life is a constitutional right requires changing expectations. At the lower levels, a fundamental shift in the understanding of citizenship would be required, to transform ordinary people into active, engaged participants in the policy process, rather than distanced and excluded clients of an inequitable system of resource distribution controlled by distant, powerful actors.

Challenges for representation and voice

As discussed earlier, the challenges for shaping policy processes where civil society participation moves beyond invitation and consultation and towards representative and accountable decision-making processes are played out in many arenas. In each, there are dilemmas for civil society actors, and trade-offs. How can civil society at the centre move from the politics of presence toward the politics of influence? How can accountable processes be achieved when government and civil society overlap? How can civil society actors widen the spaces for autonomy whilst remaining inextricably connected to international development actors and their agendas?

The challenge faced by the range of development actors in Uganda is to recognise not only the diversity contained within 'civil society', but to acknowledge that the spaces in which CSO participation is enacted frequently limit the possibilities for developing accountability. Designing and implementing policy according to external narratives about poverty reduction produces a profound disconnection between what is meant to happen and what does happen. Apthorpe suggests that part of the trick of policy discourse is to 'present what is intended and then to be done as unavoidably and unobjectionably necessary and correct' (1986:382). The orthodox framing of civil society actors, with the unobjectionable correctness suggested by civil society's central position in development discourse, needs to be critically questioned, on the grounds that many of its key assumptions do not reflect the lived realities of Ugandans.

Notes

1. Uganda's position as the 'golden child of the IFIs' is discussed in detail in Dicklitch (1198), while Himbara and Sultan (1995) characterise Uganda as an 'international Bantustan'. See also Chapter 2 for levels of aid dependency.
2. Of the four documents from which the quotations are drawn, only AAU's Country Strategy Paper continues with a disaggregation of 'civil society' into some of its constituent parts
3. This finding is resonant with Dicklitch (1998) who discovered many civil servants amongst the staff of NGOs in the mid-1990s.
4. Okuku (2002) argues that, despite the inclusive rhetoric of the Movement regime, Uganda is an ethnically-organised, one-party state
5. See Howell and Pearce (2002) on the role of the international development community in 'manufacturing' civil society
6. The Plan for the Modernisation of Agriculture is the GoU's plan to deliver on one of the four pillars of the PEAP. Amongst other things, it creates 'Farmers' Fora' as structures for farmers to decide their extension priorities.
7. The UPPAP report in question presents the findings of the first stage of a qualitative research exercise designed to elicit poor people's opinions and understandings of their experience of poverty
8. The term 'politics of presence' is taken from the work of Phillips (1995)
9. See Allen (2002) for a comprehensive discussion of early experiences with PMA implementation in Soroti and Kabale.
10. The majority ethnic group of Lira District
11. Pastoralists occupying north-eastern Uganda
12. See Annexe for the roles and responsibilities of different Local Councils.
13. Similarly, although some CSOs – notably the Uganda Debt Network – exist to facilitate the claiming of rights, they do not frame their own activities in terms of the rights and entitlements of citizenship.

6

Poverty Knowledge in central-level Policy Processes in Uganda: Politics, Voice and Legitimacy

Rosemary McGee

The knowledge essential for effective poverty reduction policy is in a state of flux in Uganda. As the poverty reduction policy process at central government level opens up to more numerous and diverse actors (see Chapters 3 and 5), a series of transformations are under way in the manner in which knowledge is generated and used, how, by whom, and to what effect. The image of donor agencies and national and international academia as the sole repository of knowledge for poverty policy is being superceded by a more pluralist model of academic, donor, NGO and public collaboration in knowledge production and ownership, and a growing tendency – at least at the level of rhetoric – for information to be used to exact accountability on policy goals as well as to inform policy choices from a technical perspective.

Shifting approaches to development co-operation, governance and public administration at national and international levels are driving these changes, reflected in shifts in demand for information about poverty. But at the same time as poverty reduction has become enshrined as the highest priority of the Ugandan government, knowledge about poverty has become a political commodity, both domestically and abroad. In this context, the prospects of poor people's needs and priorities being represented in the policy process in ways that make policy more responsive and accountable to them, are less straightforward than is implied by the discourses of inclusion and participation expounded by central government. Participation, like knowledge about poverty, is also a political commodity, and the spaces in which actors can participate should not be taken at face value. These spaces are in some cases offered, in other cases

113

claimed, and in many cases contested, or potentially contestable.

This chapter begins with a review of how the generation and use of knowledge in the poverty policy process in Uganda has evolved over the last decade. In doing so it discusses the actors in the knowledge landscape and the nature of their different contributions to the construction of knowledge, drawing on the discussion in Chapter 1 of different forms of knowledge and different ways of knowing. The 'opening-up' of the community of knowledge producers and users that appears to have happened in the late 1990s, holds a certain transformative potential, but although the actors, the roles they play, and the nature and use of the knowledge they bring to the policy process have become more diverse and complex, it appears that not all this potential has yet been realised. One barrier to further change is that the contestation and politicisation of knowledge in the Ugandan poverty policy process, both in the country and abroad, reflects too closely the interests of government and its close allies. The chapter considers the various implications of this and, in conclusion, looks at the prospects for improving the representation of poor people's needs and priorities in the Ugandan poverty policy process, pinpointing the challenges that this implies for pro-poor policy advocates.

The poverty knowledge landscape: contours and watersheds

This historical overview of the poverty knowledge landscape in Uganda draws on two sources: a review of the major publications on poverty over the past decade, and interviews with variously positioned policy actors and poverty reduction advocates conducted during our research. These include representatives of government, donor and creditor agencies, foreign technical assistance personnel who have worked for these agencies and members of civil society organisations.

The systematic production of information about poverty began in about 1993, when efforts to achieve economic stabilisation and macro-economic reform began to bear fruit and priorities shifted from these objectives towards a more explicit focus on poverty reduction. From 1993 to about 1996 the World Bank was clearly the dominant actor in terms of poverty-related knowledge, both producingauthoritative publications, and also funding the Uganda Bureau of Statistics (UBoS) and the Economic Policy Research Centre (EPRC) at Makerere University.

The two landmark publications of this era are the country study *Uganda: Growing Out of Poverty* (World Bank 1993) and the report *Uganda: The Challenge of Poverty Reduction with Growth* (World Bank 1995). Growing out of Poverty mirrors closely in its structure the World Bank's two-pronged strategy for poverty reduction, as set out in the World Development Report 1990 (World Bank 1990). A first section profiling poverty in Uganda is followed by a second which is split into 'Accelerating Economic Growth', 'Labor Market Policies for Poverty Reduction', 'Providing Key Services and Safety Nets', 'Institutional Framework Delivering Essential Services' and finally 'A Strategy for Reducing Poverty in Uganda', covering how to accelerate growth, how to deliver social services and how to establish safety nets for the most vulnerable. Thus the study clearly starts from the World Bank's (1990) universal poverty reduction policy prescription and fits the Ugandan case to it, rather than starting from reality on the ground in Uganda and devising policy prescriptions accordingly.

A look at the sources used in different chapters of the study gives an indication of what kinds of information on poverty were being produced by different actors at the time, and what priorities and associations were attached to each by the Bank. The first chapter, 'A Profile of Poverty', cites only quantitative data from UBoS surveys. The second, 'The Poor and Vulnerable', uses six examples, of which four derive from a specially conducted Rapid Poverty Appraisal, and cites NGO and academic sources. Chapter 3, on gender, uses mainly NGO and UN and, to a lesser extent, government and World Bank sources. Chapter 4, 'The Impact of Adjustment on Poverty' resorts to Government and IMF statistics. The lengthy section on NGOs in Chapter 8, 'The Institutional Framework for Delivering Essential Services', casts them entirely as service deliverers, and the remainder of the study cites few sources. An annexe shows children's depictions of poverty, gathered in the Rapid Appraisal. The capacity of NGOs and the public to contribute to knowledge for poverty policy is, then, seen as minimal and limited to the provision of illustrative examples of vulnerability and extreme poverty; 'real' knowledge in this study is that derived from household surveys and the international financial institutions' sophisticated analytical machinery.

This predominance of the international agency's poverty reduction narrative and ex ante application of a blueprint set of solutions to national reality changes somewhat by 1995, at least at the level of rhetoric. The 1995 report *The Challenge of Poverty Reduction with Growth* drew on consultation with NGOs. A technical adviser to the World Bank stresses that 'a deliberate effort [was made] to get NGOs around the table [...]', as a source of perspectives and knowledge, rather than constructing them only as welfare service deliverers; 'this was seen as very innovative and unprecedented' (*ibid*). The report self-avowedly focuses on taking stock of the economic reform programme and identifying the next generation of reforms needed; only the annexe looks at distributional questions, and then briefly. An apologetic paragraph on the economic nature of the analysis mentions a background report by Bevan and Ssewaya (1995) which furnishes a sociological dimension to poverty in Uganda. Despite being commissioned as a background paper, this seemed to have a negligible influence on poverty analysis in the Bank report.[1] Again, the central issue in the report is how Uganda can stay on track with the World Bank 1990 two-pronged strategy for poverty reduction.

A major problem in the poverty knowledge landscape at that time was the impossibility of comparing the only two survey data sets available (from Household Budget Survey 1989-90 and Integrated Household Survey 1992-3). These surveys used different ways of recording consumption as a proxy for income, and thus provided poverty headcount figures which could not be compared and which were inconclusive on the question of whether a greater or lower percentage of Ugandan households were living below the poverty line in 1992-3 than in 1989-90. Analysis of the incompatibility, funded by the UK's Overseas Development Administration (ODA)[2] showed that the apparent decrease in consumption over the period – interpreted as an increase in poverty – was spurious. This finding was welcomed by the World Bank, and the analysis undertaken has been fundamental in subsequent monitoring of consumption poverty trends, which now indicates a consistent decline in the national poverty headcount since 1992.

In the mid to late 1990s, then, the dominant producer of poverty knowledge was the World Bank, with UBoS and EPRC as its heavily subsidised clients. ODA followed behind it. Other sources tended to be eclipsed by these. In particular, NGOs and the public, and the sort of understandings of poverty that they promoted, were not yet considered valid contributions to knowledge for the poverty policy process. A poverty study led by the Ugandan NGO Community Development Resource Network (CDRN 1996), drawing on poor people's perspectives to construct a challenge to the rosy contemporary orthodoxy of falling poverty rates, suffered from a similarly low profile when published, although its authors were called upon to play central roles in the Uganda Participatory Poverty Assessment just a few years later.

The major demand for knowledge for poverty policy in the mid to late 1990s came from the very actors who supplied it. A technical assistance provider from that time notes that whereas initially the data used to be produced by and for the World Bank, 'to see what had happened to poverty and measure the performance of its own policies in Uganda', they are increasingly produced for the government. NGOs, despite producing small-scale studies, seem not to have been significant knowledge consumers. Actors at lower levels of government appear not to have been significant users of poverty knowledge either, perhaps due to their limited planning and budgeting competences at that time, low capacity, or the highly aggregated nature of most poverty knowledge produced, which made it scarcely relevant to them.

Some breaks with the past occurred in 1996. The World Bank, in producing its Country Assistance Strategy (CAS), went to some lengths to consult poor communities, including some outside Kampala, about their needs and priorities. The first Uganda Human Development Report was produced (UNDP 1996). While this was linked to the UNDP's global Human Development Report (HDR) initiative, it was conceived, according to a respondent in UNDP, as 'a corporate advocacy tool', intended to 'reactivate the national debate on human development' (UNDP 1996: vi). In contrast with the publications which had dominated up to then, the HDR contained sharp questions on the distribution of the benefits of growth. To present a knowledge publication as an advocacy tool was, in itself, a major new departure. Judging by how much they are cited and how widely known, the Uganda Human Development Reports[3] seem to have been less influential among government, donor, academic and technical assistance actors than the World Bank publications. They offered no new information, as they used the same data sets as the Bank and UBoS, but analysed them from different perspectives. Yet they filled important conceptual gaps by prioritising issues such as environmental sustainability, political empowerment and the redressing of regional imbalances, as facets of poverty reduction.

A further change occurred in 1997. DFID emerged as a major knowledge player by instigating and funding the Uganda Participatory Poverty Assessment Process (UPPAP). Like the Bank's CAS, this was an example of knowledge for poverty policy being constructed with the direct involvement of NGOs and the public. And like the UNDP's Human Development Report, it was explicitly intended to serve as an advocacy vehicle, around which, it was hoped, a more diverse and engaged poverty policy community would cohere.

UPPAP began in 1998 as a three-year programme funded by DFID and UNDP, with Government of Uganda contributions. It later received support from Sida and the World Bank and was extended for a further three years.[4] Its aims are to enhance knowledge about the nature and causes of poverty and to generate and apply strategies for poverty reduction; to enhance district government capacity to plan and implement poverty reduction strategies using participatory methods which would be applied in extensive fieldwork in poor communities; to develop systems for participatory and qualitative poverty monitoring; and to establish capacity for participatory policy research in Uganda (MoFPED 1997; Yates & Okello 2002). DFID played a major role in designing UPPAP and securing support for it. The researchers and trainers who carried it out were drawn mainly from Kampala NGOs and research centres. The Government of Uganda recognised that the kind of knowledge that could come from a participatory poverty assessment (PPA) would be a vital complement to the available macro-economic and sectoral data in explaining why Uganda's economic growth did not seem to be reaching the poorest (Yates & Okello 2002; MoFPED 2000). Thus, there was a predisposition among key government figures to adopt the different perspectives on poverty that a PPA might offer.[5]

As this attempt to diversify producers and users of knowledge got under way, UBoS continued to conduct household surveys annually,[6] with technical support from particularly the World Bank and DFID. From 1999 onwards, some interaction was established between them and the other forms of poverty-related knowledge that were emerging. This was at times positive, harmonious and mutually enriching, as appears to have been the case in the co-operation between UBoS and UPPAP over the second PPA, starting in 2001; and at times so full of conflict as to reveal in all its complexity the battlefield that is poverty knowledge. An example of a conflict situation is the conference on the Comprehensive Development Framework that took place in Uganda in November 1999, where UPPAP staff presented preliminary findings that suggested that poverty, as defined by poor people, was increasing, and the World Bank's technical adviser presented the then latest headcount figures which showed that consumption poverty was steadily decreasing. This apparent divergence prompted some prominent World Bank and Government figures to dismiss and undermine UPPAP findings.[7]

The poverty policy community: a promising cast

By the end of the 1990s, with UPPAP having delivered its findings and fed them into major policy statements such as the Poverty Eradication Action Plan,[8] Uganda stood out on the African continent for the diversity and crowdedness of its poverty knowledge landscape. UPPAP seemed to confirm the hypothesis that was to become a central plank of the Poverty Reduction Strategy framework emanating from the World Bank in Washington in late 1999: that broad-based participation of civil society actors in poverty policy processes, as well as generating a new kind of knowledge that was useable for policy purposes, also promises further-reaching transformative impacts which increase the effectiveness of poverty reduction policy. These potential impacts of opening up the poverty policy community are summed up in a study on the impact of participatory Poverty Reduction Strategy Paper processes in African countries:

> [...] civil society participation in Poverty Reduction Strategy Paper (PRSP) processes in all countries is leading to a broadening and diversification of the actors who engage in poverty discourse and the policy process. The traditional dominance of technocrats and their expert knowledge is being challenged and enhanced by a range of different kinds of poverty knowledge, including experiential knowledge. Increased interaction has led to changes in government officials' attitudes towards CSOs and their ability to contribute to policy processes. The galvanising effect of PRSP processes on civil society, and the measures taken to increase CSOs' capacity for advocacy, have been critical in enabling civil society to prove itself in these new arenas.
> The broadening of the poverty policy community is likely to enrich the substance of the discourse, but in itself, the opening up of the policy process to a wider range of interlocutors, including advocacy organisations, is a progressive outcome which suggests improvements in government responsiveness and in the chances that the concerns of the poor will be voiced and heard (McGee et al 2002: xiii).

At first glance, Uganda seems to have the conditions in place for the full potential of this opening-up process to be realised. Among today's diverse set of poverty policy actors, 'old' can be distinguished from 'new'. The 'old' ones are international creditor and donor agencies, the units of government nurtured by them, and expatriate technical assistance and a handful of Ugandan academics contracted by them. Historically, it is the data and influences of international creditor and donor agencies that have dominated: what we called in Chapter 1 'industrially produced knowledge' with associated constructed narratives and discourses. Which parts are these actors playing now, in this post-PRSP world in which they are supposed to take a back seat?[9] However much has been said about country ownership of policy reforms and the information associated with them, donor and creditor roles remain dominant, although relationships between them and the Ugandan government may have altered somewhat in quality. The World Bank, which until 1999-2000 was only providing funding to the UBoS household survey, has since become more involved in running it, in some respondents' opinion because this enables it to pursue its own research agenda. The Government's capacity to conduct poverty analysis, in the Poverty Monitoring and Analysis Unit of the MoFPED and in UBoS's own poverty monitoring unit, has greatly expanded, yet there are still few outside UBoS and expatriate technical assistance circles who have the capacity to use the poverty data produced.[10]

The 'new' actors, coming onto the scene in the late 1990s, are poor people, or more accurately, NGO personnel and non-governmental researchers who claim to represent them. Their positioning, while precluding them from producing knowledge on the scale and of the kind that the 'old' actors do, enables them to 'know' poverty in different ways from the donor and creditor agencies: through observation of poor people's experience and the use of participatory techniques to co-construct particular and authentic versions, rooted in discussions with poor people. There are thus several distinctive knowledge-related roles these 'new'actors could play: giving voice to their own or their poor constituents' perspectives; representing these constituents' experiences and priorities; bridging between local-level realities and national-level policy processes; and using these other forms of knowledge to contest the narratives of powerful actors and hold them accountable. How far do they perceive themselves as performing these functions, and to what extent does their performance match their self-perception? How can we explain any dissonance between these, and assess what potential is lost in that dissonance?

Many central-level CSOs claim to voice poor people's realities and interests, but do so largely within the parameters consolidated by UPPAP, which, as a partnership between CSOs, government and key donors, comes with certain inbuilt constraints. They cast themselves as representatives of poor people's realities and priorities, but few demonstrate their credibility or legitimacy as such. The majority do not constitute bridges between central and local levels, but operate at the central level and centripetally. Despite the strong and donor-inspired discourse of civil society as agents of accountability, few Kampala-based organisations are effectively playing this role, with the notable exception of the Uganda Debt Network. Civil society actors at the central level in Uganda currently appear to be reactive, simply taking up invitations to enter spaces – such as those offered by UPPAP – that government has created in the poverty knowledge landscape, and playing tame parts.

In summary, the transition which has taken place in Uganda's poverty knowledge landscape since the beginning of the 1990s has meant that particular poverty actors and the kinds of knowledge with which they are associated have risen and fallen over the decade. The World Bank moved from a position of virtual hegemony to being one among several knowledge producers and users, still very powerful in UBoS and other government institutions both financially and technically, but only a very minor funder of UPPAP. While still influential, it is now less visible. DFID, initially a relatively minor producer and user, saw both its visibility and influence increase when UPPAP took centre-stage, becoming the main funder and proponent of this new departure, and a vital advocate in getting the outputs of UPPAP 1 taken up in important national-level government policy processes in 2000-2001. Civil society organisations, having been minor and fairly unacknowledged producers and constructors of poverty-related knowledge previously, became involved in large numbers as researchers in the UPPAP initiative and thus strengthened their role as knowledge generators. Curiously, though, this involvement with UPPAP has not led them to become major users of its outputs, ideal though some of these are for poverty reduction advocacy purposes.

The cast is indeed diverse, and at first glance the full range of players look set to reap all the potential benefits of the opening up of Ugandan poverty policy processes. Yet a closer examination reveals constraints on the transformation process. The opening-up has only been partial so far, and has only happened at the central level. Moreover, the entry into the poverty policy process of more actors and of diversely constructed kinds of knowledge does not mean that all are regarded as carrying equal weight or enjoying equal legitimacy; nor does it mean that all entrants use the opportunity to the same extent. In particular, although these changing constellations of actors seem to have favoured civil society organisations by affording them more space in the process, CSOs remain a relatively weak set of actors in terms of their contribution and application of knowledge.

Poverty knowledge: hard figures, politics and legitimacy

This section explores the assertion that knowledge for poverty policy processes in Uganda is a political commodity and looks at some of the implications. It relates these to the observation arising from our research that, although civil society actors remain a relative weak set of actors in the knowledge arena, few of them are working strategically to become more effective in their approach to knowledge or to take its political dimensions and potential into account.

The most obvious political dimension of knowledge for poverty policy is that the government has staked so much on poverty reduction that it feels it may virtually stand or fall according to the size of the poverty headcount. In the words of one respondent, 'Everyone knows that 35% figure' – and none so well as government. The Ugandan government now 'listens' to a broad range of poverty-related knowledge,[11] but it is over the poverty headcount that it feels itself to be held accountable at election time. Used thus, the poverty headcount functions as both a legitimising mechanism for the government, which can claim to be achieving a key aim of its own and of the Ugandan people; and confers on the poverty headcount the legitimacy that comes from frequent citation as a 'headline' item in official documents and pronouncements and in the media. On the other hand, the people-centred, bottom-up understandings generated by 'new' actors in UPPAP field research have certainly proved important in earning the government credibility both internationally, where Uganda has been in the vanguard of the promotion of participation later associated with Poverty Reduction Strategies (PRSs) and domestically, where 'listening to the poor' offers government benefits of a populist political nature.

Our research suggests that three factors determine the degree of mainstream legitimacy attached to particular kinds of knowledge for poverty policy. One factor is the methods selected to generate it, ostensibly a technical and epistemological issue, but also a political one. It is no longer true that in Uganda only statistical or quantitative information, gathered by the UBoS using questionnaire surveys, is considered a valid basis for policy. Knowledge derived at the micro level using qualitative methods and co-constructed by researchers with ordinary people in participatory processes is now viewed as more legitimate than it was, although not always as useful as generalisable information obtained from random samples. But some of the NGOs involved in UPPAP assert that the government's apparent conversion to qualitative and PPA data is only partial, needing a great deal of reinforcement if it is to be sustained (see Chapter 3); and that the conversion, such as it is, can be attributed as much to the populist political benefits offered by UPPAP's participatory, grassroots approach as to any commitment to democratising knowledge for and transforming the poverty policy process.

A second factor is the political acceptability of the policy messages to which particular knowledge, and particular interpretations, give rise – an issue which is at heart of mainstream legitimacy. The nature and political acceptability of the policy implications emerging from PPA and qualitative research seem critical in determining which of these are taken up in policy debate and which are left unpublicised and unheeded. UPPAP findings seem to have been treated selectively. Some of the findings that were given considerable weight patently posed no political problems and offered easy political gains – for example, the finding that water provision was not given adequate policy attention, which resulted in the much-acclaimed increase in government spending in its effort to provide clean water for everyone.

Other UPPAP findings were more problematic. Potentially embarrassing and controversial findings on bad governance and corruption are said to have been swept together under the broad heading of 'Governance' and discussed only at the most general level, so that they never caused government the embarrassment they threatened. Similarly, views expressed by the rural poor consulted in PPA research amount to a resounding plea for the restoration of state agricultural marketing boards and price controls. These voices did not lead to the serious consideration of this as a policy option, presumably because they were obviously in conflict with the ideology of liberalisation and deregulation of agricultural markets that dominates contemporary national and international thinking and practice and is pioneered by key creditors and development partners of the Ugandan government. In this case, an item of knowledge, arising empirically from the Ugandan grassroots, appears to be accorded less validity in decision-making circles than the dominant orthodoxy coming from outside the country.

Evidence of socio-economic disparities between districts, regions or ethnic or other social groups can be politically acceptable, politically taboo or politically manipulable. In the case of the UNDP's Human Development Report, 'Parliamentarians [...] are always reading the statistics [in the HDR] that concern their district. That is a very important thing, because they go on to ask questions that concern their districts. [These data] are also used by different donors.' Despite this observation, UNDP feels that the HDR, as the only alternative source of disaggregated data available, is not used as much or as well at district level as it could be. Although regional disaggregation of poverty data is now technically feasible, data is rarely analysed and presented so as to demonstrate statistically the levels of marginalisation and resource deprivation of certain districts and social groups in northern Uganda. Conversely, the Buganda Cultural and Development Foundation (BUGADEV) takes issue with official poverty statistics which reveal that the Buganda kingdom is relatively well-off compared to the rest of the country, and has considered launching an advocacy campaign based on its own information to disprove this and reorient central government resource allocation away from more sparsely populated areas in the north towards the Buganda kingdom.[12] Gender-disaggregated poverty data, and other kinds of information which look at poverty from a gendered perspective, are also a great deal less prominent than current levels of data availability and technical competence suggest that they could be. This has contributed to the persistent difficulties encountered by women's organisations advocating for gender equality in the provisions of the Land Act in 1995-1998 (Goetz and Jenkins 1999).

The political acceptability of messages from civil society advocates can critically affect the advocates' standing in the poverty policy community. For example, over the years, the Uganda Debt Network has experienced a major turnaround in its relationship with government. In the mid-1990s it was regarded as a nuisance, a small but vocal lobbying organisation placed far outside government and using information from the international Jubilee 2000 movement to campaign for debt relief alongside other poor, highly-indebted countries. Its positions and accusations were frequently dismissed as ill-founded. In 1999 UDN submitted unsolicited but systematic comments to government on the draft version of the Poverty Status Report which assessed progress against PEAP targets. These comments, drawing on alternative information sources, offered a perspective on the findings of the Report that the Government considered enriching. The subsequent Poverty Status Report, produced in 2001, draws on far wider-ranging information sources than the earlier one, including UDN. In the meantime, UDN has become such a respected actor in government circles that it sits on the MoFPED's Poverty Action Fund (PAF, see Glossary) monitoring committee. It brings to that central government policy table the quarterly outputs of a civil society PAF monitoring network which it co-ordinates and which operates in parallel to the government monitoring system.[13] Significantly, the transformation in the UDN-government relationship happened at a moment when governments were being heavily encouraged by the IFIs to engage constructively with civil society; and the government's attitude shift revolved around its recognition that the information UDN was providing could be utilised to Uganda's advantage in its attempts to secure debt relief in its negotiations with creditors.[14]

A third factor determining the legitimacy of poverty knowledge is the identity of its source. Who commissions or conducts research, who originates or 'sponsors' a particular kind of information output or knowledge construction process, has implications for its legitimacy and acceptability. An official research institution such as the Economic Policy Research Centre is seen as virtually beyond question, at least when its contributions to revising the PEAP essentially endorsed government's preferred macroeconomic strategy. What would have happened had it contested this is a question that can only be pondered on, in the absence of any examples of EPRC fundamentally challenging the government line, and in the light of what happened to politically unfashionable findings of UPPAP.

A significant indicator of the overall recent changes in attitude towards the boundaries of mainstream poverty knowledge is the recourse to the poor at the grassroots as a source of legitimate perspectives on poverty. International donors such as the EU and DFID have given currency to the belief that civil society organisations with close contacts to the grassroots can bring in these perspectives and thus help to shape appropriate and effective policies. It was this tendency, coming through international channels, that gave rise to UPPAP and which, partly as a consequence of UPPAP and its high profile, has been strengthened and spread widely in Uganda. The change in treatment of poor people's voices is most obvious when one compares how much the first and the second versions of the PEAP reflect grassroots perspectives. The 1997 version drew on very limited consultations, held largely with intermediary organisations in Kampala, whereas the 2001 version draws heavily on UPPAP, in which extensive field research was conducted in thirty-six poor communities throughout the country; and on a series of public consultation workshops in all four regions, in which draft versions were critiqued and discussed by participants. More recently, the World Bank, main funder of the Northern Uganda Social Action Fund, based the programme's design on extensive micro-level consultations in the north, in which they found that 'the poor know their priorities very well'.

However, even among those who value grassroots participatory research, a common belief is that what the poor say they want is not necessarily what they should actually get. Traditional 'expert' intervention is viewed as necessary to translate their expressed wishes, emerging through Participatory Rural Appraisal-type exercises, into policy-friendly, trustworthy outputs. Knowledge which originates at the grassroots and is gathered or co-constructed by NGOs has often been treated as invalid, irrelevant or not even worth finding out, even when it holds the key to policy failures. When the Uganda Women's Network (UWONET) produced a qualitative study on the effect of structural adjustment on women (UWONET 1995) its legitimacy was undermined by heavy critiques from the World Bank on methodological grounds. More recent qualitative research conducted in the context of the Structural Adjustment Participatory Review Initiative (SAPRI), in which the Bank participated as a partner alongside civil society organisations, generated similar findings about the negative impacts of structural adjustment on the poor. The SAPRI findings and their messages from the grassroots about the failures of previous adjustment instruments were not summarily dismissed, but neither were they incorporated by the IFIs in the design of the Poverty Reduction Support Credit and the Poverty Reduction Growth Facility (Nyamugasira and Rowden 2002).

Despite the diversification of the poverty policy community, then, there appear to be some continuities in terms of whose knowledge counts. In the examples cited above, the gatekeepers of orthodox poverty knowledge appear to be the World Bank – still – and the government, whose embracing of alternative perspectives seems, in fact, to be functional to political interests and the imperative of maintaining good relationships with key creditors and donors. The legitimacy of knowledge constructed or advanced by civil society actors remains weak. It appears paradoxical that UPPAP's outputs, originating in part from civil society organisations, have enjoyed (selectively) high profile and legitimacy; but this can perhaps be explained in terms of the opportunities they offered for government to gain domestic political capital, by the strong role played by DFID and UNDP as funders and by the Bank as a legitimator of research processes incorporating 'the voices of the poor' (Narayan et al 2000).

What is perhaps more paradoxical is that UPPAP has not been strategically used by most of the civil society actors involved in it, either in terms of application of its findings, or in terms of maximising or sustaining the advocacy opportunities their involvement in the process afforded them. Why, in the aftermath of UPPAP, are so few civil society actors – still relatively weak actors in the poverty knowledge landscape – trying systematically to develop a more political, power-conscious and effective approach to poverty knowledge? Are they not conscious of the power that attaches to knowledge? Do they feel under-equipped or afraid of exposing their relative lack of expertise in knowledge construction and management? Do they feel that the one who pays the piper – the donors – should call the tune? Are they shying away from a challenging undertaking, preferring to take the line that the 'old' experts know best? Do they see this landscape, and UPPAP as one part of it, as all belonging to someone else altogether, with only small plots made available for them? Do they simply doubt, given the existence of both indications and counter-indications from UPPAP, whether it is evidence that leads to policy change, rather than other factors altogether?

If knowledge for the poverty reduction policy process is a political commodity, then the abilities to generate, use and own it become important and contested areas. This may partly explain both civil society actors' reluctance to acknowledge limitations to their capacities and to seek to enhance them; and the rigidity of criteria for legitimacy, by which civil society's capacities rank consistently low. It does not explain, though, the apparent reticence of CSOs in taking due ownership of the information arising from UPPAP. Does this suggest that in civil society there persists a fundamental but unstated unease about being in partnership with government? Does it indicate that 'poverty reduction', rather than being an indigenous discourse, is an external narrative that does not easily fit what most Ugandan CSOs do but gets taken up by them in the course of their funding relationships, and handled uneasily? Is it explained by the dependent, nurtured, cowed position that civil society has traditionally held vis-à-vis government (see Chapter 3)?

As a political commodity, knowledge can be used to redress power imbalances, both between those engaged with each other in the poverty reduction policy process, and, on a wider scale and in a less immediate sense, beyond the policy process: between poorer and less poor Ugandans. As we have seen, it can also be used to political ends which are nothing to do with redressing power imbalances but more about maintaining them – at the most literal and obvious level, to help keep the Movement in power.

As knowledge relating to poverty has gained political currency, so has participation in policy processes (see Chapter 3). Civil society actors could capitalise more on their identification as the new poverty policy actors, seizing the initiative by developing a more power-informed, strategic approach to poverty knowledge. The first step would be to recognise the valuable political currency they command as poverty policy actors and the presumed guardians of the 'holy grail' of participation. The window of opportunity to do this is fast closing, however, now that government has assumed such strong and widely-acclaimed ownership of the terrain.

Attaining knowledge-ability: the challenges facing civil society poverty reduction advocates

What can be concluded about the prospects of poor people's needs and priorities becoming more adequately represented in the policy process? If civil society actors developed a more politically astute and strategic role in constructing and using knowledge for the poverty policy process, this could ensure that they got more space at the table of poverty reduction policy-making.

That in itself would not ensure better representation of poor people's needs, or a more responsive, accountable policy process. It could contribute to this objective, however, if civil society actors used this space better. They could, for instance assume coherent and responsible positions on advancing the legitimacy of certain kinds of knowledge; they could guarantee their suitability as representatives of the poor and their validity as their advocates; they could manoeuvre into additional spaces in the poverty policy process which are currently less crowded and contested and where they might be considered to hold a comparative advantage vis-à-vis other actors. Our research suggests that they need to use their existing space at the policy table to assert and demonstrate the usefulness and validity of different kinds of knowledge including those which, although considered weakly legitimate by some, reflect the poors' realities in ways which could enrich policy process and content. At the same time, they need to look over their own shoulders to see who is 'lining up behind them',[15] questioning their own legitimacy as the 'new poverty experts' and representatives, and addressing weaknesses in this regard. Perhaps most strategic of all, civil society actors could focus on those spaces at the lower levels of the policy process where knowledge is constructed and applied, where government's grip and capacity is less pervasive than at the centre and where NGOs, church and community organisations have some entry-points and allies not available to government actors.

It would be facile to suggest, however, that any amount of strategic manouevring by civil society would alter the balance of power in knowledge for the poverty policy process. Donor and creditor agencies have tended to foist upon civil society the role of exacting accountability from government. Current calls for this, and stated commitments to building civil society capacity in this regard, are undermined by the apolitical analysis – among donors and civil society alike – which tend to underpin them. Donors could genuinely enhance the scope for this by themselves developing a more political analysis of the policy process, and of knowledge as one powerful force field within it. This would enable them to contribute to civil society's efforts to build a more strategic approach, including enhancing its capacity so that it can enter the political arena of poverty knowledge with greater confidence and legitimacy and use the spaces available there to better represent, or facilitate the direct presentation of the needs and priorities of the poor. It might also push donors onto ground hitherto seen as too political, such as backing their civil society partners against their government partners in cases where the latter wields its power to cow civil society into acquiescence or passivity.[16]

The evolution of the poverty knowledge landscape in Uganda in the past decade has generated a situation in which government prides itself on listening to diverse forms of knowledge for poverty policy. It has done this to its own electoral advantage, and gaining electoral advantage might well be taken as an indication of political responsiveness. This chapter has argued, though, that there are subtle yet vital differences between political responsiveness and policy responsiveness that, in the case of Ugandan poverty reduction policy at least, need to be laid bare. The next hurdle is for government, encouraged by a reinvigorated and regrouped civil society and its donor allies, to move from listening to being held accountable on the basis of diverse knowledges, prioritising reasons other than its own electoral advantage.

Notes

1. Despite the scarcity of non-economistic analyses of poverty in Uganda at the time, Bevan and Ssewaya (1995) did not become a much-cited source in its own right either.

2. Now the Department for International Development, DFID.

3. Further Uganda Human Development Reports were produced in 1997, 1998, 2000 and 2003.

4. It has since been extended for a further two years.

5. For further details of UPPAP see the website www.uppap.or.ug; MoFPED 2000 or Yates & Okello 2002. For more on PPAs in general, see Norton et al 2001.

6. With the exception of 1997-8 when no funding was available, they have been annual since the early 90s.

7. See McGee (2000) and McGee (2003); Collier (2000).

8. And, from 2000 onwards, into the developing Plan for the Modernisation of Agriculture.

9. The 1999 World Bank policy document that set out the PRSP framework and its implications for the Bank, outlining the rationale behind the PRSP approach, asserts that: '[...] donors now emphasise the importance of having governments in the driver's seat for increasing the impact of development assistance in general' (WorldBank 1999: 21).

10. A continued strong donor and creditor involvement in producing and using poverty knowledge does, of course, have its positive side. Strong

government commitment to the diversification of poverty knowledge, in the form of its backing of UPPAP, would not have occurred or sustained itself without this continued donor and creditor role, and offers many opportunities – some unexploited to date – for innovations in the production and democratisation of poverty knowledge.

11. A Movement spokesperson interviewed elaborated on his position that 'policy should originate from the bottom' with the claim that in processes of formulating local development plans, the national PEAP and the national Plan for the Modernisation of Agriculture, 'people come and they are encouraged to speak'.

12. There has been much mention in recent years of 'equalisation grants' as the means by which government would correct regional imbalances in poverty and wellbeing, but little information on how significant these grants are: in fact they are worth less than 1 per cent of total funds going to all districts, so will make little difference in any case.

13. For further details on the PAF Monitoring Committees in Bushenyi and Lira, see Brock et al. (2003)

14. These events pre-dated HIPC II, the debt relief initiative launched in late 1999 under which Uganda qualified, in any case, for relief on production of a satisfactory PRSP.

15. Borrowing from the metaphor common in Ugandan parlance which refers to 'who is lining up behind' leaders. The metaphor itself draws on the traditional system of voting in Uganda, in which the electorate stood in rows behind their chosen candidate to be counted.

16. Chapter 3 mentions the closure of *The Monitor* daily newspaper for publishing false information which the government considered could give support to anti-government elements, 'giving comfort to the enemy'.

7

Context, Rules, Participation and Exclusion: Spatial Dynamics at the District Level and below

Karen Brock

This chapter examines some of the policy spaces encountered during the course of the research at the district level and below in Uganda. It reflects on their origins and their boundaries, and the impact these have on the agency of different actors in the policy process. What opportunities do different kinds of spaces offer for the elaboration of policy which responds to poor people's needs and priorities? What constraints exist on the representation of the needs of those living in poverty? What can be learned from the dynamics of existing spaces that can help construct better ones, in which the rights of poor people can be articulated, and influence exerted on the decision-making processes about resource allocation and the structure and delivery of services which are embedded in the policy process at the district level and below?

The source of many of these questions can be found in the narratives of poverty reduction policy that emerge from central government, which suggest that successful implementation of poverty reduction policy depends on the decentralisation of many processes of resource allocation and service delivery. Such a narrative rests on the logic that the spaces of lower levels of government lie in arenas within reach of citizens; and that citizens, through the Movement system of government, may be expected to feel some ownership of the spaces of local government. In this context, therefore, spaces have both geographical and political meanings.

Lessons from processes of decentralisation in other countries suggest that the relationship between poverty reduction and decentralisation is, however, far from the straightforward one presented by these simplified narratives. Crook and Sverrison (2001) argue that the impact of poverty reduction policy depends not only on an ideological commitment to pro-poor policies by central government, but on central government's willingness to engage in local politics by challenging local elites to ensure the implementation of such policies. Robinson (1998) suggests that the institutional design of decentralisation must be mirrored by conscious political intervention 'from below' if the participation of poor and excluded citizens is to succeed. Both these positions, and a range of others (Blair 2000, Gaventa 2001) suggest that the success of poverty reduction policy depends far more heavily on local political dynamics than is apparent from a reading of Ugandan central government poverty reduction policies. Further, the suggestions of contestation, conscious political interventions and challenges to local elites implied by these positions urge us to look beyond bland, inclusive language towards the politics of dissent and challenges to dominant orthodoxies.

The concept of space provides a useful lens through which to view the everyday politics and practices of actors who are engaged in the policy process, and to examine how their agency is enabled and constrained. As noted in other chapters, there are marked differences between the centre and the peripheries of theMovement government. While mandated processes for bottom-up planning are formulated by government in Kampala, their implementation requires these new processes to be accommodated in the configuration of existing spaces at the lower levels. As Cornwall notes, 'New ways in old spaces can transform their possibilities, just as old ways in new spaces can perpetuate the status quo. Asking whether the processes or institutions created to enhance participation challenge or reproduce existing structures and meanings is thus critically important.' (2002:7)

Asking questions about the new and old ways of the policy process involves an examination of the micropolitics of space at different levels of meaning. Who created this space, when, and why? Who speaks and who does not? What are the existing assumptions and meanings that create and constrain the participation of different actors? The spaces in which poverty reduction policies are implemented at the lower levels of government are those which are closest to where Ugandan citizens actually live, and it has been argued that here their voices stand the greatest chance of being heard. It is necessary, however, to ask whether the positive aspects of geographical proximity and physical reach are mirrored by the boundaries and political dynamics of spaces. Identifying what supports and enables participation in spaces at the lower levels of decentralised governance is a key step in solving the puzzle of responsive and accountable policy.

This chapter examines these issues from two perspectives. First, it asks 'What governs spaces?' Drawing on lessons from all three districts where the research was carried out, it identifies some broad issues which govern spaces in the policy process at the district level and below, and some of the new methods which may be necessary to make real the participation of poor people and their representatives.

Secondly, it looks in closer detail at the dynamics of three spaces in Lira District – one firmly anchored within the legally established processes of district governance, one of an 'invited' space, a district planning event, and one an example of a 'claimed' space, where a small group of actors has created a space in which to hold government officials accountable.

What governs spaces?

Conceptualising the policy process as a series of interlinked, overlapping spaces in which a range of actors engage in order to influence and shape policy outcomes not only allows us to see policy as complex and political, but provides us with a lens through which to view dynamic power relations between actors as they are played out in practice. Asking 'What governs spaces?' allows both an observation of the factors which enable or constrain the agency of particular actors, and an understanding of the way that policy spaces are anchored in the wider systems of rules and norms which govern all relationships between different social actors. As Jones notes, spaces are not just neutral backdrops to social activities, but are an 'active and interactive context in which social relations and structures are produced and transformed over time.' (2002:36)

Every discrete policy space is governed by a series of implicit and explicit rules and norms which create boundaries around the different actors, and delineate processes and behaviours of public decision-making. All policy spaces, however, are also governed by broader social codes and practices which emerge from the adjacent and overlapping social spaces in which the policy process is embedded, and are thus also part of networks of spaces which are connected. Different levels of analysis are necessary to examine discrete spaces and networks of spaces, but they have some features in common. As Mahmud suggests, 'forms of inequality that reflect social relations in the "private"sphere of family, kin and community are reproduced in the "public" sphere and constrain what people are capable of doing to influence public action.'(2002:6) This suggests that while it is important to look at the rules, norms and practices of formalised, discrete spaces and networks of spaces, it is also important to consider the broader social dynamics of the 'everyday' spaces which exist alongside, overlap with, and 'push in on' policy spaces (Jones, 2000). This, as Cornwall argues, is particularly important if we are to examine the ways that policy spaces are 'occupied, negotiated, subverted and mediated'. (2002b:7).

Language and the rules of the game

Some of the spaces which make up the poverty reduction policy process are located firmly within a formal domain of governmental decision-making, part of the machinery of constitutionally-mandated structures of governance; examples of these include councils and committee meetings. Within these spaces, particularly at Local Council V[1] level, but also to some extent at Local Council III, respondents repeatedly noted that the question of language is a critical determinant of participation. When proceedings are conducted in English, as they often are at LCV level, many of those attending, particularly women, are excluded. While this problem is widely recognised,[2] and some district councils conduct bi-lingual proceedings, findings from Lira suggest that the more powerful have an interest in maintaining the status quo of spoken English. One female district councillor narrated her view of the process by which the Council adopted English-only proceedings:

When the issue of language came up, a decision had already been made outside the Council. When the issue was tabled the speaker gave very few people the opportunity to speak. Thereafter he made a ruling. Yet the majority of the people were not in support of the motion, they knew Apac District Council uses both Luo and English. This decision has blocked so many people from participating. It is not only women who are quiet, some men are equally quiet.

The rules governing the space represented by Lira District Council meetings are, in this example, shaped by a dominant minority in order to silence a disempowered majority. We also observed such exclusionary practices at lower levels in Bushenyi where, during focus groups conducted for the research, if a powerful individual wanted to dominate a group discussion, he or she would switch to English, with the effect of silencing the opinions of the rest of the group. Several respondents expressed the opinion that the government's Universal Primary Education programme would one day help to resolve the broad issue of exclusion-by-language, but none suggested shorter term solutions.

Alongside the language in which a meeting is conducted, adherence to the established 'rules of the game' shapes participation in certain spaces. An example is the making and application of agendas, which often provide opportunities for political machinations. While the established rules of agenda-setting might lend a sense of equality, because they apply equally to all participants, they are actually used in different ways by different actors. Equally, norms about expected behaviour constrain certain actors and enable others. A sub-county veterinary technician gave an example of the way that the type of space represented by council meetings is shaped:

> In the council meetings we [technical staff] sit apart and do not talk. It is only the councillors who do the talking; we only participate if there is something that relates to our sector and they need clarification about it. Me, at times I forget and I sit with them, and then they tell you that you have sat in the wrong place and you have to move.[3]

It is not just physical space that is subject to such rules. A district councillor from Lira summed up the opinions of a range of respondents when she outlined the socio-political space in which the agenda of council meetings is arrived at:

> The business committee that comprises the secretaries and chairpersons of the different committees prepares the agenda. Other members are free to add on the list. But this depends on the Speaker; at times if he does not support an issue or he has been lobbied prior to the meeting then the issue will be frustrated. So before you present an issue for discussion you should lobby.

It is crucial to note that even the relatively small range of actors included in this process do not have equal agency. The process of lobbying is far from equitable, and many kinds of people are excluded because of gender, or ethnicity, or their lack of connections to the networks of the powerful.

A similar process of agenda-setting was outlined at the sub-county level in Bushenyi, with the additional difficulty that, because of lack of funds, the committees themselves do not sit as often as they should, giving relatively more power to the LCIII executives, which sit more frequently. A sub-county councillor in Tororo District details an agenda-setting process which, like the one outlined for the Lira District Council, is dominated by a single powerful individual – here the LCIII Chairman – who controls the agenda, but also in this case acts specifically to exclude certain opinions and inputs:

> The Chairman prepares the agenda for the meetings. [...] Those issues that he does not want, do not appear. For instance, for me I go to the villages and collect information and take it to the LCIII meetings but it is never utilised and so nothing comes out of it.

Whilst some formal behavioural norms, like agenda-setting, exclude certain actors and information, some have developed as a response to the exclusion of a particular kind of actor. This seems particularly true of technical staff. One district technician from Bushenyi observed that:

The Chair is biased against some of the things the technicians want to bring up so doesn't let us talk. So there you have to bring up the issue with a councillor beforehand; the councillor then brings it up and you can be called on to talk about it.

This is an example of a mechanism which has developed in response to a perceived exclusion of one actor by another: by calling on a third actor, the excluded actor regains the opportunity for participation.

What these examples about the process and procedures of legislated policy spaces suggest is that the status quo favours more powerful actors, who are usually able-bodied men, well-versed in the arts of lobbying, and often of a dominant ethnic group. While few respondents were directly reflecting on whether such spaces contain the opportunity for making pro-poor policy, their remarks suggest that considerable structural obstacles exist to incorporating the views of groups who are socially and politically marginalised in the discussions that take place in the meetings which are so important in deciding policy priorities and resource allocations.

Gender Relations

An overwhelmingly uniform finding of our research concerns the gendered nature of public arenas. In particular, in all three districts, at all levels, women talked about the ways in which they are excluded from those spaces traditionally associated with policy and policy-making.

There was widespread agreement amongst respondents that women do not participate fully in policy spaces, either in terms of numbers, or in terms of the quality of their participation. One female district councillor in Bushenyi pointed out that education of girls is high on her agenda partly because of this problem: there are simply not enough women 'able to do the work'. One village woman in Lira, who had been trying to follow up an apparent misuse of funds, said 'You know, education also helps; if you try to tell them, they just say to you "I know more". I am also younger, so I fear.'

While in some cases the 'ability to do the work' of engaging in a policy space is concerned with educational levels or age, it is also often the work in which women engage outside the public spaces of governance which excludes them. This exclusion is sometimes very site-specific: in Tororo, on the Kenyan border, cross-border smuggling is a livelihood strategy predominantly taken up by women, and both the illegality and the time-consuming nature of the work prevent them from engaging in processes connected to the formal, legal world of government. In Bushenyi, meanwhile, one women's councillor observed that in her culture, the workload of women is such that it is difficult to find time to become a councillor, and that if one has a family, which most women active in politics do, 'it is very prohibitive'. She did observe, however, that husbands used to be an obstacle in this regard, but that this is beginning to change.

This note of optimism from Bushenyi was unique in the study. In a range of other comments, particularly from Lira, it is possible to see how cultural norms of household relations and the role of women pervade the public spaces where women try to participate. In particular, one educated, articulate male opinion leader in a Lira village, when asked why so few women had attended a public meeting to decide village priorities, cited 'laziness, and lack of commitment'. Two male church leaders in a Lira village, when asked a similar question about parish meetings, also pointed out how lazy women are, adding 'They do not come because they feel they will not be paid for coming.' When asked why they might feel this, one of the men replied, 'Because they like money.' A male community development officer in Tororo held the opinion that 'women always feel that they should be under men and so they are always submissive and they do not urge for their rights.' It is no surprise, given the common nature of narratives such as these, that – in the words of a village woman from Lira – 'most women fear talking among men.' As Mahmud (2002) observes, the low value placed on women by society impinges on women's belief that they can act as citizens.

Such an apparent lack of participation in the formal policy process, however, must not be confused with a general lack of social participation. Women are certainly very active in poverty reduction activities in the social arenas which overlap and underpin formal policy spaces. This highlights the fact that their lack of participation in the formal spaces is due to the structure of those spaces, and the dominant narratives of gender relations which they mirror rather than to any 'laziness and lack of commitment'.

Social context

What, then, of the dynamics of participation in the spaces of the private sphere, of family, kin and community? How do these dynamics affect what goes on in the policy process? While these private domains remained outside the scope of this research, there is much evidence to suggest that the way policy spaces are governed is directly related to what goes on in private. This includes overwhelming evidence of the continued importance of kinship, patronage and ethnicity in local politics.

One example of the private spaces which underpin and overlap the policy process was frequently discussed by research respondents: the bars and drinking places of villages and towns. A village elder from Lira District observed:

> There are a lot of ethnic issues – if you don't drink and you aren't of the dominant ethnic group, you don't get elected. More decisions get made at the drinking group, not in the formal place, and election results are decided before the elections even happen. There is a lot of ethnicity – that is why they never elect people who are knowledgeable. There is no space to vote the right people.

The drinking group as a place where relatively powerful local actors meet and make decisions was frequently mentioned in Lira and Tororo; here, different actors argue and make points which they would be unlikely to make in a formal space. One notable example of this emerged when two researchers interviewed a respondent at a drinking place one evening. During an interview earlier in the day, the respondent had been praising the pro-poor, egalitarian nature of UPE; in the bar, he was heard to ask 'Why bother with these UPE schools? Let poor people send their children to these schools; we can send ours to academies in Kampala.'

While these drinking places are nominally 'public', their doors are closed to some, and they are a significant site for networking and politics. Although it is almost impossible in research like this to comment on exactly how what goes on in these semi-private, informal spaces might affect what goes on in the formal, public spaces traditionally associated with policy, it is clear that the two cannot be disconnected in the search for entry points for representatives of poor people to spaces where they can act effectively.

Legislation, invitation, and claiming: establishing spatial boundaries

The way that a space comes into being, and therefore who feels ownership of it, is of central importance both in shaping what goes on within it, and in determining the degree of influence it might have on the overall policy process. In this section three types of space are discussed: legislated, invited and claimed. Participant observation of an example of each type of space allows us to reflect on the dynamic relationships between the actors within them.

We turn first to a district production committee meeting, an example of a legislated space within the formal, governmental policy process, set firmly within the boundaries of what is conventionally identified as the policy process, in which bureaucrats, technical staff and elected politicians meet in an effort to oversee the planning and implementation of policy. While a binary narrative is formally applied to these actors, whereby formulation is framed as the job of elected politicians, with support from professional bureaucrats, while implementation is the job of 'technicians', our example shows their actual relationship as far more complex and contested.

District Production Committee meeting
Extract from researchers' notes

Six district councillors are present at the meeting, of whom three are women, as well as five male Technical Staff, including the Head of Production, and a male representative of the Private Sector Development Centre.

Chair of Meeting (Councillor): This is a long and tedious process and we have been briefed about the difficulties.

The Head of Production is invited to give a presentation. He says that year's budget is going to be more representative of the needs of the sub-counties than previous ones. There has been a planning workshop bringing together farmers, technocrats and NGOs – and the workplans have come from the grassroots.

The department was told some months ago that budget planning should start in order to be ready for today, but the budget ceiling was not released until late last week, and only yesterday further instructions were received. He suggests that, because of the late changes to the budget ceilings, the nitty-gritty of money looks as if it is going to defeat this committee.

Head of Production Department: If you look at the Actuals you will see that our budget is a paper tiger. We don't carry out activities because we can't be funded. We haven't been able to access the money. Yesterday we were told that some money had arrived – but now we have five weeks to consume the money of two whole quarters.

Chair of Meeting (Councillor): The government is commanding us to be bottom-up from the SC, and that the budget has to be 'bottom-up'. But how can we reconcile budgets with the lack of activities? Why have you been unable to access the funds?

The Head of Production replies that the requirement is that implementers have to submit a report of activities, account for funds, and submit a workplan for the next quarter. The Production Department submitted, but the district did not. Other departments didn't do it, so the district didn't meet the necessary requirements.

Chair of Meeting: You have done your best to defend our department. Will the money come later? Or will it disappear?

Head of Production: You do not want to be confident. There is a likelihood of not getting it released at all. Other departments have not spent – this is why we are crying. Other departments get a bigger ceiling, and they have not spent.

Secretary: There is a need for us to be very firm in defending our budget, because we have used all the money. Let us be firm to defend it! It is upon us!

Head of Production: Even if you defend, we are already beaten. Last year, we were accused of politicising the budget by saying it was too small; this year, we do not need to be ready to defend, because we are not on the offensive [...] In this district, one person sits in a room and decides budget ceilings. And if you question it, they say you are politicising the budget. [...] The Technical Planning Committee sat yesterday for the first time this financial year. They made it very clear that the Production Committee is fond of politicising budgets, and we were warned against doing it again. We will follow the chain of command, but the people who will miss out most are the people in the rural communities.

Technician: The burden rests with the politicians to sort this out. It is imperative that you sort it out. This meeting itself is very absurd: you allocate yourself money that you can't use. It needs to be discussed by the Executive Committee. Our Secretary, our Minister, you are here.

Secretary: I have taken note of the issues about access to funds. I hope I will take it to the next meeting and cause changes for the better.

The first key point to emerge from this extract is the extent to which, in this legislated space, the different actors present have explicit identities, attached firmly to an anticipated course of action. According to the technicians, it is the burden of the politicians to sort the problem out; according to the Chair of the meeting, it is central government who are 'commanding' a particular way of doing things.

There is a strong sense of idealised roles which are discordant with practice, and of the constraints placed on actions which are seen as being roles ascribed from outside.

Second, while difficult issues are discussed at length, and passionate proclamations made about the need to defend the department, nothing was actually done to try and solve the issues arising during the meeting, apart from a very generalised resolution from the secretary, who throughout the course of the meeting had taken no notes of the detail of the discussion. This is highly resonant with other research on policy spaces in different contexts (eg. Coelho 2002). [4] Such examples indicate invisible power at play: each of the key actors in the extract has internalised a version of the policy process in which they have no effective agency outside the boundaries of a particular space, and thus the discussions within that space are rendered ineffective.

Moving to examine an 'invited' space, a sub-county planning meeting, we see similar constraints on the agency of actors to affect a wider process, together with a far greater gulf between the invited and the inviter.

**Sub-County Planning Meeting,
Extract from researchers' notes**

The planning meeting was in its third day out of four – and was at the stage where district staff were presenting 'situation analysis' of different sectors to the gathered Local Council I, II and III representatives, as well as technical staff, and CSOs.

One of the facilitators spoke to us briefly when we arrived. He described the function of the meetings as to tell the sub-county representatives what government policies are, so that they can 'correct' their sub-county plans according to these guidelines. As we were walking over to the meeting, the Vice Chair of LCIII – a woman – tells me that formerly, policy was made by central government, but that sub-counties are now having to learn how to make policy, and are trying as hard as they can to catch up.

We entered the meeting –about 120 people of whom perhaps 10 were women – sitting in classroom-like rows facing a raised platform on which several officials – all men – were seated. The person in charge of the meeting was keen to emphasise that this was a 'bottom-up policy planning process' in action – later he referred to it several times as a 'participatory planning process'.

We observed presentations of situation analyses of two sectors – water/sanitation and health – which were 'factual' presentations of the status of these sectors in the county – which were to lead to small-group discussions of 'why things are as they are'. For both presentations, the relevant technician stood on the platform and addressed the audience, writing key points on flip-charts in writing so small it could not have been seen from the second row back.

The water/sanitation presentation was virtually inaudible from the front, and was completely in English. The presenter observed that 'there is a part the community is supposed to play' – in terms of contributing labour and materials, which he described as 'mobilised community participation'. Government policies, he continued, are now supposed to be firstly privatised, and secondly, demand-driven. He observed 'the community has to express their demands by making some contribution.'

At the end of this presentation, questions were invited and one man stood up to inquire (almost inaudibly) about the status of two boreholes in his sub-county which were in disrepair – what can the government do about this? He was very abruptly asked, 'have you made any contribution? do you really want this water?' – to which he was unable to reply, and sat down again. At this point, someone attempted a second question and was completely ignored.

The person in charge of the meeting summarised 'the main purpose of us being here is to own these problems. After owning it, you ask yourself why. Maybe you don't have the capacity

> [...] how do we share the responsibilities? who should do it? how do you get that person to do it? Exposing ourselves arouses our answers.'

Perhaps the critical point emerging from this extract is the range of interpretations of the term 'bottom-up planning'. Clearly the planning and technical staff, who have invited the other participants because central government has mandated a particular form of planning, retain a strong control over what is open for discussion, what the meeting might achieve, and the meaning of the key words they are using. The way the physical space of the meeting was set up as a classroom reinforced the dynamics of control. The suppression of questioning from the audience is a further illustration of the respective power of participants. 'Bottom-up planning' is thus concerned with the existence of the space itself, and the composition of the invited audience; but it has very little to do with the opportunity which that audience has to influence the proceedings, or the process by which participation is achieved.

A second important point is the way in which the space – even though it is constructed as participatory – becomes a stage for a particular development narrative: that of 'demand-driven' service delivery where participation is in the form of communities providing labour and resources for development activities, rather than in the form of communities making decisions about resource allocation priorities. Thus the invited space of the bottom-up planning meeting becomes an opportunity for the more powerful to rehearse a dominant way of doing things, legitimised by their identity of expertise and superior knowledge.

The question of knowledge, and access to information about the proceedings of the policy process, is central to issues of accountability. It is an important dimension of our third example, which looks at a space claimed by a young man who chairs a parish youth council. He called a community meeting in an attempt to hold sub-county officials to account for their distribution of remittances from the collection of graduated tax.

'Meeting on the 25%', extract from researchers' notes

The meeting had been called because irregularities have been observed in the way that the 25% of Graduated Tax remitted from LCIII to villages was being spent. The Chair of the Parish Youth Council had convened the meeting by sending letters to a range of people asking them to attend to discuss the matter.

We were seated on chairs under the tree, slightly to one side of a central cluster of men, also on chairs. These were some staff of the district who had been invited by the convenor. Two women were next, on a mat, and opposite, on a large log, were another group of men. The men on chairs quickly went into a protracted huddle about how the meeting should be run.

It became clear that the sub-county staff were trying to persuade the meeting convenor that the issue of the 25% could not be discussed because the money was still at sub-county level. They regretted that they had not taken the opportunity to meet beforehand to make sure that they had documentary evidence for their position. The accounts book was not there.

Throughout this process, people had gradually been arriving and it slowly became clear that we are waiting for the Parish Chief – the person who is to be held accountable. During the conversation the Accounts Clerk, though in the inner circle, has sat slightly to one side, clutching a book on how to run parish meetings. At this point he interjects at length about the correct way to conduct a planning process. He seems to be telling them that they are in trouble because they have not followed the right process. Eventually, the meeting begins.

Audience member (male): I have heard what you tell me, my leaders, but we feel we should come and knock at your door – we are not happy about the use of funds. In my place, the construction of the school is not happening.

He goes on to ask the Parish Development Committee Chair and the LCII Chair if they are competent to manage these funds.

LCII Chair responds, that the 25% was divided up between the four schools, and given out – then they realised that the money was being used by individuals, not committees, which is against the law. He claims the mistakes were corrected.

The older woman sitting on the mat requests to speak and is ignored.

A long discussion ensues about exactly how the money is being 'eaten' by different contractors, officials, and elected representatives.

Audience member (male): It is bad to mismanage public funds. It is better that you give us the money and we drink it. It is useless. You are saying that the one responsible is not here. The other day we made bricks for the school, but the rain spoiled the wall because there is no roof. We made all the effort to fulfil our role. We will come again. And we are not happy.

Dates for rescheduling the meeting are discussed.

Audience member (male): You will dodge us! You will not come! You leaders – you call on us to leave our homes and problems, but when we come, you are not here – nothing comes out. Assure us that you will try and give reminders. Help by passing information to all the people expected to come.

None of the 'leaders' replies.

Despite the origins of this space – created through an attempt by an elected representative to hold a bureaucrat accountable – it is notable that those who have been called to the meeting to be held to account are those who end up controlling the agenda and the process. They also make various attempts to shift the 'blame' of what has gone wrong onto those who have called the meeting, without ever answering the accusations made against them.

Perhaps what is most notable in this example is the degree of powerlessness of those who are seeking accountability in this space.

While the very existence of the space is an achievement, within it participants are able to do very little, lacking either the knowledge or the influence to claim their rights as citizens. It is almost as if the effort of convening and attending the meeting has used all their influence; but it is also clear that there is little experience of which questions to ask, or of how to transform the dynamics of power and powerlessness.

Spatial reform for pro-poor governance?

This chapter has begun to describe the dense and complex patterns by which spaces in the policy process are governed. Crucially, while the internal governance of spaces is influential in shaping who participates and how, interfaces with other spaces are just as important. How can this understanding be used to create pro-poor, accountable, responsive policies, and by whom?

One answer is to look towards a more explicit acknowledgement that these dynamics matter, and that some of the rules and norms of policy spaces could be changed through a critical awareness of their dynamics. This, however, is micro-political work which would imply institutional learning and change within and outside government on a massive scale, and engagements, perhaps involving conflict, at the interface of the private and the public. It may also be interpreted as threatening to the extant political status quo. In spite of the showcasing of Uganda as a model for the resolution of political and ethnic conflicts, to appear to threaten the status quo remains dangerous to some degree, and in unpredictable ways.

Another potential route to change would be to focus on developing a culture of accountability, in which citizens would see the possibility of bringing powerful figures to account. While some CSOs have invested significant resources in, for example, anti-corruption campaigning, it is essential that some of this work be carried out at the peripheries of the state, as well as at the centre. A challenge here might be how to best locate this work in spaces that are separate from the state, how to work with actors located in "sites of resistance", those spaces that people fashion for themselves, those in which they come together in forms of collective action.' (Cornwall,

2002b:26). Particularly in Uganda, with an omnipresent and decentralised state, and a history of the state absorbing such sites of resistance (see Chapter 3), growing a culture of accountability from the bottom up is a huge challenge.

Looking across the range of spaces suggests some starting points and directions in the search for responsive and accountable policy. For those advocating for pro-poor change, there are choices involved about whether and how to occupy particular spaces; between entering a space and acting in it or about choosing not to enter a space at all. The challenge is how to make such decisions informed by issues of representation and accountability, rather than solely issues of survival, budgets and politics. Further, the challenge is one of how to evaluate and analyse different spaces, and one's own role as an actor within them.

As noted in the discussion of the dynamics of the production committee meeting, there seem to be few opportunities to use the spaces on offer to create solutions, rather than to carry out a ritualised series of exchanges between a narrow range of actors. Coelho (2002) notes that what identifies spaces in a deliberative or participatory democracy is that they are solution-driven, rather than driven by formalised debates between actors with frequently-rehearsed, entrenched positions. While the language of deliberative processes, increasingly used in the North to describe spaces constructed with the aim of making government more responsive and legitimate (Bloomfield et al 2001), may seem out of place in a state like Uganda, it is one way of describing what might be required if responsive or representative policy processes are to have a chance of emerging; and a way of launching discussion and analysis of whether such requirements are feasible.

What the examples in this chapter suggest is that despite definite differences in the ways that spaces come into being, one common theme is the extent to which different actors adhere to their prescribed roles. The less powerful internalise their position, severely restricting their power to act; and the more powerful internalise theirs, thus ensuring the perpetuation of their relatively influential positions.

Occupying a position of dissent in the political culture of

contemporary Uganda, where non-conformism has a high cost, inevitably means that attempts to reform spaces will be slow and incremental, and would need to involve coalitions of more and less powerful actors in critical reflection about the way that they work. Ensuring that adequate spaces exist, distinct from the omnipresent structures of the state, may well be key to nurturing arenas where the rules of the game are subverted, and where marginalised and excluded people can acquire some of the skills and understandings they will need in order to effectively influence the way that policy processes are currently managed and controlled.

The challenges this raises are not only the identification of the existing spaces at the margins of the political system where exclusion and lack of accountability are currently being questioned, but to provide effective support to strengthen them.

Notes

1. LCV is the district level of decentralised governent, while LCIII is located at the sub-county. See Annexe for an explanation of the different levels of decentralised government in Uganda, and their responsibilities.
2. See Ahikire et al, 2002 and Goetz 2002 for discussions of language and other mechanisms by which women are excluded from political participation. See also p.82 for relevance of language to donor participants.
3. Technical staff are civil servants and do not participate in the deliberations of the council because they are not elected. Their role is to provide information and advise the council and to implement the decisions and policies of the council.
4. Coelho's research on Municipal Health Councils in Brazil notes that 'councillors are always denouncing problems, but don't find ways to organise themselves in order to advance solutions to them.' (Coelho 2002:11)

8

At the Confluence of Two Streams: Poverty Reduction Policy at the Federal Level in Nigeria

Karen Brock and John Gaventa

The Federal Government of Nigeria encompasses a variety of actors, each bringing its own agendas, interests and narratives to the policy process. The presidency itself, presidential advisors, the legislature and executive, a range of committees, the national planning commission, sectoral ministries, political parties: all have a role to play in shaping poverty reduction policy. They represent the political and bureaucratic mechanisms at the centre of a divided and conflict-ridden Federation, and many of them have structures which extend to the individual states and below. International donor and creditor agencies increasingly play an important role, often relying on a logic and approach different from that found within the state. Some civil society actors have an increasingly prominent role in many policy processes, although as we shall see, their direct engagement with a policy agenda specifically constructed around poverty reduction remains very limited.

In this chapter we examine this range of actors, asking what part they play in the current unfolding processes of poverty reduction policy. In dealing with a political arena as complex as the Nigerian state, we cannot hope in a short chapter, based on fieldwork at one moment in time, to give more than a snapshot into the poverty policy process. In so doing, we focus on two distinct streams of federal poverty reduction polices and their confluence. On one hand the National Poverty Eradication Programme (NAPEP, see Glossary) has emerged from the federal government's process of 'institutional streamlining' as the umbrella institution for poverty reduction initiatives. NAPEP is overseeing the implementation of a series of job creation and skills strengthening initiatives, via a tentacular national structure which stretches from the federal centre to local government monitoring committees at the LGA[1] level. On the other hand the

Poverty Reduction Strategy Paper (PRSP, see Glossary) process, initiated by the World Bank and taken on by the federal government, is engaged in an attempt to produce a national poverty reduction strategy which embraces a range of stakeholders in formulation and implementation.

Building on the information about Uganda and Nigeria in Chapter 2, we turn first to locating the issue of poverty policy in the current political context. We point to the conflicting domestic and international pressures which the federal government faces and which have given rise to the two distinct streams of poverty reduction policy. We look in following sections at how these streams have emerged historically, and how history continues in the current confluence of politics that surround the National Poverty Eradication Programme and PRSP.

Setting the policy context: poverty and the contemporary Nigerian state

Poverty and poverty reduction are themes that have preoccupied the Nigerian political discourse since at least the beginning of the 1970s. The discourse on poverty is highly contested, and deeply entwined with a wide range of issues that are frequently framed as poverty-related. These include the hotly debated question of federal resource control and allocation, which is in turn linked to issues of ethnic division and regionalism; the growing gap between the rich and the poor, linked again to the astonishingly skewed distribution of oil wealth; and expectations that the emergence of democracy will translate to a tangible 'democracy dividend'.

Just before Obasanjo's election in 1999, one newspaper article (Punch, 10th February 1999) observed that 'by the time civilians mount the rostrum on May 29th, if they do, it will surely dawn on Nigerians that if we must be ruled then we must be poor. Unless the progressive, radical politicians seize power, we may end up in the den of those who share the philosophy of impoverishment as a strategy for political domination ... Poverty, being dynamite, has its own latent potency ...'

As illustrated by the strength of the rhetoric, Obasanjo, and through him the federal government, are under huge pressure to deliver on the poverty issue. At the same time, they face enormous obstacles. The legacy of the military regime which ruled Nigeria for more than thirty of its forty post-independence years has entrenched authoritarianism, and left little historical experience of democratic policy processes (Agozino and Idem 2001). On the other hand, years of military rule did much to benefit a politically entrenched and wealthy elite, who are likely to resist significant economic change. Corruption is rampant, further undermining perceptions that the government would be able to deliver real benefits to the poor. Cutting across all of these pressures, the growth of ethnic and regional conflict has increasingly led observers to raise again the historical question for Nigeria: can it indeed be thought of as a nation? (Abah and Okwori, 2002)

For many observers of the newly emerging democratic state, the issue of poverty underlies many of the other tensions in the federation. To quickly put in place an effective poverty alleviation programme has been seen as a necessary and critical step for upholding the new democracy. As one scholar put it, 'the government is torn between the pressures for the restructuring of the federation and the fear of disintegration, between the need to fight corruption, on one hand, and the need to maintain political loyalists through patronage for its own political survival on the other hand, between the need to resuscitate the economy and consolidate democracy, and the intensification of economic and social pressures that threaten the state itself' (Durotoye 2000:26).

As if these internal pressures were not enough, the Obasanjo government also faced large external pressures to address the poverty agenda. Because of its oil wealth, at one level Nigeria does not have the same economic dependence on donor funds and international financial institutions as Uganda. At the same time, in its search for the legitimacy provided by the economic seal of approval necessary to attract outside investment and in order to play the role Obasanjo wants to play as a regional political power-broker, it has been critical to obtain support from international institutions. The mainstream discourses of these institutions mandate that governments must demonstrate commitment to poverty reduction, improved governance and wider economic reforms. Reflecting a recurring theme, for instance, the Executive Board of the IMF in January 2003 again expressed its worries about worsening poverty in Nigeria, and argued for a series of changes in macroeconomic fiscal policies, while also noting that addressing issues of good governance, transparency and corruption 'would be crucial for strengthening both domestic ownership and investor confidence' (This Day, January 7, 2003).

While perhaps giving the Obasanjo government a lever for change, such external donor pressure for reform could also be seen as a two-edged sword. Within Nigerian political history and discourse, poverty policies are often seen as imposed from outside, and reflecting the imbalances and injustices of the international economic system. Virulent critiques of Structural Adjustment and the IMF were prominent features of the political discourse of the early 1980s, often conducted in the language of class politics and struggle. An article entitled 'The Way Out of Poverty in Nigeria' (Nigerian Tribune, 20th April 1981) is a good illustration of this: 'The advanced nations often use their economic and diplomatic power to force us to frame our national policies in a way that will favour them, even if it is to the detriment of our nation.' Similarly, an article in the same paper a year later observed that 'the poverty condition has made a group of "privileged" people the errand boys of the multinationals' (Nigerian Tribune, 14th April 1982). Opposition to the IFIs remains, and a discourse concerning their 'evil' and 'wicked' activities persists in the popular press, exemplified by a comment by the leader of the Jubilee 2000 Africa Initiative who observed that 'the IMF are now hell-bent on squeezing the last drop of blood out of a new democratic government' (cited by Woodroffe and Ellis-Jones, 2000). [2]

Durotoye argues that these competing domestic and international pressures to deliver on the poverty agenda, and the political complexities that surround them, lead the Nigerian state to be at a 'critical juncture'. He contends that despite the new democratic openings:

> by and large, the nature of the Nigerian state ... remains essentially the same, perhaps at varying degrees. What this means is that efforts at taking the country out of the critical juncture will continue

to be constrained by a lot of extraneous factors both internal and external to the Nigerian state. To be sure, the conflict of interests between the government and the external actors, and between Obasanjo's desire to resuscitate the country and at the same time to maintain his own political survival, and the interests of a power bloc within the ruling class which is to resist change and make the government affairs to be business as usual will have great implications and eventually lead to a confusion of agendas which will exacerbate the critical juncture (26).

As we shall argue in the remainder of this chapter, perhaps nowhere are these competing pressures and resulting confusion of agendas seen as clearly as in the recent efforts of the Nigerian state to develop and implement a coherent set of poverty reduction policies. On the one hand, NAPEP seeks to respond to domestic political pressures and social unrest, while at the same time remaining captive to the historical legacy of the very state it wishes to change. On the other hand, there are the politics surrounding the early stages of the PRSP. The PRSP is attempting to create a more consultative, evidence-based approach to policy but is an externally driven donor-initiated policy process which is also meant to be 'owned' by the problematic state it is meant to influence. Through further exploring the dynamics of these two initiatives, we can see how their competing sets of actors, with different interests and narratives concerning poverty, interact to produce not a single national poverty policy but a confused confluence of initiatives and debates that appear from below to be largely disconnected from the realities of the people living in poverty.

The historical context of poverty policy: the story of two streams

Continuities in the domestic stream: the state in action

Despite an overwhelming façade of reform in poverty reduction policies after the return to civilian rule, underlying the rhetoric are institutional and individual continuities which anchor current policy processes in past ones. Nigerian political history is littered with a series of high-profile, discrete poverty reduction programmes. While each emerged under a different political administration, they show many common features. While some of these commonalities are structural – a tendency towards large programmes of capital investment and direct material gains for 'beneficiaries' – there are also personnel continuities, with particular individual actors and their close networks moving through the poverty reduction programmes of successive regimes.

Poverty reduction programmes in this tradition have frequently been publicly criticised as failures, providing several clear examples of the crisis of state ownership noted by Osaghae (2001). Operation Feed the Nation, a programme of Obasanjo's 1976 military regime, was deemed to have failed because of implementation difficulties, and because it was 'largely superficial ...diversionary... and did not in any way address the structural contradictions and deformities of the Nigerian social formation, particularly the question of ownership and control of the Nigerian economy' (Ihonvbere and Shaw 1998). Similarly, the 1997 Family Economic Advancement Programme (FEAP) of the Abacha regime, which focused on micro-credit, was perceived as a notoriously corrupt entity, said by one respondent to be 'based on the attitude that "we tell you what you need"'. Another commented that 'no one sees things like the FEAP as poverty alleviation, they see it as their way of getting their own share. It becomes part of the booty.'

Traditional policy programmes such these were embedded in the 'command and control,' top-down style of military governance, and the bureaucracies associated with them. Although bureaucracies are a central part of any policy process, bureaucrats are seen as having particular importance in the context of Nigeria's dynamic and unpredicatable history of regime change. During the Gowon regime (1966-75), 'Super Permanent Secretaries' were said to be running the country because of military ignorance of politics and planning. Firmly located in this heritage, bureaucratic culture in Nigeria remains rigidly hierarchical, and an environment in which 'inferiors'are never able to challenge 'superiors'. One respondent noted that 'if you tell a big man what he doesn't want to hear, he'll find someone else to tell him what he does want to hear.'

Within such a political culture, poverty reduction policy has historically been seen to be driven by political expediency, not on the basis of evidence-based policy research or deliberation. Academic researchers voice strong disillusionment that policy is not built on analysis, but exclusively on political interests. While policy and political interests are inevitably connected, in the context of the Nigerian state, political interests are frequently personalised and tied to patronage.

The weak relationship between research and policy can be illustrated by the institutional heritage of 'advisers', powerful individual policy actors whose expertise is frequently unrelated to their advisory field, and whose motivations are often highly political, particularly with reference to resource distribution along ethnic and geopolitical lines. The historical and contemporary characteristics of such advisers, whose influence began to be felt during the military regimes of the 1960s but which continues to date, is indicative of a policy process which includes the purchase of political support through patronage, using federal poverty reduction resources, rather than through demonstrated outcomes.

In addition to problems with implementation, the structure of poverty reduction programmes created important templates for the relationship between citizens and states. Osaghae (2001) notes the phenomenon of 'the state as Father Christmas', deliverer of material gifts at no cost. There is also the powerful phenomenon of 'First Ladyism' illustrated by the Better Life Programme, an intiative of First Lady Mariam Babangida, and by many others at both the federal and state levels. Such initiatives are a particular form of a far broader cultural tradition of wealthy individuals with political position giving patronage within a frame of altruism and charity; these efforts are seen as being closely linked to elite political networks and political parties.

Such historical perceptions and experiences become deeply embedded in political culture, in several ways that are relevant to poverty reduction policy. Firstly, they frame the 'beneficiary' of the state's largesse as a bystander, rather than as full participant in a development process, with rights and control. This fundamentally undermines the ability of ordinary people to claim the entitlements of citizenship over the entitlements of patronage. Secondly, they frame the ways in which current debates about poverty reduction policies and programmes are popularly understood, in the context of mistrust by citizens of the state.

These emergent themes are important in understanding how poverty reduction policies are perceived in contemporary Nigeria, particularly since they represent a traditional approach to poverty reduction that has been replicated by the policies of the current regime through the NAPEP.

Contemporary donor agendas

This historical understanding arising from domestic experience with 'poverty reduction'stands in sharp contrast to the interpretation of poverty reduction policy introduced by the contemporary donor agenda. Sometimes intertwining with, sometimes apart from the domestic poverty programmes, the emphasis by donor agencies and international financial institutions here – as in other countries – has been on the need for evidence-based poverty policy, informed by consultation with a range of stakeholders.

It is impossible, of course, to put all donor strategies and interventions for poverty reduction into one basket. There are important differences among the international financial institutions, as well as among a number of bilateral and multilateral donor agencies that have increasingly emphasised poverty reduction in the post-military regimes.[3] At the same time, for almost all there is a consensus that the primary agenda, poverty reduction, is linked to issues of governance – transparency, accountability, and administrative reform.

One of the key entry points for several international agencies[4] has been to support activities which may result in a more evidence-based policy model, to counter the government's own patronage driven model. This effort is hampered by the deficiencies and unreliability of official statistics, which come from a range of sources. The Federal Office of Statistics, which has responsibility for the national census and the national household survey, is said by many to be chronically under-funded. The Central Bank collects and analyses macroeconomic data, which appears regularly but is limited to the formal economy. Sectoral ministries are supposed to have departments of planning, research and statistics, but one respondent noted that these are thought of as a 'punishment station' in the civil service and are poorly staffed. The National Planning Commission has a mandate to produce economic statistics: it was described by one respondent as 'moribund', whilst several others pointed out that it had been chronically under-funded and faced with an unreasonably heavy but not always clearly delineated work burden.

This under-co-ordinated and under-funded mixture of efforts is in part a result of the widely noted detachment of research from policy. What it means in effect is that almost all the poverty data on Nigeria that does exist is provided by international donor and creditor agencies. In 1993 the World Bank made poverty assessments a condition of lending. The report which resulted, *Poverty in the Midst of Plenty* (1996), presented a mixture of findings from qualitative and quantitative research and was credited by one World Bank staff member as having sparked a major realisation in the federal government about rapidly growing levels of impoverishment. The most frequently quoted quantitative data on poverty in Nigeria come from the related World Bank-funded initiative to produce trend data from the 1992 and 1996 household surveys, but the impact of HIV-AIDS alone in the intervening years makes these figures dangerously out of date.

Other donor-resourced strategies for constructing poverty knowledge have bypassed the household survey, notably two DFID-funded initiatives, the Voices of the Poor study,[5] and the development of a rapid survey instrument, the Core Welfare Indicators Questionnaire (CWIQ). The Voices of the Poor study tried to strengthen capacity for qualitative research in the NPC, while the CWIQ was being piloted as the interim-PRSP (i-PRSP) was being drafted and looked likely to feed information into the proposed later stages.

Many donor respondents emphasised that the majority of their activities were carried out away from the domain of federal poverty reduction policy. When they do engage directly at this level, however, they exercise influence not only through dialogue with key federal players, but through supporting the production of the kind of information about poverty which can feed into the evidence-based processes advocated by the PRSP approach. As such, the messages of 'externalised discourses of poverty reduction' shape action, and influence domestic actors and processes.

Analysis of national poverty reduction policy documents from the 1990s reveals that the federal government's stated position on poverty reduction has long mirrored mainstream donor positions. The statements contained in policy documents have seldom, however, impinged on the implementation of poverty reduction initiatives in the traditional style outlined above. As a donor respondent suggested 'up until now, the production of papers on poverty, to serve a short run function, seems to have been the main focus for government. The strategic content has tended to take a back seat. ... consultation and participation outside government has not really featured at all.'

It might be added that one reason for this failure of strategy is the persistence of the traditional approach to poverty reduction policy-making, and its co-existence and intertwining with externalised discourses and approaches. The contemporary challenge – the resolution of the critical juncture, and the navigation of the convergences between the two streams – is aptly illustrated by the evolution of the NAPEP (domestic) and the PRSP (donor). Examining the unfolding dramas of these two processes reflects the endeavours of the Obasanjo government to negotiate its way between their often competing, but sometimes intersecting, demands.

The current situation: competing versions of poverty reduction policy?

As defined in Chapter 1, policy spaces can be conceptualised as 'moments in which interventions or events throw up new opportunities, reconfiguring relationships between actors or bringing in new ones, and opening up the possibilities of a shift in direction' (Brock et al, 2001:22, citing Grindle and Thomas 1991). The period since Obasanjo's election and new attempts to deal with the poverty agenda, have given rise to a multitude of such moments. Yet, as we have seen, the continuities of the domestic and donor streams shape the opportunities represented by these new spaces, and the confluence of the two streams has continuously been a zone of turbulence and confusion.

Both streams involve many of the same actors, but in the spaces provided by each stream, these actors have different relationships and agencies. In the 'domestic' stream, international actors are rendered spectators, speculating on how outcomes will affect their own strategies. In the 'donor' stream, government agencies and non-governmental stakeholders are under pressure to produce and own a new version of poverty policy which will be both 'country-owned' by domestic actors, and acceptable to the donor community.

Continuity in the domestic stream: NAPEC and NAPEP
When Obasanjo was elected president in 1999, he was faced with an immediate need to do something about poverty, especially as reflected in the rising militancy of unemployed youth, sometimes organised in youth militias. The processes he set in motion, beginning with the creation of the Poverty Alleviation Programme (PAP), whilst simultaneously initiating a complex process of streamlining the multitude of government institutions with a poverty reduction mandate,[6]led eventually to the emergence of the NAPEP.[6]

Many familiar criticisms were levelled at the PAP: rapidly constituted, with little consultation, it distributed 10bn Naira from the national budget to programmes of job creation and material benefits to communities. By late 2000, the PAP was widely acknowledged as a failure, and in November Obasanjo announced that it was to be scrapped in favour of the Youth Empowerment Scheme (YES). This was targeted at reducing the scourge of youth unemployment, increasingly being linked to the incidence of civic unrest and urban insecurity; the YES in turn became one of the four programmatic pillars of the NAPEP.[7]

The NAPEP has the ambitious goal of 'the eradication of absolute poverty in Nigeria,' to be carried out in a series of stages, from 'restoring hope' to 'wealth creation'. It aims to achieve these aims by co-ordinating all poverty eradication efforts in the federal government through one agency, the National Poverty Eradication Council (NAPEC); relating with CBOs and NGOs through partnerships; and facilitating the involvement of international donor agencies and the private sector. While the federal government is responsible for co-ordination, implementation is at the state and local levels. In each state, a State Poverty Eradication Committee (SPEC) is established, and at each local government, there is a local government monitoring committee and a NAPEP office.

While officials in the Obasanjo government have constantly held this programme up to international donors, the press and others as demonstration of a federal commitment to poverty alleviation, to many observers the NAPEP is a continuation of the old-style poverty programmes from previous regimes. This continuity is illustrated by the presence of powerful actors from the poverty reduction programmes of previous regimes on all three committees which were set up to define with the new poverty programme, and who were seen as trying to guarantee a future for their own institutional interests.[8] The initial character of the committee process, which was framed as open and consultative and headed by an individual identified for his 'neutrality', quickly reverted to a process of deliberation which took place behind closed doors, with existing actors defending their access to and control of resources.

One key player in NAPEP was the former manager of Obasanjo's campaign for President,[9] giving the agency a distinct image of being linked with the People's Democratic Party (PDP), the ruling party. This was reinforced by NAPEP's subsequent employment of thousands of staff at the lower levels, many of them PDP stalwarts. In addition, many saw NAPEP as being driven by the vice-president's office, which is also seen as the power behind Obasanjo's throne, at least on domestic affairs.[10] In general, NAPEP was viewed as a 'highly political animal', deeply associated with party politics and, as it unfolded, largely concerned with delivering patronage to consolidate the government's position before the 2003 presidential and parliamentary elections.

This very top-down political positioning reduced the chances that NAPEP would become in any way the bottom-up initiative implied by its multi-level structure and stated commitment to include a range of non-governmental actors at the state and LGA levels. This perception is vividly symbolised by the fact that many state and local NAPEP offices were physically in the same building that had housed the FEAP and the BLP of previous regimes. Patronage was seen to extend not only to the appointment of state and local co-ordinators and committees, but also in some states to the distribution of benefits – who you knew and whether they were in power was seen as the major criterion of eligibility.

The mood surrounding the implementation of the NAPEP has often been stormy and controversial. In Bayelsa State, where youth are known for their militancy, and where resource distribution issues are particularly volatile, armed guards surrounded the NAPEP office when the federal officer arrived to take applications and determine eligibility. In Jigawa State, where the state government has its own poverty policies (see Chapter 12), NAPEP was criticised for taking its definition of poverty and target groups from the centre, which prevented it from becoming supportively involved in state poverty reduction policy. Of the five states in our fieldwork, only in Ekiti – a state not controlled by the ruling party – did we find some perception that NAPEP had the possibility of reaching the intended beneficiaries. Here the state co-ordinator was a widely respected leader who stated that NAPEP was to be seen as a national programme for all Nigerians, irrespective of party affiliation. He placed this in the context of maturing democracy, suggesting that 'we are all stakeholders in this national project'. Even here, however, significant obstacles to implementation have emerged (see Chapter 11).

Despite the volatility surrounding NAPEP and critical reports in the press and elsewhere, NAPEP's Permanent Secretary insisted when interviewed that, 'there is no resentment about what we are doing – there is a consensus. This consensus has come about because whoever is doing something has to make consultation, and in this area of poverty eradication, the consultative approach was in place right from the beginning. At all levels, there have been regular briefings, a flow of information up and down.'

Thus, there is a duality of narratives concerning NAPEP, between its stated functions and the actual processes of implementation. While NAPEP ostensibly offers a new approach to poverty policy, it is firmly set in the mould of previous federal poverty reduction interventions, and is firmly anchored in established policy spaces open only to those actors with federal political power. Such historical continuities have current potency, and many suggest that they affect the degree to which civil society organisations choose to engage or not in the policy process, and how poverty programmes are perceived and implemented at the local level. A common perception is that while 'the words have changed, the actions have not.'

At the same time, the questions of who owns and controls NAPEP become particularly apposite in the face of the objectives of the PRSP to develop a 'country driven, nationally owned' process. The NAPEP is an entirely Nigerian creation, and thus to some degree more 'country-owned' than the externally-stimulated PRSP could ever be; indeed, donors were not kept informed of many of the stages NAPEP's evolution, and many were surprised when the programme was announced. However, the model of poverty reduction which the NAPEP puts forward is not congruent with the donor script, and 'country-ownership' is limited to powerful individuals and institutions with political agendas, and their clients.

The PRSP process: new invited spaces?

While NAPEP is widely seen as 'business as usual' politics, the PRSP in contrast is deeply embedded in a set of external narratives about building broad ownership of policy through the consultation and participation of multiple stakeholders. The PRSP process has become another important 'theatre' in which poverty reduction policy is played out in Nigeria. The two processes have unfolded alongside each other, each being enacted in a distinct series of spaces, but intersecting in terms of some of the actors who are involved. As such, the PRSP can be characterised as the projection of external discourses of poverty reduction onto an already complex and contested terrain of domestic poverty reduction policy which conforms to a different model. Terms like 'national', 'country-owned', 'participatory' and 'consultative' define the template for a process which is located in a highly politicised, top-down, heavily bureaucratised and exclusionary policy landscape.

When the idea of a PRSP was first introduced to Nigeria by the World Bank, the National Planning Commission (NPC), which has formal responsibility for introducing all donor interventions, initially became the secretariat for the new process. Subsequently, however, a lengthy period of negotiation between different government actors ensued over who should lead the PRSP process. Struggles between different parts of government were fed in no small part by backstage interventions of donor agencies, who sought to develop alliances with and provide support to their own champions within federal government. Both the World Bank and DFID continued their investments in the NPC's capacity for evidence based and consultative policymaking.

During late 2000 and early 2001, at the same time as the NAPEP was being established, there was a hiatus of activity in drafting a PRSP, during which backstage negotiations for control of the process prevailed, beyond the control or influence of donors and creditors. During this period, the Economic Policy Co-ordinating Committee (EPCC), a new agency housed outside any existing ministry, and reporting directly to the vice-president's office, emerged as the most powerful contender for the 'driving seat' of the PRSP. This even seemed to surprise the NAPEP, who had also made an ultimately unsuccessful claim to become the channel of international funds for the PRSP in June 2001. Even the chief economic adviser in the NPC expressed his frustration that he been unable to assert authority over the process.

The emergence of the EPCC was seen by some as strengthening the hand of those who favoured the orthodoxy of liberalisation, privatisation and the reduction of the role of the state as the overarching approach to poverty reduction. Though Nigerian, the head of EPCC had been recruited from Kenya on secondment from the IMF, into a position funded by the macroeconomic policy office of USAID. World Bank and DFID officials, who had until that time perhaps been the most influential leaders in the PRSP process, found themselves relatively constrained. In all the institutional jockeying, little time was given to crafting the policy itself. As one senior academic commented, 'Federal politics is all about who's in and who's out – with all this they do not have time to make policy. It's almost as if policy itself is an alien form of politics.'

While struggles were taking place over where the PRSP process should reside, the mandate of a more inclusive policy model shaped a sporadic drafting process. A drafting committee, the National Core Team, was selected and convened by the NPC in the early days of the process, including a range of actors representing federal ministries, some state governments, and some LGA officials. In addition, five of the fifty members of the NCT were selected as 'civil society representatives'; their names were taken from a list provided by the National Centre for Women and the International Co-operation Department of the NPC, and selected according to geographical spread and whether or not they had a female representative. In July 2001, when a small drafting team of 20, 'the Core of the Core', was convened, there was only one civil society representative present, who is also a full-time civil servant. The remaining members were all from federal government agencies, ranging from the NPC and NAPEP to the Central Bank and the Federal Office of Statistics. The team that eventually drafted the first version of the interim-PRSP was a sub-set even of the 'Core of the Core'.

The National Core Team is led by an academic, head of the Nigerian Institute of Social and Economic Research, who commented that 'the donors don't want to drive the process, the government doesn't want to be seen to drive it, and somebody has to drive it!' He suggested that his perceived 'neutrality' as an academic rather than a politician or a bureaucrat may invest the process with a degree of protection from the danger of political capture; others observed that they thought his freedom to act, particularly without clearance from the EPCC, was very limited. Another leading academic resigned after one of the first meetings, claiming inordinate donor interference and control.

During the parallel processes of early drafting and intra-governmental contestation, some donors expressed frustration at how best to exercise their influence, without abusing the principle of building country ownership. One World Bank staff member was led to observe, 'We have the dilemma of how to help them, without just coming out and telling them how to do it...maybe it is best to let them muddle through it, rather than feeding it to them. Maybe they have to chart their own course.' Another encapsulated the difficulty of standing back to allow country ownership to develop: 'We can't do a Country Assistance Strategy without a PRSP– but if we close our eyes and accept, and they do a bad PRSP, how can we build our CAS on quicksand?'

The i-PRSP which eventually emerged from these bewildering political processes was seen by many donors as an inadequate document, which, as with previous policies noted above, was weak in analysis, lacked evidence, and failed to link poverty reduction to broader concerns of macroeconomic reform, public expenditure review, or more transparent and accountable governance. Responding to criticism, the EPCC, now housing the drafting process, convened a series of consultations with a wider audience, including civil society actors and donors. These consultations mostly took the form of extremely large public gatherings to witness the presentation of the i-PRSP, but with no mechanisms for ensuring that participants' comments were taken into account by those responsible for drafting. The presentation of the i-PRSP in this way in some senses marked the closure of this first phase of the PRSP process, marked fundamentally by a period of contesting ownership by government, and opened the strategy to wider input, albeit in a highly constrained set of spaces. [12]

Increasingly, however, as civil society actors began to hear about the PRSP process, and with the encouragement of some donor agencies, debates began about how civil society engagement could be made more real. Entering the constrained spaces of the PRSP process is a huge challenge for the majority of civil society organisations, not only because of the legacies of previous poverty policies, but also because of civil society's own nature, history and priorities.

Other fears were expressed about the fate of the PRSP once it entered the proposed later stage of 'regional consultations'. Many differently positioned respondents suggested that regional workshops would deteriorate into battles for resource allocation, and that the spaces they opened would be captured either by political parties or by bureaucratic interests.

At one level the donor emphasis on a more inclusive process of poverty policy, based on national ownership and widespread consultation, offered the possibility of going beyond the historical model of poverty policy in the Nigerian federal context. At another level these spaces, created according to an externalised, normative logic of the way the policy process works, projected onto existing complex realities, provide inevitable political challenges. For example, the notion of 'national ownership', projected onto the Nigerian context, allowed space for competition and conflict among competing political elites over resources and legitimacy that only questionably would reach or benefit the poor. In a county as divided and diverse as Nigeria, the very idea of a single national policy – built on consultation with a range of actors who themselves were either excluded from the political game or very heavily in conflict within it – seemed at best to be a daunting prospect.

Conclusion: poverty policy at the confluence

A review of the politics of two contemporary poverty policy processes at the federal level in Nigeria gives us insights both into the challenges for the Obasanjo government, as well as into the dynamics of the policy process more generally. While the federal government has made efforts to deliver on the poverty agenda, our historical and contemporary review shows how those efforts are pushed and pulled by competing political pressures and forces. On the one hand the domestic heritage of poverty politics as a form of patronage shapes the delivery of the National Poverty Eradication Programme. On the other, demands for more consultation and inclusion by external donors, and the need for legitimacy from the international financial community, lead to a parallel process, in which yet other actors are brought in, and in which various donors compete for influence. The resulting confluence is an often inchoate and swirling policy process, enacted in a diverse range of spaces.

At a broader level, this snapshot into the federal poverty policy at the national level in Nigeria reveals further insights into the policy process itself. New policy spaces, such as those created by the PRSP, cannot simply be grafted onto existing actors and institutions regardless of historical context. Political cultures of previous poverty policies and programmes, continuities of powerful interests, and a strong gap between the policy discourse and its implementation all shape how new spaces are used, by which actors, and with whose knowledge. Invitations into new policy arenas cannot merely be announced – more democratic and inclusive processes must be constructed over time for invitations to be taken as real.

The challenge of inclusion is made even greater in a country as diverse and divided as Nigeria. In this context, notions that there will be a single national poverty plan in which all will be included is a powerful mirage which quickly evaporates as one takes a closer look at the conflicting interests across federal and state levels, between rich and poor, amongst regions and ethnicities.

As we shall see in the chapters that follow, a range of others arenas exist outside the federal machinery, in which there are other more autonomous spaces for organising around poverty issues, created from below through independent forms of social action, political opposition and resistance. Although such spaces are extremely important in Nigeria,[13] their visibility at the federal level, where nearly all activity is defined by its relationship to government, is very limited. While there is a possibility that civil society participation in the policy process might provide linkages to such autonomous spaces, and thereby provide a channel for alternative versions of poverty and poverty reduction to influence policy, to some degree civil society is shaped by the same historical and contemporary forces which affect the state that it seeks to engage.

For donors seeking to promote a more inclusive approach to the policy process, the irony is that the very act of holding out the invitation for others to enter the federal policy space intensifies the mirage that effective federal poverty policy can or does exist. Requiring entry into this space in the name of democratisation may in fact serve to weaken the influence of those very actors who are being invited in, who derive their legitimacy from poverty knowledge and policy spaces far removed from those located behind the closed doors and in the consultative conference halls of Abuja. In the confluence of the domestic and donor-driven poverty policy streams, there appears little space for the poor themselves.

Notes

1. See Annexe for a description of the different levels of decentralised government in Nigeria, and their responsibilities.
2. In interviews, contrary to the popular perception of their power, IMF staff emphasised that there is less opportunity to impose conditionality on Nigeria than on other countries, because of Nigeria's relative wealth and because the Fund does not have a direct stake in the country's debt. The IMF itself holds none of Nigeria's debt, most of which is held by the UK government. The only thing a relationship with the IMF absolutely guarantees the Federal Government is access to the Paris Club, and therefore the potential for negotiation on debt forgiveness.
3. The World Bank has a 'three-pillared' strategy to the programme it re-established in 1999: economic governance, private sector led growth, and community driven development. This programme however remains an updated Interim Strategy, rather than a fully-fledged Country Assistance Strategy (CAS). The Bank hopes to base their CAS on a government-led PRSP. All Bank staff interviewed noted the considerable shift in Bank activities, towards 'empowerment', poverty reduction and community driven development; in the Nigerian context this is reflected by the flagship Community Based Poverty Reduction Initiative (CBPRI), a social fund established in twelve states. In addititon to the IMF and the World Bank are a large range of agencies of multilateral and bilateral co-operation, with UNDP, the EU, DFID, and USAID amongst the largest. For UNDP, for instance, the main focus because the National Programme on Governance for Sustainable Human Development. While DFID argues that 'everything we do is poverty focused', governmental reform is seen as the most important mechanism for poverty reduction. USAID also echoed this approach, arguing that the main strategy needed was to get the government to use its own resources for poverty reduction; 'the resources of all the donor agencies are miniscule compared to the amount the government fritters away every year'.
4. Most particularly, DFID, the EU and the World Bank

5 . Funded in Nigeria by DFID in connection with the World Bank's WDR 2000/01

6 . This initiative eventually took the form of three committees, the Joda Panel, the Ango Abdullahi Committee, and the Borishade Committee. A fourth and final committee was convened to 'harmonise' the findings of the first three committees, and resulted, in January 2001, with the publication of 'A Blueprint for Schemes', and the establishment of an institutional structure, the National Poverty Eradication Council (NAPEC), which in turn was to oversee the National Poverty Alleviation Programme (NAPEP).

7. The others are the Rural Infrastructure Development Scheme (RIDS), the Social Welfare Services Scheme (SOWESS) and the Natural Resource Development and Conservation Scheme (NRDCS)

8. Indeed, the individual who emerged as the director of NAPEP entered the committee process as director of the FEAP, served on all three committees, and emerged with the most powerful appointment in the federal poverty reduction field.

9. He also served as Special Advisor to the President on the Organised Private Sector.

10. The National Planning Commission, by contrast, is associated with the President's office. As Obasanjo focused increasing attention outside of Nigeria, the Vice-President's office was seen as the key place for domestic policy.

11. Subsequent phases, which we might see as civil society contesting ownership of the PRSP, are discussed in Chapter 9

12 .Considerably more important than they are in Uganda.

9

Civil Society Engagement in the Federal Poverty Reduction Policy Process

Karen Brock, John Gaventa and Olusade Taiwo

The story of civil society engagement in the federal policy process is one in which actors located in a diverse, vibrant, regionally-differentiated arena have slowly and tentatively begun to enter newly opened invited spaces in order to contribute to poverty reduction policy. It is also the story of a new type of engagement with the state being offered to civil society actors, influenced but not controlled by the donor community. New engagements, taking place within a political discourse of democratisation and of partnership between civil society and the state, present enormous challenges in terms of overcoming the ingrained patterns of patronage found in 'business as usual' relationships between the federal state and its citizens

Civil society organisations across Nigeria are marked by a tremendous range and diversity, spanning social movements, institutions of self-help and mutual aid, development NGOs, human rights groups and trades unions – to name only a few. Across this diversity of CSOs, it is possible to trace two long-term historical trajectories which shape current experiences of civil society participation. Both trajectories have emerged in response to years of corrupt military rule, and the historical weaknesses of the federal state in Nigeria. On one hand, the exit of citizens disillusioned with state functions into parallel systems of self-help and governance, many of them in rural areas, has built on existing structures to embellish and diversify what Osaghae describes as 'embedded' civil society (Osághae 2001). On the other hand, a history of political opposition and resistance to military rule has given many urban-based civil society organisations a legacy of activism around a range of rights abuses perpetrated by the state.

The co-existence of these historical trajectories has several important implications for the potential engagement of civil society actors in contemporary federal poverty reduction policy. Perhaps the most important concerns representation of a broad spectrum of civil society. Decision-making in federal policy processes is of essence centralised, and is in many ways disconnected from the localised social and politcal processes in which many civil society organisations are embedded. The window of opportunity for civil society participation provided by these centralised processes is very narrow, compared to the breadth and diversity of rural and urban civil society. Usually, those positioned to take advantage of the narrow, invited spaces on offer are urban-based CSOs, often those with connections to government or international development actors. Actors from exit-based, embedded CSOs are seldom present at the policy table; and seldom are they closely connected to those who do take a seat. This challenges the frequently made assumption that civil society participation in invited spaces automatically confers 'country ownership' on a policy process. It also presents a challenge to civil society actors themselves, concerning the dynamics of representation of the interests of the poor.

Given that the recent history of active civil society in Nigeria has largely been either in opposition to the state, or in response to the absence or inadequacy of the state, for most civil society actors inclusion in the policy process is a relatively new phenomenon. While federal government does have a history of government consulting selected civil society organisations, the terms of invited participation have greatly widened under the democratic dispensation. Experiences of engagement under previous governments, however, have led to expectations and assumptions of what the consultation of civil society by government might consist of. Government and civil society actors are often mutually suspicious of one another's motives. Until very recently, this suspicion has been a major inhibiting factor in civil society participation in policy.

Nonetheless, civil society participation in poverty reduction policy is expanding, taking place in invited spaces which open around major policy initiatives like the Poverty Reduction Strategy Paper and sectoral policies like Universal Basic Education, often with donor prompting of government. This participation takes place in the context of a range of expectations and assumptions. Particularly important here are the assumptions of civil society actors based on historical experiences of engagement with government; and the assumptions of mainstream development discourse, transmitted through donors, about partnership, governance and the right of poor people to be represented in policy-making.

An important element of this development discourse is the poverty reduction agenda itself. The idea of an integrated, national, strategic poverty reduction policy is almost entirely a construct of this discourse. While the federal government itself has a mass of programmes and processes that impinge upon poverty reduction – sectoral programmes, co-ordinating structures, Poverty Eradication Programmes, national and state budgets – they have not had a coherent identity as 'poverty reduction policy'. Similarly, civil society actors are engaged in poverty reduction processes in a range of ways – campaigning for workers' rights, providing micro-credit, maintaining community infrastructure – but few if any would identify themselves as 'poverty reduction advocates'. In this sense, the recent experience with participation in the PRSP represents new terrain, and a new headline agenda which sometimes seems to encompass everything and nothing.

In order to further explore the dynamics of civil society participation in the federal policy process, we first examine the diversity of contemporary civil society, and look at the challenges faced by those CSOs who might be expected to engage in policy. We then turn to dicuss historical experiences of engagement with policy processes, and the expectations of federal government to which they have given rise. Finally, we move from issues of broader engagement to focus on civil society efforts to engage in the later stages of the interim Poverty Reduction Strategy Paper process,[1] examining the dynamics of invited spaces and some of the expectations of civil society participation.

Diverse composition, diverse challenges: the landscape of civil society
The diversity of contemporary Nigerian civil society owes a great deal to the phenomenon of exit from the state – the tendency of

citizens to view state organisations as irrelevant to their lives and so to separate themselves from these – and from any responsibility they feel towards state institutions. Particularly during the last 15 years, exiting citizens have built on the foundations of a rich existing civil society to create 'parallel sites of self-governance' in Nigeria (Osaghae 1998 p.1). Concepts of citizenship are often rooted in one of these parallel sites, in conjunction with regional, religious or ethnic identity, rather than in the state (Jones 2003). The modern era of exit has coincided with social change and modernisation, and the result is a huge diversity of parallel structures, both formal and informal. Some can be characterised as political – such as ethnic identity-based movements which challenge the federal state – while others are socio-economic, like hometown associations (HTAs).

The forms which civil society organisations take are regionally differentiated, with HTAs particularly common in the east, development NGOs in the south-west, and religious organisations in the north. Walker (1999) notes that in the south-east, south and Middle Belt,[2] CSOs are numerous and more likely to be involved in advocacy, democracy and governance issues, and have closer links with donor community. In the north, CSOs are more likely to be based on traditional structures and associational patterns, and less formally organised.

The example of HTAs is illustrative of some of the dynamics of exit-based CSOs in poverty reduction. Mohammed's study of HTAs (2000) shows that in most cases, their formation was precipitated by the feeling that government could not be relied on to develop towns. It was widely possible for local leaders to unite different groups within a community around issues of infrastructure. Some HTAs have been successful in meeting their objectives of local development, which often have an indirect impact on poverty reduction.[3] Mohammed notes that the more successful HTAs are, 'the more they draw the attention of different political forces with different agendas who may want to manipulate them to achieve certain political objectives' (2000:29).

For the HTAs, in common with the range of exit-based CSOs, direct engagement with the state in policy processes represents a new approach. Previous federal governments have sometimes provided state support to self-help development activities, based on the rationale that poverty alleviation will occur through partnership with and funding of parallel structures.[4] Such efforts represented invited participation in provisioning, which did not give options for actually hearing the voices of the poor or using citizen knowledge in defining poverty alleviation policy. They have largely failed to address basic problems, particularly distrust and lack of confidence in the ability and willingness of the state to protect citizens' rights or interests. They have in some senses reinforced an almost complete disconnection between embedded, rural civil society and the spaces and discourses of federal policy.

While HTAs are only one example, research in Ekiti, Benue, Jigawa, Kaduna and Bayelsa states (this volume) suggests that the experience of disconnection and mistrust of government advances is a common one. From the zakkat committees of Jigawa State, to the committees of radical youth in Bayelsa, to the community development associations of Benue and Ekiti, exit-based civil society organisations are dislocated and distant from federal decision-making and indifferent to offerings of federal poverty reduction policy.

Despite this dislocation, there are CSOs engaged with federal government, some of them also active at the level of state governance. Though many of these are not well connected to local, exit-based CSOs, some, like the Nigerian Labour Congress, are national structures with a mass membership, active simultaneously in federal and state politics to forward the interests of workers. A CSO like the NLC can be seen as straddling the faultlines between the centre and the peripheries of civil society, engaging in a range of spaces in both democratic politics and the policy process.

Even within the relatively narrow slice of CSOs able to directly engage with the federal policy process, there is diversity of identity: professional bodies and trade unions, philanthropic organisations and foundations, faith-based organisations, development NGOs, the organised private sector, academics and others. Many of these have a long history of engagement in the arena of the civic public, *olu oyibo*.[5] For each, there are particular challenges associated with participation in the federal poverty reduction policy process.

In the case of labour unions, for example, there is a tension between a highly politicised history of struggle and resistance and the position of unions in the current politics of opposition to the government. The Nigeria Labour Congress is an important actor in the democratic dispensation because it acts as a major focal point for people's general aspirations. To date, however, it has not had a great deal of impact in invited spaces in the federal policy process, and this is not unconnected with its history of ideological divisions, which are perpetuated and exploited by government. Recent attempts by the NLC to float a political party are a case in point; the government has made significant efforts to arrest the move because of its likely implications for the prospect of the existing political parties. Simultaneously, however, the NLC has been pursuing a more proactive role in the later stages of the PRSP process, and has engaged in a certain amount of reflection about its role as a policy actor (Lukman, pers. comm.). The challenge here, if the NLC is seen as potentially a major driver for change towards pro-poor policy, concerns both the internal dynamics of the NLC itself, and the boundaries of legitimate action for a civil society actor engaged in the policy process.

One group of actors frequently defined as being part of Nigerian civil society is the 'organised private sector' (OPS).[6] Indeed, the OPS has a tradition of having a voice in policy in a way that other sectors of civil society have not; the best example of this is the Vision 2010 process of the last years of the Abacha regime, in which a series of public consultations between federal government and the private sector were held up as evidence that the resulting policy document was nationally owned.[7] Perhaps the privileged position of OPS actors in influencing policy has more to do with their overlap with political elites, than with any sense of their being representative of poor people's needs. While a generic commitment exists to economic growth as a route to poverty reduction, this is firmly located within the frame of neo-liberalism and does not extend to examining issues of corruption, expropriation of resources or redistribution of wealth. In the case of the OPS, questions emerge concerning definitions of civil society in theory and in practice, and the very broad assumption that civil society participation will result in policies that are better for poor people.

Given the importance of religion in definitions of identity and citizenship, Nigeria's many faith-based organisations might be expected to take an active role in the poverty policy process. Instead, we found far more common a position that 'the poor will always be with us,' leading to a lack of critical engagement with the root causes of poverty. Although faith-based organisations make occasional pronouncements on policy issues, they are not known to be proactive in engaging in invited spaces, beyond those created for inter-faith conflict mediation. It is not unlikely that their minimal action in this regard is influenced by the preferred theological position on poverty espoused by their popular leadership. For example, although the Christian Association of Nigeria sometimes takes on strong rhetorical positions on the implications of certain policies on poverty levels, it seldom pursues or follows up pronouncements with strategies that will ensure that the positions it takes are carried through; neither does it mount visible pressure on policy-makers to take its positions on board. According to one cleric, this is in part because the structure on the ground cannot support any policy advocacy beyond the level of expressing an opinion in the media.

A second reason, given the importance of religion in federal politics, may be that the leaders of faith-based organisations undertake their activities in closed, backstage spaces, rather than in public, invited ones. Similar to the questions emerging from trade union participation, some of the challenges for faith-based organisations are internal, and some concern the position they hold in the broader configurations of national politics.

Indigenous development NGOs, unlike labour unions, OPS and faith-based organisations, are a relatively new phenomenon in Nigeria.[8] Development NGO staff interviewed for the research identified functions which encompass service delivery, capacity building, social functions and advocacy. By working with and through traditional associations and embedded CSOs, development NGOs are taking on more modern functions by giving their members access to information and services available in formal public arenas.[9] This might also be seen as presenting an opportunity for development NGOs to provide a bridge between the two elements of civil society, having a foot in both worlds.

Staff of development NGOs also noted that a key challenge in their work is to better understand the synergies between their different functions so that, for example, advocacy work around rights or poverty reduction is informed by lessons and experiences encountered while carrying out a service delivery function. Possible disconnections between the different functions of NGOs are further compounded by factors of identity, particularly as international development NGOs with operations in Nigeria are far more likely to take up identities as pro-poor advocates than indigenous development NGOs.[10]

Looking at the issues raised by the experience of the NLC, the OPS, faith-based organisations and development NGOs suggests that considerable obstacles exist to fruitful engagments with government policy processes. Some obstacles are related to the internal dynamics of CSOs and the relationships between them; some are related to the positioning of CSOs in the complex, political domain of relationships between state and society. Just as many, however, are related to an enduring mistrust of the state, and a set of expectations of the way that the state will behave in a consultative encounter with civil society. We now turn to examine in more detail the expectations that arise from these historical encounters.

Consulted by government: historical lessons and contemporary realities

What happens when civil society actors take part in the federal policy process? Who is invited, and what are the outcomes of their participation? The following extract notes the observations of a staff member from an international NGO who became involved in a campaign engaging with federal education policy. It illuminates the importance of the diverse expectations and agendas which surround episodes of consultation and participation.

There was a lack of civil society input to any of the government's plans [on education]; although they said they were working with civil society, when we asked them which NGOs they were working with in which areas, we found that actually the 'civil society' input was from 'experts' – academics and bureaucrats – not from NGOs who had anything to do with the grassroots. But some NGOs had been 'consulted' so we went to them to find out what the consultation had been – and it was all about being called to a meeting and being told what the government plan was, to hear of the plans. This kind of consultation was seen as a demand of the donor community. The nature of the consultation was not one of partnership.

Even in this short account, we can see that different actors have very different opinions about what civil society is, and what engagement in a policy process might or should consist of. This account, and many others put forward by research respondents, suggest that historical experiences of what is usually termed 'consultation' have done much to contribute to the mutual suspicion that exists between government and civil society actors in the policy process. It is into this existing landscape of relations between actors with different positions that external narratives of civil society participation are introduced.

The danger lies in the possibility that, although generic objectives of a process like the PRSP might be presented as new, differently motivated kinds of consultation, in implementation they will be rendered as sterile as previous consultations by the entrenched mindsets and behaviours of the policy actors involved. Examining civil society engagement in the policy process necessitates a better understanding of the convergence between externally-driven narratives and historical meanings of consultation and participation. While the political dynamics of civil society engagement are clearly different under military and democratic governments, there are continuities of personnel and bureaucratic norms between the two which suggest that many of the historical challenges encountered shape current practice.

What, then, are some of the lessons which may be learned from previous experiences of civil society engagement in the policy process?

As already noted, different types of CSO have had more and less confrontational engagements with different regimes. Perhaps at the least confrontational end of the spectrum lies the invited participation of the Organised Private Sector, both in the Vision 2010 process of the latter years of the Abacha regime, and in the budget process.

Despite the non-confrontational nature of these engagements in the federal policy process, an official of the Manufacturers' Association of Nigeria observed that OPS contributions to the budget process were frequently ignored, the budget sometimes featuring the exact opposite of the recommendations emerging from the consultation. This account of advice sought and rejected by federal government is also common amongst academics, who discuss the demoralising nature of being commissioned by government to do research on a policy issue, only to have their research findings overlooked. This points to an underlying feature of the way that consultation is commonly understood: those who are being consulted have no guarantee that their opinions will be taken into account or acted upon. While this understanding is clearly rooted in highly apolitical experiences of consultation by a military government, it remains as a strong template for expectations of governmental behaviour in general. It also points to a widespread perception that research is irrelevant to policy.

A second historical experience, that of the Directorate of Food, Roads and Rural Infrastructure (DFRRI) under the Babangida regime, is instructive in seeing CSOs as passive recipients of top-down consultative efforts, with little or no control over outcomes. After its inception, one department of DFRRI spent a great deal of time and energy on a nation-wide mapping of community development groups and their priorities, in order to begin implementation of an integrated rural development programme. This represented a massive effort by the federal state to engage directly with local organisations, a route fraught with political controversy. According to one respondent, there was a high degree of commitment within the department to carrying the exercise out well, as it would facilitate the successful delivery of programmes responding to community needs. In implementation, however, there was an over-emphasis on capital projects, with awards of contracts to military personnel, rather than to the social projects many communities had requested when consulted.

The broader lesson here is the extent to which top-down consultation processes have been controlled to ensure that their benefits accrue to the more powerful, and the extent to which actors who are positioned in between the more and the less powerful do not necessarily have adequate agency to act on priorities identified through consultations with grassroots constituencies. Experiences like the DFFRI example have contributed greatly to the negative impressions of government officials and policies common amongst community and exit-based organisations (see Chapter 13).

A third useful example of federal government-civil society engagement comes from looking at attempts in the 1980s and 1990s to form umbrella networks of NGOs. The history of the Nigerian NGO Consultative Forum (NINCOF), a space opened in 1991 on the impetus of the UNDP in collaboration with the Federal Ministry of Culture and Social Welfare, reveals how the interests of differently-positioned actors can lead to the collapse of the space, particularly if ownership is not clear.

NINCOF was established following two earlier failed attempts at starting an umbrella organisation for CSOs. NGOs who participated in the space offered did so because many of them believed that the lack of effective networking was a serious weakness in their activities. The UNDP provided resources in accordance with its focus on strengthening relationships between government, non-governmental actors and the private sector as partners in development. The federal government collaborating in the project had an explicit interest in monitoring and , as collaborators, regulating the NGO sector, which had expanded rapidly from the mid-1980s.

The differences between these agendas are highlighted by the example of a federal government attempt, during the Abacha regime, to draft a national policy on NGOs, with the stated aim of dealing 'with the problem of how these diverse organisations can be effectively integrated into the development processes as partners with government.' The process for drafting this policy involved a series of inter-ministerial meetings attended by relevant officials and a few NGO representatives who were 'hand-picked' by the committee, including the executive secretary of NINCOF. The draft was circulated for comments among CSOs through the NINCOF office, and received a highly negative response. In the words of one CSO actor, 'the process of generating this policy is flawed and we are not concerned with tinkering with the document; rather we would be calling for a more democratic process for developing a policy that can be respected.' The disagreement and conflict provoked by different positions of CSO actors within NINCOF towards the process of drafting the national policy was one of the factors which contributed to NINCOF's decline into inactivity and eventual dismantlement.

While the lessons from this process concern the different agendas of the actors involved, which affect who participates and how, the most striking comes from reading the account alongside contemporary accounts of invited participation, such as CSO engagement in the interim-PRSP process. Such a reading reveals that many of the issues and challenges of civil society engagement in federal policy processes remain unchanged – for example, the hand-picking by federal government of civil society representatives at the policy table, and the scheduling of 'consultation' only after a policy has been drafted. As several respondents observed, it will take more than one short experience with democracy to alter some of the basic values which keep the policy process largely closed to civil society actors.

In this section, we have reviewed lessons from the past about process and content of consultation which contribute to currently held expectations of the way that government will behave. Such lessons provide obstacles to the smooth uptake of external models of participation which suggest that civil society engagement is an important mechanism for building 'country ownership' of mainstreamed poverty reduction strategies. They also suggest that home-grown models of 'consultation' are frequently superficial and laden with contradictions. Building on these lessons to create meaningful opportunities for change in the policy process is the agenda facing a range of CSOs in Nigeria today. In the next section, we turn to the example of civil society engagement in the PRSP process to see how actors in civil society organisations are pursuing this agenda, and how what they are able to achieve is critically shaped by the expectations of other actors.

The PRSP process: an opportunity to challenge sterile consultations?

Central to the PRSP model is the expectation that a PRSP should not only be locally generated and owned, but also developed through a wide participatory dialogue between the government and civil society. The process of drafting an i-PRSP for Nigeria has, therefore, had at least a strong rhetorical emphasis on including civil society actors. As we argued in the previous chapter, however, the early stages of the process exhibited many of the difficulties suggested by historical expectations of government behaviour.

The early stages of the i-PRSP process indicate that its convenors were working according to a particular understanding of participation. For the Economic Policy Co-ordination Committee, the arm of the federal government which took conrol of the process in 2002, responding to demands for better participation initially meant expanding the numbers of seats on the National Core Team of the PRSP, and continuing plans for regional consultations, planned as a series of six set-piece consultation workshops.

The i-PRSP document itself[11] bears witness to a certain type of consultative process. It claims that its preparation process 'is designed to be non-exclusive and to involve all stakeholders in each and every stage of the process.' (Economic Policy Co-ordination Committee 2002 p.2) The document backs up this claim with a long list of procedural drafting stages, intended to demonstrate the inclusivity of the process. This narrative of stages moves through the establishment of a National Core Team – although it gives no details of its composition or of how it might advance processes of participation – setting up a drafting team, forming a technical support team, and so on. Of a total sequence of nineteen steps, the tenth is 'circulation of i-PRSP first draft to all stakeholders', and the eleventh 'all stakeholders national workshop to review the i-PRSP first draft'. These two steps are the only ones which could be interpreted as broadly consultative of any civil society constituency other than the five CSO representatives on the National Core Team. Several respondents concurred that the 'national workshop', a one-day event which convened an enormous audience to hear presentations of the i-PRSP and sit in small discussion groups focused on thematic areas, had only minimal efficacy, being both time-constrained and dominated by government and donors.

One of the intended functions of an i-PRSP is to provide a road map for the greater civil society participation in the full PRSP process. The Nigerian i-PRSP makes an explicit commitment to 'a participatory approach being instituted' (2002:46), suggesting both a media campaign of sensitisation to the PRSP, and six zonal working groups, composed of:

> appropriate ministries and agencies of the federal government, officials of the National Orientation Agency, the National Poverty Eradication Programme, the National Population Commission, staff from at least one University in each zone, opinion leaders such as teachers, business people, religious leaders and leaders of community based organisations. (EPCC, 2002:48)

Experience from previous processes of consultation are relevant to the potential fate of the PRSP once it enters the stage of 'regional consultations'. A standard model of consultation exists in Nigeria, held to be the minimum necessary for political acceptability: six zonal workshops, corresponding to the six geopolitical regions of the country. Many differently positioned respondents suggested that such regional workshops in the context of the PRSP would deteriorate into battles for resource allocation. One respondent who had organised a national consultative process around electoral procedure asked:

> If there was a consultation about poverty, who would come? The PDP would hijack it and transport people there. Every State Governor, or State Governor's First Lady, has a pet NGO, and they would be well represented [...] It would be spoiled before it was started [...] You also have to remember that half of any

consultative forum is ceremony; that the opportunity to speak will be limited for most people, and that most of the comments will be lengthy, elaborate critiques from distinguished people, which will reduce the space open to the people you really want to hear from.

Creating alternatives to the kind of sterile consultation implied by this account of regional workshops has come to preoccupy a range of non-governmental actors engaged in the PRSP process. There was, however, remarkably little discussion amongst federal government actors of what participation was for and how a consultation could be approached, planned, or made more accessible to a wider range of actors.

The rationale of PRSPs suggests that CSO engagement with the policy process is sought because CSOs are nearer to poor people than the state is, because many of them work with or through the poor in different ways, or have poor people as part of their membership. Consulting CSOs is therefore held to be one route to make policy both more relevant and more widely owned. As we have already seen, this is not necessarily a valid interpretation of civil society. Even so, it is important to ask how CSOs import the knowledge and information that their position gives them into invited policy spaces like the PRSP: which talk are they talking, and is anyone listening?

CSOs have been found to understand poverty mainly in terms of basic needs (Gass and Adetumbi 2000) and there is increasing evidence that many development NGOs now generate their own micro-level poverty data for the purpose of identification, targeting, monitoring and evaluation in their interventions. Whilst these sets of data are sometimes produced using sophisticated methodologies, they are localised data, largely driven by the demands of international development actors to measure how well a project could perform in terms of objectively verifiable indicators. While all these examples are important attributes of CSO operations, there is a broader point to consider here: the poor may be able to tell CSOs who they are and CSOs may be able to do piecemeal project impact assessments, but how easy is it to aggregate this kind of information for use in the wider context of the policy process? This remains the daunting lack of connection between CSO project context and the state policy context.

There is, however, a second and equally daunting lack of connection which, rather than being exclusive to CSOs, affects the whole policy process: the lack of connection between systematic research and policy. This challenges the assumption that CSOs are invited to participate in federal policy processes because of their ability to represent poor people's poverty knowledge, and suggests that other motivations are as important. A wide range of respondents pointed out the influence of international development actors in this regard, in both persuading federal government to open some spaces in the policy process, and in driving the agendas of civil society organisations through funding. Some civil society actors, however, pointed out that while their arena of engagement may be dictated by the direction of funding, their intention was to exploit invited spaces to critically engage government, and make demands for 'empowered participation rather than sterile consultation' and that 'macro-economic policy decisions be subordinated to clear anti-poverty goals.'[12]

Some urban-based NGOs, particularly international NGOs, have developed advocacy and campaigning agendas to make demands both within and outside invited spaces, although these tend to be focused on narrower poverty-related issues such as HIV-AIDS, or education. Here, however, expertise is largely concentrated in a highly educated urban minority of NGOs – particularly those with a history of political engagement around human rights abuses and electoral reform – who are said by some to be disconnected from a predominantly rural constituency of poor people. A different view of advocacy comes from those outside these pockets of activists, where policy influencing via 'lobbying' – an important part of the advocacy process – if understood through the Nigerian meaning of the term, is equated with 'bribery'or 'gratification'. As we have suggested earlier, many CSOs concentrate on service-delivery and may not be familiar with the skills and tools of advocacy, or with terms imported from international development discourse. If, however, civil society participation in the policy process is held to bring decisions closer to ordinary people, such CSOs should provide vital spaces for representation. Building their capacity for advocacy may provide the bottom-up pressure necessary to strengthen vertical connections with civil society actors who are directly engaged in invited spaces closer to centres of power.

As well as the rights advocacy and international NGOs at the centre there are others who seem only loosely connected to programmes of pro-poor or rights-based activities. One CSO member of the expanded National Core Team of the i-PRSP, after observing that CSO representation in government policy-making is just 'window dressing', claimed that most of the time it is a 'man knows man' factor that determines who is invited, rather than any criteria based on objective considerations. In the view of the respondent, some of the CSOs in the i-PRSP process had not been attending regularly due to poor communication, had little understanding of what the process was about and were unknown to development networks. Various considerations influence which CSO actors are invited to the government policy spaces, but one appears to be that the CSO sector is not well known to the government, and that there is no neutral reference point such as an CSO umbrella network or viable CSO directory where information about CSOs can be easily accessed.

In contrast to the CSO representatives invited to the PRSP process, the group of 31 CSO representatives who convened to strategise about the PRSP in Abuja in February 2002, had a great deal of discussion of what 'improved participation' in the i-PRSP process might consist of. For these actors, participation was something more complex than a series of workshops; they called for both 'a reconstituted, empowered and effective co-ordination mechanism for the PRS process which has multi-level representation of the full range of stakeholders' and 'a process that ensures greater knowledge and information parity among all levels of stakeholders.'[13] The latter calls resonate with challenges for participation identified by many CSO research respondents.

The call for 'knowledge and information parity' is related not only to access to existing information, but to the legitimacy of different kinds of knowledge in the policy process. The civil society representative on the drafting team of the PRSP emphasised the importance of his 'being able to make a good argument' during meetings in order to be taken seriously, and that this relied on access to information. Another civil society actor observed that 'part of the battle is about what you know. You may occupy the space but what you bring to the table is very, very important. You will only be respected if you talk the talk.' Very often, the 'talk' that is expected and legitimised is speaking the language of poverty reduction as central to development and is discordant with other narratives of development that may arise from different spaces.

Subsequent to the February 2002 meeting, a range of civil society actors working with bilateral donors and international NGOs, undertook to develop a clear agenda around which to engage in the PRSP process. This coalition has weathered its own internal political difficulties to reach a position of informed criticism of the PRSP process. At a consultation event for a revised version of the i-PRSP, coalition members handed out leaflets to participants explaining flaws in the process. The coalition, despite its donor backing, has remained wary of becoming directly involved with organising the regional consultations for the i-PRSP, choosing instead to focus its activities on issues of state-level budgets, and the implementation of the National Poverty Eradication Programe. This development suggests that the interim-PRSP process may have created an invited space which provided a catalyst for action – but not perhaps the action intended by the initial invitation.

Conclusion

Looking across the range of agendas and institutions which fall under the name of civil society in Nigeria, there is a remarkable complexity of form and function. In examining similar complexity in Ugandan civil society, Lister and Nyamugasira (2003) argue that many CSOs undertake several functions simultaneously, only some of which are related to direct engagement in the policy process. The same is true of Nigeria, where many CSOs pursue a number of objectives at one time, as well as being shaped by the funding of external actors and the conditions attached to resources. The challenge posed by this diversity of form and function is to understand what influences the particular combination of functions that CSOs adopt. Are they reactive or proactive choices? Do the choices differ according to the kind of space on offer for CSO participation? What are the best strategies for engaging with the invited spaces on offer?

In addition to the challenges posed by the diversity of civil society are those presented by the different ways that people understand the very agenda of poverty reduction. While the examples drawn on in this chapter provide broad understandings of the dynamics of civil society engagement in policy areas relevant to poverty reduction – the budget, rural development programmes, education – it is notable that none of them concerns policies which involve a mainstreamed, explicit focus on providing a strategy for poverty reduction. Indeed, many civil society respondents noted that the issue of poverty reduction itself – rather than the dynamics of the policy process – raises particular challenges for their participation. One civil society activist observed that 'poverty as a term has been abused. Major scams wore the cloak of poverty. The word doesn't mean anything.' Another said 'poverty is like mercury: it just goes all over the place and you can't get hold of it.' The head of the Nigerian Poverty Eradication Forum goes beyond this: it is not just the term 'poverty' that causes difficulty, but the government's interpretation of it: 'a refusal to look into the Pandora's Box of the causes of mass poverty in this country can only come from class wickedness, self-exempting religious fatalism, a neo-Malthusian criminality of spirit, or simply pure and unadulterated sadism.'[13] All three perspectives reflect the contemporary reality of civil society's suspicion towards federal poverty reduction policy processes.

Notes
1. See Chapter 8 for an account of the evolution of the PRSP
2. The Middle Belt is a term used to describe the central region of Nigeria, one of the six geopolitical zones.

3. On the role of CBOs in poverty reduction, Francis et al note that although CBOs often provide some support for 'the indigent', generally they aim to provide benefits at the community level rather than the level of the individual poor person.
4. For example, the Babangida regime's programmes under its Directorate of Food, Roads and Rural Infrastructure (DFFRI).
5. See Chapter 2 for more discussion of Ekeh's (1975) civic and primordial publics.
6. The phrase 'organised private sector' (OPS), used far more commonly in Nigeria than in Uganda, signifies both a distinct sub-section of civil society, and the actions of individual entrepreneurs as communal champions, closely tied to the politics of patronage (Francis, Pers. Comm.).
7. The Vision 2010 Committee had 248 members organised into 53 sub-committees, considered 750 memoranda from the general public and held 57 external workshops (World Bank 2002).
8. Of a sample of development NGOs in Taiwo's 1997 study, 70% of the sample were founded after 1986, the year of the first structural adjustment programme, with the majority formed after 1990.
9. NGO Networks for Health 2001 and Taiwo, 1997
10. For many, the identity of international NGOs is defined by their position as part of the donor community.
11. Federal Government of Nigeria, Interim PRSP, First Draft 2001
12. Communiqué from 'A workshop on Enlightenment and Empowerment for the Poverty Reduction Strategy Paper (PRSP) process' February 26th - 28th 2002, ActionAid Nigeria and the Centre for Public-Private Co-operation (CPCC).
13. Dr Arigbede, *Nigerian Tribune*, 7 July 2000.

10

Contesting Control of Resource Allocation: Power Relations, Actors and the Policy Process in Bayelsa State, Nigeria

Peter Ozo-Eson with O. Owei and U. Ukiwo

Bayelsa State, the smallest in Nigeria, lies in the extreme south of the country, on the delta of the Niger river. It produces oil, and this fact is probably the most defining single feature of politics and livelihoods in the state. While oil is at the centre of Nigeria's enormous wealth, Bayelsa's inhabitants are deeply impoverished, and their livelihoods, based on the exploitation of natural resources through farming, fishing and palm-tapping, are threatened by the environmental degradation which arises from oil extraction. Definitions of poverty in Bayelsa are always made with reference to the oil industry, whether in terms of the inequalities of distribution which see huge quantities of oil wealth disappearing from the state; or in terms of the employment practices of oil companies which import labour but ignore swathes of unemployed local youth; or in terms of environmentally destructive practices.

As well as being a producer of oil, Bayelsa is home to a range of ethnic groups. Within the context of the Nigerian Federation, all Bayelsans come from minority ethnicities; within the context of the state itself, a majority group, the Ijaw, dominate the multiplicity of smaller groups. Ethnic identity, intertwined with the politics of oil, therefore underpins the political process in Bayelsa. This chapter examines how these complex factors impact on the way policy is made in Bayelsa, by looking first at government, and then at the dynamics of oil companies and the youth organisations that protest against them.

There is a range of ways that government actors engage in making policy in Bayelsa, which suggest that many of the classic features of the neo-patrimonial state (see Chapter 2) influence the policy process, particularly the personalisation of political power and the concomitant importance of backstage spaces. In addition, absentee local government, co-option of local elites, the importance of policy entrepreneurs and crisis-focused consultation, all militate against the possibility that poor people's needs and priorities will be represented in policy.

As in other states in the federation, government is seen by many of Bayelsa's citizens as remote and corrupt (see Chapters 11, 12 and 13). While in other areas this perception has given rise to widespread exit from the state into organisations of self-help, in Bayelsa exit from the state takes a subtly different form. The presence of oil companies provides a focus for political dissent and violent protest, but also makes them an alternative site where claims for the provision of services can be staked. In many ways, the oil industry provides an alternative to the state, and one which may be more susceptible to various forms of pressure from ordinary people and their organisations.

Each of the unique range of actors that engage in the policy process in Bayelsa creates and occupies a different space: from the official spaces of the formal policy process occupied by government, to the invited 'stakeholder fora' established by the oil companies, to the action spaces created through the protests of ethnically-identified social movements. As this chapter shows, these spaces overlap and interlock, and at their interfaces are opportunities for the creation of change.

An overview of Bayelsa State

Bayelsa State was created out of the old Rivers State in 1996 by the embattled regime of General Sani Abacha as it looked for ways to broaden its shrinking support base. While the regime used state creation for self-legitimisation, it no doubt met the genuine desires of the political elites in the region. In the military period, revenue was allocated on a state-by-state basis across the country, regardless of where it actually originated. The elite realised that this inevitably favoured those areas that had more states (Gbóyega 1998). With 107 electoral wards, the smallest number of any state in the country, Bayelsa does not command many votes in the national legislature.

Size also has implications for resource allocation: between 1997 and 2002, Bayelsa State received the smallest allocation from the Federation Account to local government councils of all states.

Bayelsa is predominantly an Ijaw state, but the population also includes several minority ethnic groups, including the Biseni, Epie, Nembe and Ogbia and Epie-Atissa. The minority groups continue to protest the dominance of larger groups, thereby making the state one which has to grapple with problems of minorities within it. Simultaneously, however, the political identity of Bayelsa state in relation to the rest of the federation is fundamentally shaped by its minority status with respect to the nationally politically dominant ethnicities, Hausa, Fulani, Yoruba and Igbo.

While the politics of the state are underpinned by issues of ethnicity and minority, they are also fundamentally shaped by its status as an oil producer. Oil companies such as Shell, Agip, Chevron and Consolidated Oil prospect for oil in Bayelsa where they maintain oil rigs, flow stations and oil terminals. Their headquarters are usually located in far-away Lagos, with regional offices located in either Port Harcourt or Warri, two Niger Delta towns where there is a high concentration of firms in the oil and gas industry, due largely to the existence of better infrastructures.

The people of Bayelsa, living alongside the industry which extracts oil from their land, are principally fishers and farmers. Subsistence agriculture is, however, constrained by problems of coastal erosion, land acquisition and the environmental pollution caused by oil exploitation. A considerable proportion of the population is also involved in trading, crafts, oil palm milling, lumbering, boat building, mat weaving, palm wine tapping and local gin brewing. Poor transportation and communication networks have adversely affected livelihood activities. The state and its capital Yenagoa are accessed by a single road, while flooding, erosion and the growth of water hyacinth have combined to make water transport, the alternative to roads, hazardous and costly.

Social amenities are grossly inadequate in Bayelsa. For instance, it is the only state in the federation that is not served by the National Electric Power Authority (NEPA). In the education sector the state is also lacking, with only 98 secondary schools and 337 primary schools in 1991 (Okoko and Owugah, 1997). Though the state and federal governments have in recent times established new schools, the state is still educationally disadvantaged, and many communities do not have primary and secondary schools. A similar lack of infrastructure prevails in the health sector, where 180 comprehensive health centres are a far cry from the needs of the numerous isolated communities that do not have even primary health services.

There is virtually no tertiary industry in the state apart from the oil rigs, platforms and flow stations, owned by multinational corporations that litter the state. The result is acute unemployment, especially among young men. The state civil service, which is the main employer of labour, has reached its maximum of 17,000 from 4,800 when the democratically elected government took over in 1999.

This picture of inadequate infrastructure and disappearing sources of livelihoods explains why most of the people interviewed described themselves as poor. It also puts in perspective the incessant uprisings, agitations and intra- and inter-communal conflicts that are endangering security. Given the abundant deposits of oil and gas in the state, which constitute the mainstay of the Nigerian economy, the people of the state believe that the principles of allocation of revenue regardless of its primary origin have bred poverty across the land. Thus from youth groups to women's groups, traditional rulers to civil society organisations, leaders of thought to government officials, there is consensus that a critical way of addressing poverty in Bayelsa State is resource control.

Formal policy processes in Bayelsa: the arena of the state

While the way that policy is made in Bayelsa is rendered exceptionally complex by the presence both of oil companies and of politicised, ethnically-identified social movements, formal responsibility for making policy continues to lie in the hands of government actors. In this section we examine the dynamics of governance in the arena of the state, and discuss the connections and disconnections between different levels of government.

The Bayelsa study buttresses the increasing realisation in the literature that the policy process is complex, embracing a range of actors who are sometimes not aware that they are making or influencing policy. It shows that relationships between actors within and outside the formal policy structure constitute the 'processes of inclusion and exclusion, of contestation and consensus, through which particular policy positions are shaped' (Brock et al, 2001:4).

At the state level, State Governor Chief DSP Alamieyeseigha is the major actor. Although the formal structure of policymaking places the governor at the top of a hierarchy of officials from whom policy is expected to emerge, he also has the constitutional powers to reject or accept any recommendation that gets to his office via bureaucratic actors like commissioners, permanent secretaries, etc. Programmes may also emerge through the legislature via individual members' bills in the state legislature. Once such bills pass through the first, second and third reading and are taken as a resolution of the house they are forwarded to the governor for assent. If the governor objects, the house may review his objections and, after consultations, pass it into law by a two-thirds majority.

This model represents an ideal version of how policy should be made, according to the constitution. In practice, the governor looms even larger in the state policy process than even his constitutional role might suggest. While this can be traced to the operative presidential system that emphasises the principle of individual responsibility, it is also due to the fact that Bayelsa's government is a complicated coalition in which various vested interests have to be catered for; all too often this leads to deviations from the ideal process. Within the context of the zero sum character of politics, regime or personal survival take precedence over policy or ideology (Ake 1996). There is an endless quest to maintain legitimacy in the eyes of different interest groups, which launches the governor into various populist programmes and projects outside the formal government structure. In the circumstances, manifestoes and ideologies of political parties are sidelined or manipulated into the service of the political survival of the governor. Poverty alleviation programmes are no exception, being rooted not on the need to improve on the standard of living of the poor, but to enhance the governor's political survival. Groups that can support or destabilise the regime become the key actors in the poverty alleviation policies of the state.

One example of this is the governor's adoption of an ethnic-based political identity over a party-based one. While downplaying the platform of the Peoples Democratic Party (PDP), the governor advertises himself as a representative of the Ijaw people, irrespective of creed and state of origin. After part of Bayelsa State was invaded by soldiers of the Nigerian army, the self-declared 'governor-general of Ijaw nation' broke ranks with the PDP-controlled federal government. According to him:

> It was not because I love confrontation but because the interest of the Ijaw man was at stake. And in such situation, I always choose to be on the people's side... Any problem that faces an Ijaw man, be he from Akwa Ibom or Edo State, is our problem.

A related factor that explains deviation from the formal structure is the personalisation of power, a classic characteristic of the neo-patrimonial state. Senior government officials painted a picture of utter helplessness when the governor is involved, thereby suggesting that the chief executive is accountable to no one. This personalisation is illustrated by a tendency to attribute all successes to the governor. While commemorating his mid-term, for example, the governor was reported as saying that:

> the state was in a near state of hopelessness when he took over, with youth restiveness which had virtually stagnated oil production and made governance a nightmare. Two years on, he has been able to touch the hearts and lives of the people in all sectors (*The News*, 2001).

An extension of this tendency is that if a policy is likely to give credit to a political opponent, the governor can veto it by refusing to release funds for it even though the programme in question may have been approved by legislation already. This is equally applicable if the policy in question was introduced by a previous administration. The whole idea of government as a continuous process is undermined in the quest for publicity; the result is a litany of abandoned projects.

A further deviation from the idealised norm of government structure is seen in the considerable interventions of informal actors, such as politicians and close associates of the governor, in the formal structure. These seem to wield more influence on the governor than formal actors like commissioners; they may have funded the governor's campaign, or be power brokers whose support the governor feels is crucial to his regime survival. Adept bureaucrats utilise the good offices of such actors to carry out programmes. A commissioner in the state shared his experiences:

> Fortunately, we have politicians and contractors who come to us and say they want to supply this equipment. Since they have the clout to get things approved, I love them. So when they come with ridiculous equipment that we don't need, and because I know that all they want is money, I can sit them down and say to them. 'We don't need these but these are what we need, can you supply them?' They agree and we apply. It is their job to get it approved at the appropriate quarters.

It is interesting to understand the role of policy entrepreneurs in unwittingly influencing policy in their quest for business; as Clay and Shaffer (1984) argue 'the whole life of policy is a chaos of purposes and accidents'. Thus, formal actors disconnected from the state governor can be reconnected through the good offices of informal actors, who have the ears of the governor. Formal structures are superseded by informality; the people involved matter more than what the rule says.

Informality pervades the whole governmental structure and is not restricted to the executive arm. Even in the legislative arm, legislators attempt to confide in the governor and assure him of their allegiance before tabling a bill at the House. This process circumvents the traditional model whereby bills go to the governor only after being passed by the whole House. Formal actors in the state who ignore the informal route of getting at other formal actors are more likely to be de-linked and disconnected. A member of the legislature complained:

> The system here is faulty. The executive governor derives pleasure in approval schedules. Even if it is in the budget and he says 'I can't approve'. That is it! ... I represent a people but I don't know the project being carried out in my area. This is because while there is a budget, there are extra budgetary expenditures. The budget is not exclusively followed. It is followed at the discretion of the governor. At this level, the legislator cannot carry out his oversight functions.

Apart from the governor, state government officials use their positions and relationships with colleagues to influence policy and projects. A Permanent Secretary admitted that she was able to attract a project to her community because of the relationship she had with a commissioner. She reckoned this was the norm in the present dispensation where top civil service employment has been politicised and senior bureaucrats are expected to mobilise support for the governor from their own communities, while at the same time being expected by their communities to attract development projects with their 'connections' in government:

> Today, if you don't have somebody in government or a politician who can cause trouble for government you will be forgotten. And if you go into government without giving anything to your people, they will abuse you. I got a health centre for my community and when a commissioner for public utilities close to me was appointed, I asked him to site a jetty in my community, which he did. That is the way it operates here. We have not yet reached American democracy.

Consequently, it is not so much the formal structures that matter but informal relationships with relevant government officials. The formal policy making process is lubricated by informal networks among formal actors playing informal parts. Aspirant politicians and ethnoreligious leaders take advantage of this to become critical actors within the state policy realm in their quest to ensure that their own ethnic or communal groups benefit from the state cake.

A number of non-governmental actors enter the state policy arena on the explicit and formal invitation of the government. These range from consultants and advisers to civil society organisations and professional bodies. There are several mechanisms through which the participation of such actors is articulated. The House of Assembly, for example, invites memoranda and holds public hearings in the course of legislation. In addition, members of the House are financially empowered to maintain offices in their constituencies, to maintain a good relationship with the people they represent. Some public policies emerge through the interactions that take place in the constituency offices. Civil society organisations, meanwhile, may get involved in the state policy arena when their members are appointed to governmental positions. Government asks for nominations for appointment as special advisers and commissioners, and some groups have lobbied for these.

It is worth noting that within the State Executive Council are representatives of women and youth interest groups. There are indications that such appointments have enabled the government to co-opt or pacify some groups as the incidence of youth uprising has reduced considerably since the inception of the elected administration. While critics say that invited actors are just window-dressing to garnish the public policy-making process, a result of the current popularity of consultation in development discourse, there are indications that consultations do occasionally enrich policy.

Federal government agencies also feature as formal actors in the state poverty arena. The involvement of the federal government is necessitated by the fact that though its programmes and projects originated from and are funded by the centre, the sites of implementation are the states. In the case of such federal programmes, for example the National Poverty Eradication Programme (NAPEP), state-based actors – politicians and bureaucrats – are appointed to monitoring and or implementation committees. In many cases, the state government appropriates policies embarked upon by the federal government to boost its own legitimacy. A permanent secretary in the state frowned at this tendency by observing that, 'Even the state government has taken credit for federal government sponsored projects. All of these things depend on politics.' Although state actors are invited into the implementation of federal programmes, the fact that they are 'users' and not 'choosers' (Cornwall and Gaventa, 2001) creates its own dislocations. Senior government officials in the state described how they were usually summoned without notice to attend federal 'briefing' sessions, and how they have to comply because refusal or inability to do so would be tantamount to the state losing its share of the national cake. Often, compliance is at the cost of state projects or resources. Sometimes it is very difficult to know precisely who is responsible for a programme as both state and federal actors fight for pre-eminence.

While federal government actors are engaged in state-level policy processes, it is also the case that, under the rubric of resource control, state actors agitate in the federal arena to bring a greater share of oil revenue back to the Delta. Bayelsa State government's campaign for control of its own resources, in concert with other South-South[1] states, is done through the quarterly meeting of governors of the South-South and representatives of social movements such as the Niger Delta Union, and through the pursuit of lawsuits between the federal and state governments over revenue allocation. In the context of Bayelsa state politics, these activities can be viewed in several ways: as a populist strategy linked to the political survival of the governor, as an articulation of popular discourses on attacking the causes of poverty in the oil-producing areas, and as a marriage of convenience between a range of actors whose interests do not always coincide in other areas.

As well as engaging federal government around issues of resource control, the state government agitates to bring federal agencies and projects to the state. In spite of the political difficulties which arise when such agencies and projects are in place, they are seen as another potential route to accessing a more generous portion of federal largesse. The state government, for example, fought for the location of the headquarters of the Niger Delta Development

Commission (NDDC) to be in the state. The NDDC was established by the Obasanjo administration to deal with the agitations in the Niger Delta over marginalisation and underdevelopment, after the failure of previous agencies, especially the Oil Minerals Producing Areas Development Commission (OMPADEC). Although this lobbying was not successful, it is nonetheless illustrative of the relationship between the state and federal governments.

Thus far, our discussion of the government arena has focused on state-level actors, and their upward linkages to the federal. The lower layers of the decentralised system, however, may be held to be the most important in terms of connecting the people of Bayelsa to the official spaces of policy-making. The mechanics and processes of governance at this level are in many ways a microcosm of those already described at the state level, featuring personalisation of power and the politics of patronage.

The key actor in the local government policy arena is the local government chairman, who occupies a similar position to that of the governor at the state level. Although he heads a council made up of elected councillors, he is not accountable to it, because he holds office through direct elections by the people of the whole local government area. While he represents the entire Local Government Area (LGA), the councillors represent the wards that make up the LGA. The chairman is responsible for awarding executive portfolios to the councillors. This power and his control over LGA resources enables the chairman to wield enormous influence over the councillors. He is also the chief security officer of the LGA and therefore has access to the means of coercion. The councillors constitute another layer of formal actors within the local government level. They are the ones who propose to the chairman what projects they want the council to carry out in their wards. Communities therefore give credit to their councillors for attracting projects.

Within the local government arena, other actors also operate. These range from traditional rulers to community-based organisations. Traditional rulers, for instance, attempt to influence policy at local government level through advice. Since the traditional rulers receive their salaries from the state government through the local government councils, the councils also influence the traditional rulers. On the other hand, in several cases where the traditional rulers are powerful they influence who gets elected into the councils and therefore exercise a degree of control over them. In fact, powerful first class traditional rulers also exert influence beyond the LGAs, on state actors.

While LGA officials and traditional rulers are closely intertwined, each influencing the other, there is by contrast a considerable disconnection between elected officials and those they are supposed to represent. The phenomenon of absentee representatives was mentioned by many research respondents. One traditional leader described an attempt to raise an issue of salary arrears with his LGA chairman:

> We met in council and invited him. He refused to come. We went to his office he was not available. We wrote and copied the governor. He called us, but did not come to the meeting. We planned the last attack, the last straw, and he called another meeting. We have decided that he will pay all the arrears when we get there or everybody will hear about it. [...] That's a typical politician.

This example is illustrative of a range of incidents concerning elected representatives who are absent, difficult to contact and almost impossible to meet. In this case, the traditional leader narrating the story is a relatively powerful actor, with access to a telephone and able to write formal letters; but even he experiences extreme difficulty gaining access. For ordinary people, the problem of access to elected representatives is infinitely compounded.

Gaining access to those with the power to make changes is not only an issue between citizens and their elected representatives, but also between different levels of government. One LGA official observed that relationships between LGA and state levels are almost entirely problem-oriented:

> His Excellency came because there was a serious crisis over the

road and bridge construction. The youths rose and there were some accidents. So the workers fled. The bridge is His Excellency's baby because it is going to his home town and the federal government's eye is on him. So when there is a problem like that he comes to us. But for real decisions on policy-making and execution we are dispensable, they can do without us.

Crisis orientation and lack of access are two issues that are part of a wide range of factors which cause ordinary people to be estranged from the government which purports to represent them. A third is exclusion on the grounds of ethnicity, particularly given the presence of many small minority groups in the state. A participant in a focus group discussion in Yenagoa noted that:

Our town is a peer kingdom, made up of 17 villages. The state government came but in terms of appointments, government has operated through nepotism. We have a House of Assembly; we have councils where elected people should give voice to the people, however appointments only go to the Ijaws. Nothing goes to our clan.

Alongside exclusion is the issue of lack of accountability; this was linked by some to a generalised atmosphere of violence:

Nigerians, when they get to office, want to keep power. Our experience shows that nobody can be recalled, one would be killed if you tried, the level of thuggery is there and unless you are prepared to get killed, you cannot bring about change.

While exit from and mistrust of the state is a widespread phenomenon all over the country, it is particularly acute in the Delta, where government is widely held not only to be corrupt and virtually useless in the arena of service provision, but to be complicit in the extraction of the region's wealth. While such mistrust of government persists, however, the presence of oil companies provides another set of powerful actors to which people can turn in their attempt to claim compensation for the degradation of the natural resources on which their livelihoods depend. A complex set of spaces has come to exist outside the formal policy arena, occupied by non-governmental and governmental actors, in which claims for the means to reduce poverty are made and acted upon. It is this arena that is the subject of the next section.

Outside the arena of the state: hegemonic oil companies, dissenting youth

The complexity of relationships between communities, oil companies and government is daunting, and cannot be fully covered here. In this section we focus in on two particular sets of actors, oil companies and youth groups. Youth militancy in the Delta, closely connected to the issue of unemployment, has emerged powerfully in the last decade as a channel of dissent. Youth groups, often with strong ethnic identities, have raised the stakes of dissent and confrontation, and as such represent an extreme on a broad spectrum of engagement with oil companies. The companies themselves, on the other hand, have been pressed to find a range of ways to engage with the different actors with whom it is necessary to maintain a functional relationship in order to continue to do business.

Oil companies as actors

Given the significant role the petroleum industry plays in the socio-economic life of the state, oil companies are important actors in the state policy arena. They enter into the policy sphere through two principal routes.

The first is as invited actors. State government officials admitted inviting the oil companies to collaborate in the provision of basic services. Partnerships where the state provides some facilities while the oil companies provide others are worked out. For instance, in the health sector, there are several health centres, which were built by the state government but equipped and managed by the oil companies. Oil companies are also expected to contribute to the funding of the health insurance scheme and the training of public health workers. The role of oil companies as invited actors in the state policy arena is, however, constrained by fundamental differences in their motivation and that of government. State officials, for instance, fear that the powerful multinational corporations are capable of nipping a policy in the bud if they feel it is not in their long-term interest.

The second route of engagement of oil companies is as autonomous actors whose role has almost led them to be regarded as constituting an alternative government. With state failure to provide amenities and the exit of citizens from the state (Osaghae 1995) several communities turned to the nearest oil companies to provide goods and services. The companies are targeted partly because they are seen as agents of government, and partly because they are the ones who actually exploit oil and gas resources. A community leader in Oporoma put the issue in perspective when he observed:

> We don't know the government. We cannot get them. Even the local government Chairman moves around with mobile policemen. All we know is that when we want something, we march to the Shell flow station, shut it down and our demands will be met.

The result of the scenario is that Shell, as well as other oil companies, has been forced to take over the role of provision of social amenities. It is consequently possible to see Shell 'communities' where every social amenity is provided by the company. Oil company staff confirmed the extensive role of the companies in community development. They said this is necessitated by the fact that they need to have a social licence – the consent of the people – to operate beyond the official commercial licence issued by government. While the companies do not cherish the burden of being seen as an alternative government, they cannot escape it either. A community development staff of a major player in the industry confirmed this dilemma:

> It is a big question of trying to manage and endure it. Would you not do it because you don't want to be seen as government? The communities will not see it that way. They tell you, you took so and so number of barrels of oil. Even when you tell them that of all the oil revenue, only a certain percentage gets to the oil

companies, they don't want to hear. They even have statistics that you do not have.

In some cases, oil companies have been summoned by the state House of Assembly to explain certain areas of their operations. They are given certain directives, such as providing employment to youths or paying compensation to communities, or cleaning up areas affected by oil spillage. While such directives cannot be enforced by the state government, given the nature of the joint venture agreements, many oil companies tend to abide by them because they value the efforts of government officials to intervene during crisis moments.

Oil companies frequently hold consultations with a range of actors including government officials, community development committees, youth, women and civil society organisations, under the framework of stakeholder fora. While some participants in these fora do not believe they influence the policy of the oil companies, recent community development efforts by the oil companies indicate that they may have taken account of some of the issues raised by stakeholders. Apart from the projects they carry out in the communities, the oil companies have also become a medium for channelling the needs and views of the communities to the government. An oil company staff said:

> In the Stakeholders Forum for instance, the communities want us to be their voices with government. They believe we can influence government to do certain things for them.

While it is undoubtedly the case that oil companies have become involved with communities in a range of ways, and do in some areas provide services, this type of engagement is restricted to those places where there is a direct relationship with the company. It is far from the fundamental reversal of power relations which would be needed to overturn the inequalities of oil extraction.

Youth as actors
While poverty in Bayelsa is widespread, it is amongst unemployed

youths that its impact is perhaps most keenly-felt and vociferously expressed. As a member of a youth group in Onyoma commented:

> The youths are not employed in the state, local government or Shell. We are jobless. This is the cause of youth restiveness. We are not working class people. We riot against oil company and all they do is to give us casual work for a short period of time [...] I live under our parents, and still depend on them for food.

Resentment about widespread impoverishment, unemployment and lack of access to education has, since the 1990s, led to the emergence of youth movements all over the Delta, and especially in Bayelsa. Such movements are becoming entrenched as policy actors.

They have become involved in policy through two principal routes. The first is as invited actors to government or oil company consultative arenas such as stakeholders' fora. This route, which is becoming more common, is, however a dividend from the autonomous spaces that the youths have created for themselves through action, often of protest or dissent. Actions such as the closure of flow stations and the vandalisation of multi-million dollar equipment have forced oil companies to open some invited spaces in their internal decision-making structures. Here, the youth groups have successfully influenced the employment and community development activities of oil companies.

The youth movement operates at many different levels, and this is one of the keys to the successes it has achieved. As well as being active in the community, youth groups also engage LGA, state and federal government, and have an apex body, the Ijaw Youth Council (IYC). The IYC was formed to mobilise Ijaw people against violent repression, marginalisation, neglect and ecological destruction allegedly orchestrated by the federal government and oil companies.

In response to the repressive attitude of the federal military government, youth groups have adopted violent means to achieve their goals (Ikelegbe, 2001:11-117, ERA, 2000:153). They have succeeded in sacking local elites and stopping oil production. The emergent political leadership in the state, realising that it was in its interest to co-opt the popular IYC, decided to do so. Consequently, a few months after the inauguration of the Bayelsa House of Assembly in 2000, IYC visited the House of Assembly. They called for the leaders to meet them outside, handed over the resource control bill, which they themselves had drafted, and demanded that it be urgently passed into law. The resource control bill is derived from the Kaiama Declaration in which the Ijaw youths in December 1998 called on oil companies to vacate Ijaw land. Although the military authorities ignored the challenge and arrested several youth leaders, the IYC remained resolute in its demands and decided to forward them to the elected government. Consequently, as noted above, Niger Delta politicians have identified themselves with the resource control debate.

By 2002 the Resource Control Bill had advanced to the third reading in the House and the governor has also indicated his assent, following his radical rhetoric in favour of resource control. This appropriation of populist rhetoric is a survival strategy by the ruling class, which Claude Ake (1976) described as defensive radicalism. Since it is unlikely that the politicians are fundamentally committed to these ideals, the marriage of convenience may not last. In recent developments, the IYC, believing that the politicians were only interested in controlling resources which they would corruptly acquire, and not in transforming the poor socio-economic conditions of the people, have developed their own rhetoric to advocate transparency, accountability and 'communitarianism' which provides local control of resources.

Whilst youth movements have achieved some successes, there are limitations. Firstly, many youth remain outside the organised movements, intimidated not only by the violence of government and oil company agents, but by the prospects of themselves adopting a path of violence. As a youth participant in a focus group discussion in Yenagoa observed:

Oil companies are giving jobs to other people. At the end of the day we complained but the oil companies have the police and army and they suppress us. The old men will not represent us;

the old men sell us out. In terms of politics, we had the belief that the new democracy would bring government close to us, but then we discovered that rich men get access to more wealth, poor people are becoming very angry.

Secondly, violence is not the only reason that youths stay outside organised movements. Here also the issue of ethnicity is strong. While the IYC has scored successes, non-Ijaw youth are not included in the movement, and it seems that there has been little progress amongst youth from minority ethnic groups who already keenly feel the pressures of exclusion from mainstream decision-making.

Thirdly, and perhaps most fundamentally, success is limited by the very nature of what can change. Where oil companies have made reforms in the way they behave, changes are incremental rather than broad, localised rather than generalised. As such the systemic inequalities of wealth extraction remain unchallenged, and the provision of services remains uneven and unequal.

Conclusion

The study revealed a pervasive lack of confidence in government even among very senior government officials. This lack of trust, suspicion and cynicism about government derived partly from the personalisation of power and the governmental system by the chief executive, a legacy bequeathed by decades of military rule. It is in this context that the constraints formal government actors face in influencing policy could be appreciated. The study revealed the strong influence of politicians and contractors in the policy making process: formal actors have to connect to the centre of policy-making through the good offices of the politicians-cum-contractors. Consequently, formal governmental spaces are circumscribed and invited spaces are few and not dependable. Both must be lubricated by informal actors who are well linked to the chief executive – who is apparently accountable to no one but himself. The study further revealed that the people, seeing the elections as ridiculous, do not believe that elected officials are their genuine representatives, and are therefore hard pressed to make them accountable.

There is an emergent culture where politics is seen as a fraudulent enterprise where politicians invest in elections and are allowed to recoup their profits during their tenure, even at the expense of public welfare and security. The lack of trust in government, the failure of governance and the pervasive reality that the people do not benefit from the resource revenues accruing to government have combined to force the people to turn to the oil companies to exact benefits from them. In a way, this constitutes an informal mechanism through which the oil-owning communities are able to impose a kind of resource tax levy on the companies. The active engagement of oil companies by youths and communities through actions such as closure of flow stations and vandalisation of multi-million dollar equipment has opened up some invited spaces within the oil company policy processes. Still, the so-called massive investment of oil companies in community development has not been enough to satisfy the needs of the people. Equally, successive poverty alleviation programmes have been 'full of sound and fury signifying nothing' but the further pauperisation and disempowerment of the mass public. As a result of militarisation and poverty, autonomous spaces for community development are rare, and more often than not, constitute demand-oriented spaces that are dependent on oil companies and government for actualisation.

Notes
1. One of the six geopolitical zones of Nigeria.

11

Different Narratives, different Policy Models: Whose Knowledge counts in the Policy Process in Ekiti?

Olusade Taiwo and F.O.N. Roberts

Poverty in Ekiti state as in other parts of Nigeria is regarded as a matter of urgent public policy concern, considering the generally perceived rate of increase in poverty levels in the midst of enormous national endowments. Despite this, there are few people in the state who have a strong awareness or understanding of government policies designed to address poverty, reflecting a generalised sense of disconnection from government. One of the consequences of this situation is that ordinary people lack the ability or have no opportunity to contribute to the policy process from the vantage point of their lived experiences. Another is government's ineffectiveness in formulating enduring policies of poverty alleviation.

Ekiti state is a relatively new creation, carved out of the old Ondo state in south-west Nigeria in 1996. With sixteen local government areas (LGAs) and an estimated population of about 1.75 million when it was created.[1] It has the reputation of being easily the most advanced state in terms of the educational attainment of its people,[2] but this highly educated population has not altered Ekiti's status as one of the poorest states in south-western Nigeria.

Ekiti used to be well known for its production of cash crops, especially cocoa, which helped to alleviate poverty among its people. The profitability of export crops began to decrease in the late 1970s, and structural adjustment, implemented in 1986, reinforced the long decline in cocoa production. Price liberalisation led to fluctuation of commodity prices and adverse terms of trade for primary commodity producers. Combined with the impact of the expansion of Malaysian cocoa production, cash crop production in Ekiti contracted dramatically.

The poverty situation in Ekiti arises from the context of state's unique peculiarities of economy and society. If poverty policy is to address these contextual issues, it needs to be representative and accountable, and based on a strong connection between state and localised versions of poverty reduction. This vision of a direction for reforms to the policy process implies a concern with the way that the state is able to function, both as a representative and accountable body, and as an entity that distributes resources for development.

The realities that emerge from Ekiti are somewhat discordant with this vision. A diversity of policy actors exists at various levels in Ekiti state, each having interests within and outside government, and each with different knowledge of and opinions about poverty. Although there is a complex of linkages among these actors, the weakest of which are at the decentralised levels, it is apparent that in general policy-making is still predominantly top-down, lacking both a connection with localised understandings of poverty, and an effective capacity for implementation.

The prevailing top-down approach is undermined by inherent weaknesses in the structure of the state, including the lack of integration of policies across sectors and departments. Policy spaces are crowded with a multiplicity of unco-ordinated government actors, whose effective agency is closely related to their access to resources from the federal government and from donors, as well as from state generated revenues. Spaces where the participation and the perspectives of civil society actors can be accommodated remain limited. For poverty policy presently, indications are that it is the interests of the major policy actors that are being served by poverty reduction policies and programmes, rather than those of the poor. The situation concerns patterns of governance and power relations which endure despite regime change, or the democratic identity of the current ruling party.

One outcome of this configuration of state actors is that Ekiti state government has not been proactive in distilling a definite stream of poverty policy that it can call its own; there is no 'Ekitised' poverty reduction policy based on local realities. One way of explaining this is in terms of discourse, particularly the role of external actors – in this case, both the donors and the federal government – in promulgating a unified neo-liberal discourse of poverty reduction which is at variance with the more welfarist approach to development which is deeply embedded in the manifestoes of the dominant political parties of the region and characterises state party politics in Ekiti.[3] Another explanation lies in the functions and processes of different levels of governance – federal, state and LGA – and the uneven relationships of authority and flow of resources between them. Taking either of these explanations as a starting point, the relationships between policy actors and the narratives they employ as they enact their relative agency are critical.

What follows, therefore, is an examination of the major poverty policy actors in Ekiti, and the different narratives and types and sources of knowledge that inform contemporary poverty policy. We look first at how different groups of actors – government staff from different levels, political parties, civil society organisations and donors – have an influence on the policy process, focusing on the nature of the connections and disconnections between them. We then examine the diverse kinds and sources of knowledge that these actors bring to the policy process, ranging from narratives of cause and effect, through discourses of appropriate policy solutions, to the measurement of poverty itself. Finally, we discuss the prospects for an Ekitised poverty reduction policy in this context.

Government actors: a diversity of levels and identities

On the side of government, many agencies and departments exist which have an interest in poverty-related programmes in Ekiti. These actors come from all three of the major levels of government – the federal, the state and the LGA.

Beginning at the state level, the most prominent pro-poor programme is the federal government initiative, National Poverty Eradication Plan (NAPEP),[4] which addresses financial and non-financial aspects of poverty, mainly through microcredit, graduate employment and youth education. The state committee of NAPEP claims that it finds out what people want and monitors it by 'moving round'. This 'moving round' is claimed to be linked to data gathering and storage, in terms of forms and questionnaires. In interviews,

NAPEP staff implied that it is from the people themselves that it gets information about poverty.[5] Sometimes knowledge is acquired through the instrumentality of officials who, according to the state co-ordinator of NAPEP, are supposed to know poverty when they see it by virtue of being grassroots actors. Furthermore, information for pro-poor policies represented by NAPEP is partly credited to 'the people who wrote the manifestoes of the PDP'.

The Ekiti House of Assembly, unlike some of its counterparts in other states, has no House Committee on poverty. Some top government officials consulted during the research claimed not to know about poverty policies in Ekiti State, but nonetheless routinely pointed to the existence of the Ekiti State Poverty Eradication Committee (SPEC) of NAPEP, headed by the state governor, as evidence that such policies might exist. The SPEC, however, is a legal requirement of the NAPEP, rather than an initiative of the state government. It was constituted by a guideline from the federal government which inter alia specified its composition.[6] As such, the SPEC should represent an important space for poverty reduction policy, bringing together a range of actors; but ownership of the space lies outside the state, and the SPEC is seldom convened.[7]

The SPEC is located within the Department for Poverty Reduction (DPR) in the Ministry of Special Duties, which was set up to co-ordinate all poverty-related programmes of the federal government and the donor community. As both SPEC and the DPR are externally-focused, this alone has implications for the ownership and effectiveness of poverty policy in the state.

When the Commissioner for Special Duties, who oversees the DPR, listed the series of 'modest achievements' recorded by Ekiti State in the area of poverty eradication, he pointed only to the Ekiti State Community-Based Poverty Reduction Agency (ESCOBRA), the State and Local Government Reform Programme (SLGRP) and the NAPEP. While NAPEP is an initiative of the federal government, the others are programmes being implemented by the World Bank and DFID respectively. All three of these programmes are rooted firmly in the approaches to development of their originating agencies. While state-level actors were consulted by all three programmes, and a degree of political ownership is expressed, participation has been limited, and does not equate with the introduction of indigenous interpretations of poverty or approaches to alleviating it.

Despite this broad lack of state government participation, a list of the 'proposed programmes of the Ekiti DPR' – a state department – includes the payment of counterpart funds for the ESCOBPRA and the SLGRP. The only initiative unique to the state government itself is the provision of some infrastructure, and a microcredit scheme. This reflects one argument for domestic political ownership of externally-led poverty reduction initiatives: the relative absence of adequate, non-conditional resources to conduct state-led poverty policies.

Moving from the state to the decentralised level, elected and career officers of the local government area constitute the major actors, and are traditionally regarded as 'policy makers' at this level. They include the chairman of the council who is the (political) executive head of the council, the vice-chairman, supervisory councillors and elected councillors, who have a constitutional responsibility to represent their constituencies by bringing their welfare aspirations to the policy table and monitoring the governance process in general.

These actors, as local government, often see themselves as being nearest to the people and thus positioned to assess the people's needs and provide adequately for them. Their role as perceived by the people they are supposed to serve is that of an institution in charge of the resources of the area, which should use those resources to provide for the basic needs of the people and create an enabling environment for individual growth and development. These idealised versions are, however, not really reflected by the realities of local governance, for as poverty policy actors, officials of local government seem to lack dynamism, mainly relying on personal experience and political stereotypes in their area of jurisdiction as templates for action. In addition, local government offices are heavily staffed, and most LGA income is spent on salaries, leaving little or no room for meeting either the capital or expenditure costs of development initiatives. Such revenue difficulties frequently paralyse LGAs in their day-to-day business;[8]and this is even before one starts thinking about poverty reduction policy.

Beyond these financial considerations, the political complexion of local councils and the dynamics of party politics are an important influence on the way that the policy process unfolds at the LGA level, and can on occasion compound the paralysis of government officials. It is to a closer examination of political parties as policy actors that we now move.

Political parties: machines of ideology, machines of patronage?

A discussion of state actors in the policy process – whether federal, state or LGA – cannot be done outside the context of political parties. Parties in Ekiti state are important actors in at least three key dimensions of the policy process: in influencing broad local discourses of poverty reduction, in implementation of federal policies and programmes, and in the micro-politics of LGAs.

It is important to note that historically, there was in the south-west Yoruba-speaking zone of Nigeria a strong tradition of a welfare system of governance which, as noted earlier, is deeply embedded in the manifestoes of the formerly dominant political parties of the region.[8] It has become almost mandatory for successful political parties and administrations to float, under the headline of the 'Four Cardinal Programmes', free health, free education, integrated rural development and full employment programmes. In all Alliance for Democracy (AD) states, the due implementation of these programmes was logically taken to be tantamount to a poverty eradication programme.

In the words of the late Chief Obafemi Awolowo, the leader of the defunct United Party of Nigeria (UPN) and the architect of the Four Cardinal Programmes:

These Cardinal programmes constitute the substratum, the foundation, the solid and indestructible base on which a truly dynamic, stable and developed economy can be erected. Without this substratum, any other projects, however good and grand, will benefit only a few and as such, can only at best, as hitherto, induce in us an illusion of development and national affluence, in the face of grinding poverty for the masses. (Awolowo Obafemi 1981).

Given the importance of this welfarist narrative of wealth redistribution in the political history of the state, it is little wonder that Ekiti state government cannot boast a policy that fits in with the neoliberal orthodoxy of mainstreamed poverty reduction. Taking the welfarist narrative as the base would suggest instead that in AD states all the ministries and departments relevant to the four cardinal programmes constitute important poverty policy actors. The different approaches to poverty that are taken by the AD states, with their cardinal programmes, and the federal government, with its NAPEP, highlight an inherent tension in the nature of federalism in general, and Nigeria's federalism in particular: the programmatic and political contradictions between federal and state governments. This weakness has been a major cause of popular agitation and sentiments in favour of a different kind of federalism, often framed in terms of the political debate on federal resource allocation.

The role of political parties as major actors in Ekiti state policy spaces, and the disconnection between federal programmes and the state policy processes become clearer when we observe that PDP controls power at the federal level from where NAPEP originates, and that the AD controls Ekiti state. There is partisan politics in NAPEP despite the public efforts of the PDP federal government to adhere to the principle of fair representation by allowing certain percentages for other party members in the committee structures of the NAPEP. Partisan politics fuel suspicion between federal and state government functionaries over the modalities for executing the programme. Existing suspicions were further exacerbated when a PDP politician was appointed as the Ekiti state co-ordinator of NAPEP.

There had already been some degree of apprehension about the NAPEP programme in Ekiti before its implementation began. Petitions and counter-petitions had been mounted by non-PDP and PDP politicians respectively to the headquarters of NAPEP in the federal capital, alleging the exclusion of non-PDP members from NAPEP implementation in Ekiti.

There had, however, also been widely publicised attempts amongst policy actors to close ranks in supporting the programme, for the benefit of the people. The governor even became 'well disposed' to the project, co-operating with the federal government for this reason. Although doubts linger as to the practicality of the NAPEP approach, these efforts at reconciliation across party boundaries led to the creation of a small but well-located constituency of support for the programme. This may be termed as 'qualified collaboration' in the prevailing context of partisan politics, and has been made possible by a variety of factors bordering on leadership and personality issues. Both the AD state governor and the PDP chairman, as well as members of the state NAPEP committee, have demonstrated non-partisan leadership in the matter of creating a space for NAPEP at the state level.

The creation of this space indicates some momentum to overcome the divisions associated with party politics in state politics, and to fuse different approaches to poverty reduction policy, if only for reasons of realpolitik. In other areas, notably at the LGA level, such divisions continue to abound, in many cases paralysing policy actors. For example, in Ikere Local Government, there is peculiar blend of the ruling AD and the opposition PDP. Out of the eleven electoral wards, seven are controlled by PDP while AD, the ruling party in the state assembly, controls only four. The LGA is thus managed under the dual control of an administration and a legislature under different political parties. This creates multiple dilemmas for agenda setting. At the same time the impact of federal programmes such as the Poverty Alleviation Programme (PAP), which preceded NAPEP, had been felt more by PDP members in the community, which indicates that policy implementation maybe partisan.

As this very brief glimpse shows, the dynamics of party politics are one of the factors which underpins structures of government, shaping the way that different actors relate to non-local poverty reduction policies, and how they see their own activities in terms of poverty reduction. As the Ikere example shows, party politics also shape the way that decentralisation takes effect, and the way that it intersects with policy implementation.

Political parties in the Nigerian context can be seen as both machines of ideology and machines of patronage, and party politics and affiliations spill over the boundaries of 'government'. Individual actors in the policy process often have multiple identities – one may simultaneously be a party member, have a government job and be involved in local CSOs. While on one hand party dynamics are the fabric that links different government actors, on the other they also permeate civil society, creating and sustaining the links of patronage between urban and rural noted by Osaghae (2001). Party politics transcend the constructed boundary between state and civil society actors. Nonetheless, the boundary remains intact in other ways: civil society organisations experience only limited opportunities to participate in the policy process. It is to the dynamics of this participation that we now turn.

Civil society – embedded or externalised?

Civil society actors in Ekiti state, whilst diverse, fall into two broad categories. The first are the major policy actors outside government but at the state level, agencies such as the state branch of the Nigerian Labour Congress (NLC), the National Association of Small Scale Industrialists (NASSI) and development NGOs, both national and international. The second, and more numerous, are various forms of community-based groups who, while they sometimes act at the state level, act more in the autonomous spaces of exit-based institutions and organisations.

CSOs in the first category are often part of wide structures, whether national or regional. One such is the NLC, whose officials believe that it does not merely agitate, but functions as a form of political opposition. Presenting itself as an organisation that is not for workers alone, the NLC officials argue that 'we want to be part of policy formulation' and that labour should be involved, for example, in the government's process of budget preparation. Labour leaders hence see themselves as fighting for the downtrodden masses.[9]

There is, however, little evidence that the NLC has a clearly articulated position with regard to the defined anti-poverty narratives of federal or state governments, or donors, beyond occasional national level pronouncements on the effects of low wages on poverty. Despite this, a respondent from the NLC state chapter claims that the NLC was involved in the formulation of the NAPEP at the federal level, and that the state chapter is part of the SPEC. In this case, the NLC can be seen as a CSO that, despite ascribing to a narrative of poverty reduction incongruent with that of federal government, has access to invited spaces due to its own national structure and its position of embeddedness in political networks at both state and federal levels. Other CSOs in this first group, particularly NGOs, owe their access to invited spaces to the donor funding which underpins and in some senses directs their structures and activities. Yet others, like the NASSI, are deemed legitimate participants because they were initially creations of the government.

By contrast, the second category of CSOs has its origins and networks in predominantly rural civil society. Many CBOs, such as co-operative societies, market men's and women's associations, farmers' associations, progressive unions, hometown associations, credit groups and trade guilds, are involved in activities of poverty reduction. One example is the 600 registered women groups in Ekiti state which have as one of their aims the alleviation of poverty among women. Another example is the Erelu Adebayo Foundation, an NGO founded by the First Lady of Ekiti, which focuses on vulnerable groups, especially women and children. In many similar cases, a poverty reduction focus is assumed rather than explicit; and this is one factor that prevents many of the CSOs in the second category from being recognised by government, and invited into processes of consultation.

The aims and objectives of embedded CSOs and their associated programmes and projects, directed mainly towards their members and the promotion of their economic interests, can generate the means for poverty alleviation. More often than not, these associations contribute money from which members can raise funds for their individual needs, usually in the form of loans. Many beneficiaries of such rotational credit have been able to improve on their businesses and thereby contribute to improved living standards and community development. Unfortunately, because membership is not free, only those who can afford monetary contributions are members. This means that many people in the community are excluded. Among these are the bulk of the poor, whose only choice for survival is to struggle, often without success, for space in the available programmes, or to solicit gifts from friends and relations. Thus, although many CSOs in the second category do contribute towards poverty alleviation, they are not all equally accessible to the poorest.

The umbrella or apex community/town development associations deserve special mention amongst the second category of CSOs. They have been very active in the physical, socio-cultural and economic development of their respective communities. Many of these associations enjoy popular legitimacy because people see them as their own and are actively involved in their operations. There are opportunities for individuals to participate actively in decision-making processes, project identification and evaluation. The associations play the role of bridging the gap between the government and the people, albeit with questionable effectiveness.

As with government actors and political parties, the participation of civil society in the policy process depends on networks of connections and the dynamics of engagement in a range of spaces. CSOs, frequently having multiple functions, engage in many domains; and the multiplicity of domains of engagement can lead to disconnections. For example, while Home Town Associations (HTAs) may have high levels of local ownership, the focus of their energies and activities is not directed towards influencing policy or its implementation. NLC, on the other hand, may be structurally connected to the grassroots, but faces internal and external obstacles to becoming a channel for citizens' voices.

How do these CSOs articulate citizens' perceptions of poverty? Individual perceptions of poverty at the community level vary but three aspects are discernible, namely the welfare and living standard of the individuals and the immediate household; an individual's obligations to the extended family members or neighbours; and an individual's involvement in community development activities. Welfare and living standards, and involvement in community development activities are more obvious indicators of poverty but obligations to members of the immediate family are also important variables in the local concept of poverty. With respect to individual obligation to members of the extended family, for example, one is expected to take care of the needs of those in the extended family. Social norms expect one to educate children of the first and second cousins if need be and to bury one's parents 'decently'. Someone who cannot do these is regarded as a poor person.

These understandings of poverty reveal the extent to which processes of indigenous poverty reduction are embedded in precisely the kind of civil society networks which characterise the second category of CSOs. As it is these which are least likely to be involved in the poverty reduction policy process via their existing linkages and networks, this has unsettling implications for the way that lived experiences of poverty might shape policies.

Donors: importing non-local narratives

Several donors are active in Ekiti, but the two most important are the World Bank and DFID, both of which have selected the state to be part of their flagship poverty programmes;[10] they form the focus of our discussion in this section. Whilst both institutions rely on a view of poverty as a multidimensional phenomenon,[11] their programmes suggest very different understandings of the appropriate policy solutions to address it.

The World Bank's focus on poverty reduction is generally based on three pillars, namely economic governance, private-sector led growth and community-driven development. ESCOBPRA, the World Bank designed social fund in Ekiti, aims to reduce poverty by channelling direct benefits through a fund which is administered at the state level, to which applications are made via community-based institutions. The Fund is independent of the machinery of the state, although there are various government actors on its committee structures, and local leaders – traditional and elected – at the local level are important actors in the process that shapes the priorities of community applications to it. The project expects that each community, through its Project Implementation Committee (PIC) will present its priorities to the social fund. ESCOBPRA's adoption of a closed menu of projects, however, suggests that what is said is not always what is done. While the programme relies on a view of poverty as multidimensional, a large part of the solution it supplies is in the form of material and financial benefits supplied to communities in the form of matched funding.

The ESCOBPRA relies on Federal Office of Statistics poverty data, which according to staff of the agency reflects 'structures on ground', but has been acknowledged by many to be unreliable to some extent (see Chapter 8). The most recent household survey income poverty data is from 1996; the World Bank itself funded analysis of this data, and its comparison with earlier household surveys (FoS 1999), and has been the major resource-provider for efforts to construct headline statements about national poverty statistics. DFID, similarly, relies on the Nigerian report of the *Voices of the Poor*,[12] a piece of research which it funded, and championed in the Nigerian policy community. More recently, DFID has also worked to develop a rapid survey tool, the Core Welfare Indicators Questionnaire (CWIQ), which has been piloted in the states DFID has selected to work in,[13] and which it hopes will eventually have national spread. These examples of produced poverty knowledge indicate the degree to which external actors drive the construction of national poverty data, but also point to the extent to which the operational design of their programmes is located in a generalised view of poverty and poverty reduction, rather than one which is specific to Ekiti.[14]

DFID, in contrast to the World Bank, has adopted a strategy of reforming state governance through providing support to bureaucratic champions of poverty reduction, as well as supporting sectoral interventions in the arenas of finance, health, access to justice and rural livelihoods. According to the state co-ordinator of DFID in Ekiti State, DFID has 'a synergy of interventionist efforts at all levels' but in its current 'state focus', unlike in previous ad hoc programmes, the department channels its assistance into areas where the host community will feel the impact of the intervention.

According to the Project Manager for State and Local Government Reform Programme (SLGRP), in Nigeria, DFID has come to realise that to tackle poverty, you have to tackle governance. No matter how much money you spend, if there is no good governance, nothing will be achieved. Good governance reduces or eradicates poverty. DFID recognizes this approach as a 'paradigm shift' in its own operations.

For DFID, poverty reduction at the state level is also pursued through 'support for formal knowledge sectors', including, for example, working on the design and implemenation of a Core Welfare Indicators Survey with government actors. In this sense, as well as through the focus on governance, DFID's narrative of poverty reduction makes an explicit acknowledgement that the dynamics of the policy process itself are an important part of the vision of a sustainable solution. Support for formal knowledge sectors, however, rests on an assumption that an evidence-based policy process is a possibility. Given the foregoing discussion of the complexity of identities and political agendas at play around poverty reduction in Ekiti, this assumption may be questioned.

Both the SLGRP and the ESCOBPRA were in the very early days of their implementation when this study was carried out, and cannot therefore be in any way fully evaluated here. However, we can speculate that there are distinct contrasts between the 'external' and the 'domestic' streams of poverty reduction at the state level in Ekiti, just as there are at the federal level in Abuja (see Chapter 8), and that the dissonances between the two may well inhibit the development of an Ekitised poverty reduction policy. Donors are powerful actors and their templates for knowledge construction, analysis and poverty reduction interventions are an essential part of the poverty reduction policy landscape. In order that these templates might fruitfully contribute to an Ekiti-specific solution to poverty, however, they need to exist in a productive interface with existing actors and the spaces in which they operate. At present, ESCOBPRA has interfaces with particular sections of particular communities; and SLGRP has interfaces with a particular constituency of individuals in state government. There is perhaps a danger that what will result are islands of excellence, good practice or reform, at a level somewhat removed from existing official and invited spaces for poverty reduction policy. The next section returns to the realms of government and community in order to look more specifically at some of the ways that different actors are linked, in order to further understand some of the routes and terrains that different narratives about poverty and approaches to its reduction may have to travel in order to produce a poverty reduction policy tailored to the needs of and fully involving the poor of Ekiti.

Actor networks: dense but disconnected

The diversity of narratives of poverty reduction and the multiplicity of actors engaged in the policy process lead to a multitude of related and overlapping processes which are confusing and often contradictory. These processes illustrate powerfully the lack of an 'Ekitised' poverty reduction strategy: each is owned by a different configuration of actors with a variable approach to poverty reduction, each to an extent responding to externalised narratives. Ownership of policies is based in these actor networks, and this is partly what prevents disconnections to embedded constituencies of poor people at the grassroots from being overcome.

In this last section, we present a brief overview of a few of the ways that some policy actors connect with each other in the state arena, before moving to a particular LGA, Emure, to look at the way that an umbrella CSO connects a range of actors in the community.

State level connections and disconnections

In Ekiti State, the key poverty policy actors are linked and connected in various ways. Networks of actors meet around different narratives about poverty and policy initiatives; some of the actors are involved in several networks, and this provides some sense of connection between them.

At the state level, for example, there are strong linkages and interactions between some of the poverty policy actors and NAPEP. The social welfare department, for instance, makes inputs into NAPEP in the form of recommending destitutes for inclusion in its assistance schemes. These inputs are not necessarily complementary in terms of shaping the parameters of poverty policy, as these are handed down from Abuja; they are essentially inputs for implementation. The state and the federal therefore connect through implementation of programmes. This brings a particularly hierarchical flavour to the connections between government actors with different identities, firmly casting the state actors as 'users' rather than 'choosers' of policy (Cornwall and Gaventa, 2001).

NAPEP attempts to reach out to some important stakeholders in poverty policy such as NASSI and NLC. The state chairman of NLC is a member of the State Co-ordinating Committee (SCC) of NAPEP. This connection may be characterised as taking an invited seat at a policy table, although once more the concerns of those seated are with implementation rather than formulation. The seat is available to a senior member of a bureaucratic CSO, and may be seen as largely symbolic. As we have already discussed, the NLC takes a significantly different view of the causes of poverty from that of the federal government. As such, making a symbolic connection by occupying an invited seat is a relatively minor connection in the enormous web of interlocking actor networks in which the NLC itself is embedded. Although the NLC occasionally attempts to rally other civil society organisations towards having a word in shaping the policy of the government, it has recently directed its energy towards the arena of national electoral politics in an attempt to catalyse the formation of a Labour Party which would provide alternative spaces for policy articulation in the interest of the masses.

The World Bank's ESCOBPRA, like the NAPEP, is logically linked to the federal government, as the project is a social one, financed by a World Bank credit to the federal government. The important contributors to the programme are the communities for whom the programme is meant – who are required to pay 10% as counterpart fund – and the appropriate ministries in the state. A board serves as the interface between the state government and the federal government, bringing together actors from different departments. Once more, these connections represent a relatively superficial layer of the entirety of ESCOBPRA's activities; and the spaces established to connect the programme to the government are managed according to the rules of the implementing agency. In this case, it is federal, state and LGA actors who are the 'users' of the policy, while the

World Bank sets the parameters for legitimacy about which kinds of community project can or cannot receive funds.

With the SLGRP, focused on reforming state governance, DFID makes explicit efforts to consider how to engage government actors in a productive way. Early in the process, there were 'consultative forums' where programmes were introduced to the governor and members of the state government. A series of explanatory meetings led to the formation of the Ekiti State Reform Team (ESRT); gradually a network of poverty reduction champions is emerging in Ekiti state. Notably however, despite DFID's objectives of reaching the 'state as a whole', the ESRT has little interaction with civil society, and has chosen to direct its activities towards civil service reform, arguing that:

> The ESRT in its governance reform process is saying charity must begin at home. It has therefore chosen as one area of assessment, operational reform in members' places of work, as a matter of utmost necessity.[…] the civil service is the hub of the public service and for any meaningful governance reform to be achieved the machinery to propel it must itself undergo reputation and image rejuvenation. The civil service must be transparent, accountable and efficient and must be seen to be so in its day-to-day operations. (DFID, January 2003)

The process of the SLGRP, and the kind of connections it tries to establish with different actors, represent an attempt to shape the policy process itself, as an indirect route to reducing poverty. Certainly, the relationships that SLGRP creates and supports are of a different nature from either those catalysed by the ESCOBPRA, or those established under the aegis of different federal and state programmes. Thus three separate actor networks coalesce around the key imported programmes, each catalysing different spaces in operational isolation from the other. They lack horizontal connections which would allow programmatic learning to be exchanged and shared in the hope of creating more consistent approaches which would be widely spread and owned. Further, their vertical connections are limited: while the

ESCOBRA and NAPEP do have relationships with actors at the community and LGA levels, these are again shaped by externally-generated rules; and in the case of NAPEP, embedded in inter-party political dynamics. Crucially, these limits shape the prospects for the upward flow of information and influence that would be necessary to reverse the dominant, top-down nature of the policy process.

Lower level linkages
At the community level, networks among various civil society actors are quite visible, and markedly different from the networks in the state arena discussed above. For instance, membership of the various associations in a locality, neighbourhood or village often overlaps. Those in co-operative societies are also members of market traders' associations; farmers' association members also take part in social clubs. Besides, all the associations have representatives in the apex development associations, which meet periodically to deliberate on the development of the community and individual problems in particular. One example of these is the Ikere Development Council (IDC) in Emure LGA.

IDC purposefully brings together a range of actors, each of which has a different function with regard to meeting the aims of the organisation. The IDC is organised hierarchically; at the top sits the traditional leader, the Oba, who gives ultimate approval to the decisions about development projects made by the IDC. A key figure in the IDC structure is the registrar, who liaises between the Oba, heads of lineages and quarters of the town, and the LGA. He is instrumental in identifying development projects for the town, mobilising resources from community groups, getting the support of the LGA for such projects by counterpart funding, infrastructure and technical support and removing administrative bottlenecks.

Heads of various families, trade associations and social clubs are used as contacts in reaching the people or in overseeing the equitable allocation of benefits and responsibilities for projects, whilst religious organisations such as churches and mosques are often approached for assistance. Women's organisations participating in the IDC have been a platform for receiving or asking for poverty relief action for women, and for group action to receive aid such as government loans, commercial inputs, skills acquisition, development information and so on, and for protecting the political and socio-economic interests of women.

As such, an apex community development association like the IDC encompasses a range of interests and differently positioned actors, whose own linkages and networks are relied upon to carry out particular functions with regard to the development of the town. Meetings of the IDC may be characterised as autonomous spaces, or as sites of exit where ordinary people are trying to generate their own solutions. The relative strength of this kind of association in the Ekiti context is founded on the ethnic homogeneity of the area, and thus the relative lack of ethnic conflict within communities. While a space like the IDC undoubtedly holds within it uneven power dynamics, inequalities, party political loyalties and blocked communications, it represents a significant space in the configuration of localised attempts to reduce poverty and achieve development

Where, though, does an organisation like the IDC fit into the wider picture of poverty policy in Ekiti state? While IDC membership includes the LGA chairman and other important government functionaries, the link between the autonomous and the official policy space is not strong, being personalised in the same way that, in a wider sense, political power is personalised in neo-patrimonial states. The LGA chairman himself might be seen as a linkage to other government policy arenas at the state level, but as we have seen, there is a degree of disconnection between state and LGA level which suggests this might not be the case. In spite of the routine exhortations that local government is a grassroots government, there seems to be significant alienation of the people from the activities of the government, and a significant disconnection between the networks which form around policy initiatives at the state level and those that characterise autonomous activities of self-help at the community level and below.

Conclusion

Our discussions in this chapter suggest that there are disconnections at play in the policy process which underline the incomplete participation or exclusion of some actors. In a sense, different institutional actors at all levels have different outlooks, and these are played out through the different actor networks that each creates around itself. The principal narratives and threads of poverty reduction solutions are reinforced by these networks. Those at the higher levels are the most important; and in Ekiti, the knowledge that counts most, that is considered the most valuable and legitimate, comes from outside the state.

The multiple constituencies represented in the dense actor networks in Ekiti rely on different experiences and understandings of poverty to inform their actions. Different actors have different stories to tell: some are in the form of research, information and measurement of the phenomenon of poverty, while others are embedded in the actions of poverty reduction, be they at the level of exit-based self-help, or the programmes and strategies of governmental and non-governmental institutions.

As we have seen, not many of the prevailing local narratives of poverty actually get translated into policy. There are thus gaps in the policy process. For instance there are various views on the causes of poverty. For the local government area and traditional elite, one narrative includes the problem of lack of creativity among people, so that the urge to create wealth and turn around the resources available is not there. A second narrative emphasises the lack of basic facilities and an enabling environment, which discourages people from coming 'home' to invest.

It is as instructive as it is revealing that many respondents, in and out of government, saw education as a 'cause' of poverty in Ekiti state. The state's sobriquet is the 'Fountain of Knowledge'. However, rather than translating knowledge into the means of eradicating poverty, this high level of education manifests as poverty among a highly literate people, for many reasons. Education alone cannot solve the problem of poverty. In the absence of a basic infrastructure and industrial development, the government remains the main employer of labour. State officials claim that the state government pays a wage bill almost equal to the amount of the state's monthly share of revenue from the federation account. As a result many graduates are without prospects for employment. The large army of unemployed graduates creates a burden on the family and the community, thus increasing the poverty index of the state.

During the research feedback meeting, an elderly woman painfully lamented the plight of unemployed graduates in her community, narrating that her community had just witnessed a suicide due to this phenomenon, and crying out for the creation of skilled employment opportunities. Laying emphasis on the acquisition of certificates, rather than skills, creates shortages of the kind of manpower needed to develop the potential industries in the state.

This critical knowledge, central to public discourses about poverty in Ekiti, is not translated into policy because it is not part of the dominant imported narratives connected with the federal government and the donor community. It is little wonder, therefore, that poverty policy in the state and local government is seen broadly as a welfare promoting action, whilst the donors also pursue their own agenda according to their preferred orientations, which are dictated from the capital, or from their overseas headquarters.

The weakness of the interface between knowledge base and policy formulation reduces the latter to a subject of intuitive judgement. The limited interface between research knowledge and policy needs to be bolstered by improving direct contact between the users and producers of poverty data, 'producers' being interpreted to include poor communities.

Because policy-making is still predominantly top-down, more spaces need to be created to accommodate the knowledge of civil society. If anything, it is state officials, rather than community members who have first-hand experience of poverty, who need to be sensitised and perhaps mobilised for action. This is necessary because, from impressions expressed at the feedback meetings held after the research, participants claimed that government authorities are not accessible and that they do not respond favourably when approached. It is further believed that governments never change. Official attitudes are said to be set and therefore attempting to influence government is regarded as a waste of time.

The major concern is how policies can be developed that will serve the needs of the poor and not the interests of the major policy actors. In other words, poverty reduction policies and programmes should be made more accountable and responsive to the needs of the poor. There is a need for the Ekitization of poverty policy distilled from its disparate poverty knowledge. Poverty knowledge should be translated into poverty policy as a first step towards a bargain with other poverty policy actors who have their own interests. Otherwise, its poverty reduction initiatives will continue to lack clarity and focus, and be doomed to failure.

Notes

1. http://www.ekitistate.gov.ng/ accessed 12.06.03
2. Many villages in Ekiti boast a Ph.D. holder.
3. The current ruling party, the Alliance for Democracy (AD) can trace its manifesto from the defunct AG and United Party of Nigeria (UPN).
4. See Chapter 8 for a discussion of the evolution of NAPEP.
5. This is in direct contrast with NAPEP staff in Jigawa, who claimed that all their poverty knowledge came from the federal government.
6. Nonetheless, those agencies represented on SPEC provide an indicator of which government departments are seen as major poverty policy actors. They include the Social Development Department (SDD), State Works Department (SWD) and Ministries for Women Affairs, Education, Women and Youth Development, Environment, Finance and Budgeting, Local Government and Special Duties.
7. The same phenomenon was noted in a study of Enugu state, where researchers were unable to find evidence that the SPEC had ever met (Francis and Nweze 2003)
8. See Francis and Nweze (2003) for details of this in Enugu
9. See Chapter 9 for more detail on the role of the NLC in national civil society
10. The UNDP also does considerable work in Ekiti state, principally through funding community development projects, with which it aims to 'influence policy through demonstration'.
11. This view is shaped by mainstream development discourses on poverty reduction, and is mainly informed in the Nigeria context by the findings of the seminal 'Nigeria: Voices of the Poor' (Ayoola et al, 1999) study.
12. commissioned in Nigeria by DFID as part of a 23-country World Bank

study, managed from Washington, which presented findings about poverty from poor people's perspectives. (Narayan et al, 2000)

13. Ekiti, Jigawa, Enugu and Benue

14. While both ESCOBPRA and SLGP have undertaken analyses of local information as part of their process, this takes place at the implementation and monitoring stage rather than at the design stage. As such, incorporating learning from the existing social situation requires changes in operational practice.

12

Constructing Spaces for Poverty Reduction: Politics, Religion and Poverty Reduction Policies in Jigawa State

Yahaya Hashim and Judith-Ann Walker[1]

Jigawa State was created out of the former Kano State by the military regime of General Ibrahim Babangida in 1991. At the time of its creation, 17 local government areas (LGAs) were inherited from Kano and 4 new ones were created. In 1996, six further LGAs were created by the military government of General Sani Abacha, giving Jigawa its current 27 local government areas .

Side by side with the modern system of democratic governance in Jigawa is the traditional emirate system. There are 5 emirates in Jigawa state[2] each administered by a traditional ruler referred to as the emir. Below the emir there are district heads, followed by the village heads and then the ward heads. Within this traditional system of governance, the emirs and other traditional rulers historically wielded both religious and secular authority.

Indigenously owned discourses of poverty reduction have a strong place in the policy process of Jigawa. Not only does the state government of Jigawa have its own poverty reduction programme,[3] but there also exists a complex local system of distribution of resources between richer and poor members of communities, adminstered via the emirate system, and firmly located in Islamic understandings of poverty reduction. In this chapter, we discuss elements of these indigenously owned discourses in detail, before going on to look at three policy spaces for poverty reduction which arise from them, and which present different opportunities for responsive policy.

Discourses of poverty reduction in Jigawa
Official poverty discourses:equilibrium and vulnerability
How does the Jigawa state government perceive 'poverty? What are the sources of poverty knowledge for governmental actors? How

238

do these actors use poverty knowledge and what are the effects of the different ways of using poverty knowledge?

Perceptions of poverty among government officials in Jigawa State are unusually uniform; all government officials, as well as other actors interviewed, shared a perception of poverty similar to that of the official view of the governor, Alhaji Saminu Turaki. This is a perception of poverty as general within the state, and which views all inhabitants of Jigawa as poor. We describe this as an equilibrium model of poverty, best articulated in the narratives of government officials who responded to questions of how they viewed poverty in Jigawa State by saying that: 'Jigawa is the poorest state in the Federation and therefore most people are poor.'

It is with this in mind that the address of the Commissioner of Information on the occasion of the 10th Anniversary of the state in 2001 should be viewed. The title of the address was appropriately entitled: 'Jigawa: A Decade Behind.' Interviews with government officials in critical departments such as Economic Planning showed that they often held the view that there were more poor people in Jigawa State than in other northern states such as Sokoto, Borno and Yobe.

The equilibrium model which informs government's perceptions and narratives about poverty encompasses the entire state and includes multiple target groups who are classified as living in poverty simply because they reside in Jigawa. For the Jigawa state government, the people of the state are poor because the state is poor. The state is poor because it is young and rural, and its citizens are viewed as lacking the requisite skills and aptitude to generate good incomes for themselves. This view of poverty results in the corresponding analysis, repeatedly narrated by civil servants to the research team, that 'everything the government does in Jigawa state is for poverty alleviation.'

The state government views development in terms of a modern and industrialising economy, and thus poverty is defined as the state of existence without key competences for a modern and, by definition, developed Jigawa. Descriptive narratives of poverty which emanate from the equilibrium model of the state government, revolve around notions of the poor as rural, under-productive and unskilled. Models of government action that arise from the narratives are therefore based on the assumption that a minimal level of physical infrastructure is required in lead sectors such as technology and industrial production.

In addition to the equilibrium model, there is a second narrative which also occupies the minds of government officials. In this view, poverty is the result of short-term disruptive experiences and risks such as natural disasters. In a sense this view is more about vulnerability and the vulnerable in society than it is about poverty. This point is, however, lost on the Jigawa state government which views vulnerability as itself a form of poverty. For many state officials interviewed, Jigawa's position as one of the poorest in the federation was linked to the fact that it is subject to the risks of drought, floods, pest infestations and desertification.

There are therefore in Jigawa State two sets of official perceptions and discourses of poverty, the equilibrium model, and the vulnerability model, which resonate with each other. Despite this resonance, sources of knowledge about poverty when it is viewed as inherent risk, are different from those relied on when it is viewed as a generalised phenomenon. When the state government responds to unplanned disruptive events, it does so with knowledge gained from experience and aimed at a practical outcome. For example, the Assistant Chief Executive Officer of the State Emergency Relief Agency explained the activities of the agency in terms of systematic, rational and organised efforts designed to achieve optimal service delivery. He talked about rapid appraisal in the immediate aftermath of a disaster. This, he said, is followed by an assessment by an operations team. Estimates are then made of damage and needs and relief material is acquired accordingly.

In regard to the equilibrium model of poverty, which is reflected in the policies of the state government, multiple sources of poverty knowledge are used. The introduction of a specific poverty alleviation initiative cannot always be linked to a particular source of knowledge. More often than not it appears that several different knowledge sources combine towards producing a specific project or programme. Interviews with senior government officials revealed, however, that the governor's own comparative assessments and informed opinion are the most important knowledge sources that lead to innovative poverty alleviation outcomes.

Poverty discourse in Islam: Destitution, disability, welfare and charity

In the Islamic discourse on poverty, Zakkat constitutes the central point of departure. Zakkat[4] is a charity tax which, together with five daily prayers, faith, performing the Hajj,[5] and fasting in the month of Ramadan, collectively constitute the five pillars of Islam. Zakkat is therefore an Islamic injunction and is compulsory for Muslims within the taxable bracket which lies above the Nisab, an Islamic poverty line. Self-sufficient and wealthy individuals are expected to pay their debt to the poor through this process of purification. In Northern Nigeria Zakkat is, for the most part, left to individuals to implement. In Jigawa, however, five Zakkat committees, corresponding to the five emirates, have been established.

The underlying perception of poverty in the Zakkat committees of the three emirates that this study examined was that it is a transitory state of extreme privation. This perception is informed by a particular poverty discourse within Islam which holds that while poverty cannot be eradicated entirely it can be alleviated through purposeful actions, as specified by Islamic tenets and guidelines. Because the condition of the *faqiri* (the extremely poor) and the *miskini* (the moderately poor) is seen as harsh, Muslims who have more are obliged to contribute towards the alleviation of poverty. Our study found that community members and associations generally believe that the Zakkat committees of the three emirates have been effective in targeting the poor and alleviating their poverty through charity.

The knowledge base of Zakkat is well known and has little variation. The four main schools of Islamic jurisprudence are agreed on the basic tenets that inform Zakkat, which clearly define who should give Zakkat and which wealth is 'taxable'. For example, such wealth should have been held for a year, should be in excess of basic needs and should not be encumbered by debt.

The tenets are also clear on the beneficiaries of Zakkat. These include the *faqiri,* who have no means of livelihood beyond day to day, and the *miskini,* who do not have a year's supply of food secured. The collection and the distribution of Zakkat relies on a traditional census in the community to collect data that will identify beneficiaries and contributors. The enumerators here are not trained professionals but neighbourhood leaders, ward and village heads and district heads. They move in a troupe from house to house with some support from scribes who may be local teachers or local civil servants.

Donor discourses

While the donor community in Jigawa is not large, its discourses and resources are an important part of the policy process. It is important to situate donor discourses in the context of both the programmes and foreign policy of external actors, and in some cases in the context of the methodologies of the bilateral and multilateral international development establishments. In this regard, marked differences can be observed in respect of the perceptions held, the narratives entered into and the use of information.

In the main, different donor approaches to poverty reduction policy can be classified as those used by international development organisations which buy into and try to support the existing poverty policies of the state, and those used by donors who formulate and implement their own development programmes. While the former group works within the perceptions and narratives of the state government, the latter acts according to its own perspectives and often draws from and adapts headquarters discourses of poverty to the local situation.

An example of the former approach is the bilateral support given to agriculture in Jigawa state by the United States Government upon the visit of the American Congress Delegation in November 2000. The American Congress Delegation pledged financial assistance worth $3 million from the U.S. government to complement the state's efforts towards boosting agricultural production. Support from other donors, most notably members of the UN system, comes in the form of supporting the state's own plan.

DFID's[6] State and Local Government Reform Programme (SLGRP) is an example of the second group. Instead of contributing via the state government's plans, it has designed its own pro-poor programme in support of the state's poverty alleviation policy. The SLGRP seeks:

> to enhance the capacity and effectiveness of state and local government to formulate policy, manage resources and support service delivery in the interests of poor people...The expected outputs of the programmes are... more efficient and effective service delivery ... especially to poor people; more democratic, accountable, transparent and responsive state and local government (SLGRP Briefing Note, April 2001:1).

Interestingly, despite their independent roots, there were remarkable similarities between the human resource approach of the SLGRP and that of the state government. The SLGRP arrived at perceptions of poverty and poverty reduction options that rejected actions such as construction of wells and high technology solutions, and focused instead on improving the responsiveness of the system. By equating responsive government with poverty reduction, the SLGRP seeks to support the Jigawa state government through initiatives such as improved communication between local governments and communities, and civil service training in participatory methods and techniques. Hence the following observation:

> SLGRP is therefore taking care in its use of language. By avoiding this word [poverty] in certain states, breaking down poverty-reduction into its constituent parts, and using more positive terminology, we may find that SLGRP and the state governments are actually talking about the same thing. *(Op. cit,* p. 4)

In spite of this overall level of complementarity, there are, however, conflicting perceptions of who is poor as well as disagreements over the role of human resource development in poverty alleviation. On the issue of who is poor, fundamental differences exist between the

SLGRP and the state government. The SLGRP seeks to reorient civil service through retraining in participatory needs assessment and budget analysis in order to make allocations which better serve the rural poor. On the other hand, the government's equilibrium model classes civil servants as themselves poor people who, like the rural poor, need to be targeted for poverty alleviation.

With regard to discourses of poverty reduction, the SLGRP appears to be guided by a notion that human resources can be made more effective in poverty alleviation through reorientation and retraining. The state government, while agreeing that human resources are unproductive and ineffectively allocated within the current system, considers the solution is not to retrain civil servants to be nice to poor people, since they were also poor, but to give them new skills in sugarcane production and relocate them in order to enhance their income generation abilities.[7] It has established a programme, the Millenium Village Commission (MVC) to implement this objective . Hence the observation of the SLGRP representative in Jigawa State when she states that the DFID's perspective is about enabling the government to deliver better services, while the government's own perspective focuses on income generation.

With specific regard to the SLGRP in Jigawa State, the findings of enquiries, as well as national level data, constitute the key sources of poverty knowledge for the those charged with carrying out the programmes. The methodologies, data sources, reference points and approaches employed in enquiries largely reflected participatory approaches favoured by DFID. Ultimately it is the DFID Nigeria Country Strategy Paper, which convened a series of country-wide consultative workshops, that is the key knowledge source which underpins the whole approach of the SLGRP.

Actors constructing spaces for poverty reduction

In poverty reduction in Jigawa, the state, international donors and civil society actors are engaged in the construction of policy spaces and in shaping the decisions made in these spaces. In Chapter 1, we described three types of spaces, official, invited and autonomous, which we adapted during the course of the research. Here, we discuss an example of each of these three kinds of space from the research in Jigawa, looking not only at the nature and dynamics of the space, but also at the implications of what we learned for the categorisation of different kinds of spaces.

Creating invited space for the people – the Jigawa State People's Congress

The Jigawa State People's Congress (JSPC) can be considered an invited space, defined by the state inviting the participation of civic organisations to strengthen JSPC programmes. The JSPC was conceived by the state government as an intermediary organisation, facilitating both the formation and identification of civic and development associations, and improving their relationships with branches of the state government. The idea is that the JSPC will aggregate demands and community needs through NGOs and CBOs, and will pass them over to the government to ensure that the government development programmes serve the people and meet their needs. Civil society is therefore invited to work with government in the spaces provided by the JSPC to develop and/or implement poverty reduction policies and strategies. While it is only politicians and bureaucrats who have access to official spaces, in the invited space created by the establishment of the JSPC, civil society actors not only have access, but are a major focus and target. It is important however, to note a number of interesting points about this invited space, especially when compared to the official spaces.

The first is that the state institutional actors in this space are not the primary actors in poverty policy. Although a tangential link with the Millennium Village Commission, the main poverty reduction programme of the state, was established early in the process of forming the JSPC, it has had only a minor role in the work of the congress. This raises questions about the importance of civil society participation in different parts of the state government, and defines limitations of what can be achieved in the invited space.

The second point is that there is a great deal of confusion about the space offered by the JSPC, indicated not only by the fact that its legal status is very unclear, but by the diversity of ways it is viewed by differently positioned actors. While CSOs and donors regard this space as official space or at best invited space, the state government insists that it is an autonomous space, in which civil society actors have a degree of control, and has asked the other actors to treat it as such. CSOs have expressed willingness to work with the JSPC or are doing so, but they approach it as they would approach an official body. The donors are much more reluctant to engage the JSPC, viewing it with some suspicion. Although DFID has worked with the JSPC to support it to develop a strategic vision and plan, the leap to grant-making to the JSPC, as to an NGO, has not been made.

Thirdly, policy decisions are not made in the space provided by the JSPC. Instead, the space is used to process suggestions and complaints and to mobilise civil society groups to support and understand government programmes. The mobilisation role of the JSPC is fairly obvious even to the casual observer. A twice-weekly radio programme, *Dandali* (platform) is produced and broadcast by the JSPC's leading officials. We monitored the radio programme over several weeks and our conclusion is that while it focused on mobilising people to engage with the JSPC, it also contained a strong element of political propaganda. The JSPC also organised a 'Grand Rally' in 2000, where it brought together organisations from all the twenty-seven LGAs in the state. The organisations were encouraged to set up a stall to show and explain what they do. According to a senior official of the JSPC, the governor addressed this rally and went round the stalls to talk to the organisations and to suggest solutions to some of their problems. The mobilisation represented by the rally and radio show is largely focused on problem identification and top-down suggestions for solutions, rather than making it possible for the voices of citizens to be heard and to influence government policy.

A review of eighteen[8] randomly selected complaints which were brought to the JSPC shed light on its other role, that of aggregating demands, complaints and suggestion, which are then passed on to the Jigawa government. Two of the eighteen complaints and suggestions were made by individuals while the rest were made by CSOs. Over thirty per cent came from organisations and individuals from Dutse LGA, which is also the state capital, although there were complaints and suggestions from all the five emirates. A detailed examination of the eighteen complaints showed that little or nothing was being done by the government in response to any of them.

The semi-autonomous space of Zakkat: a return to what the people know

There are no spaces in the policy process in Jigawa that are completely autonomous of government. The 'autonomous' spaces can be more accurately described as semi-autonomous or semi-official, their status being defined by the degree of their independence from the state or from powerful international and local actors. Genuine autonomy might be more of a characteristic of individual powerful actors, and these are indeed few. In Jigawa the Zakkat project of the emirates occupies a semi-autonomous space. Two major actors are involved in this space – traditional titleholders and Islamic scholars. Others are wealthy individuals and jurists. Civil society organisations other than these are not conspicuous in this space; neither are major donors, who for obvious reasons would not normally be involved in the space created by the Zakkat.[9]

The initiative for Zakkat came from the emirates, especially that of Dutse. However, official financial support from the state government and the legal status of the Zakkat under Sharia law itself suggest a semi-official space with a complex identity. The hope of the government is to encourage the setting up of a single state Zakkat committee that will co-ordinate the various emirate committees. Indeed the Emir of Dutse was approached by the government to initiate and chair such a committee, but he declined and opted for emirate-based committees.

The Zakkat committees have a structure that starts from the community and goes up to the level of the emir's council. Each level has its functions spelt out. The structure follows closely the governance structures of the former emirates. At the village level a committee under the chairmanship of the village head supervises the ward level committees who collect census data on who is eligible to receive Zakkat, and store the Zakkat collected for final distribution. The village committees are overseen by district committees. Above this, each emir chairs a main Zakkat committee.[10] The functions of the main committees are the same in all the emirates, namely the disbursement of the resources of the committee, the determination of its general policies and the supervision of the whole Zakkat programme.

Alongside this emirate-based committee system, a local government committee has been created to co-ordinate all the districts in a Local Government Area. This is a deviation from the traditional governance structure of the emirates, and a member of one of the committees confessed that it was actually created to co-opt the Local Government Council. As he puts it 'transport, petrol and such little things are critical to the logistics of a programme such as Zakkat therefore having the LGC's financial support might be critical for implementation.'

By all accounts in Jigawa the outcome of the Zakkat structure is successful, although this success is not evenly distributed between emirates. In Dutse, 93% of those identified in the beneficiaries' census as being in extreme poverty were reached by the Zakkat project in its first year, while 36% of those identified as needy were reached. Drawing from the experience of the best practice represented by Dutse, the apparent success of the Zakkat is attributable to certain pertinent factors, which include transparency in policy implementation, information-based policy design, a system of incentives to implementers to perform, strategies to overcome anticipated obstacles and a non-political approach.

Transparency is evidenced from the distribution of Zakkat in public. At publicised open meetings in the communities in which Zakkat was collected, the names of all contributors are read out. The beneficiaries are given the Zakkat at the same meeting. The rule is that Zakkat should be distributed in the communities in which it was collected, except when it is necessary to balance off a surplus in one part with a shortage in another. Two members of the Dutse Zakkat committee told us that at first there was reluctance to give Zakkat because the contributors said their wealth was going to be siphoned to the state capital to give to the rich. They therefore wanted to continue to give their contribution to whoever they chose privately. The system of open distribution changed this. Members of the community had started to ask why some names were not mentioned when they knew that they were eligible to pay Zakkat. The givers also wanted the public recognition of their social contributions.

The design of the Zakkat project was preceded by the collection of the basic information needed for setting targets, identifying type of beneficiaries and estimating contributions. In addition, information on anticipated obstacles was compiled and strategies developed to overcome them. For example, it was anticipated that since the *ulamas*[11] had been the ones getting all the Zakkat to distribute before and had not done so effectively, their support for the new system might be difficult to gain. An advocacy plan was therefore developed to win their support, and with the open community-based approach the Zakkat committees felt they would be able to contain the *ulamas*. This indeed succeeded and ulama support was built; some of the *ulamas* were involved in committees and others were legitimate Zakkat beneficiaries themselves.

A system of incentives was also built into the Zakkat project. The public mention of contributors was an incentive to them to give. Indeed during interviews mention was made of contributors who had privately paid Zakkat before because they were suspicious of the new Zakkat project but who gave again publicly because they were now happy with the openness of the new system. Generous prizes were also set as incentives to the best collecting district, village and ward heads. The voluntary workers on the project were also given allowances to take care of their expenses. So everyone had an incentive to work in implementing the policy.

Finally the non-political nature of the project and the promise of heavenly reward implied in the activities made many of the actors feel that they were involved in something that was virtuous and honourable. This motivated the actors and, with the other factors mentioned, combines to make this semi-autonomous space different from the others.

The weak impact of federal might: the official space of the NAPEP
As in other Nigerian states, the federal government's National Poverty

Eradication Plan is an important poverty reduction initiative in Jigawa. The Jigawa State NAPEP programme co-ordinator explained that the NAPEP was a federal programme which took its definition of poverty and target groups from the federal government. In implementing it in Jigawa, a standardised approach was used to ensure consistency with the other states. The co-ordinator explained that in view of the programme design, no specific data derived from Jigawa was used.

When asked about the innovative poverty reduction schemes of the Jigawa state government, the difficulties being experienced in these schemes and the possibility of NAPEP supporting them, the response of the co-ordinator was as follows:

NAPEP has no involvement in sugarcane projects of the state. We know that the sugarcane projects are a big problem and many people are losing income, but NAPEP is a co-ordination body of the federal government and has a standard approach to poverty alleviation which must be implemented throughout the country, it therefore cannot get involved in the sugar cane projects of the Jigawa State government. For now NAPEP is limited to youth empowerment schemes; there is no direction to go into the sugarcane scheme.

In response to further probing about the possibility of the NAPEP programme collaborating with and developing supportive links with the state poverty alleviation programme, the co-ordinator affirmed:

The industrial attachment scheme under NAPEP and the skills acquisition centres are the only links with the Jigawa State programme. We willingly pay the government for the use of the centres. Instructors are government workers so no payment is made to the instructors. There is no other area of co-operation.

The sources of poverty knowledge for the formulation of the NAPEP programme were also federally determined. The programme was designed at the federal level, and NAPEP documentation refers to data and information from all states of the federation. When the NAPEP co-ordinator for Jigawa state was asked whether the knowledge base of the NAPEP programme addressed the peculiarities of poverty in Jigawa, he cited his inability to identify and place unemployed graduates in Jigawa. Because of the low literacy rate in this state most graduates are employed – 'I cannot even find unemployed male graduates, let alone female graduates'. From this, he seemed to be suggesting that indeed the peculiarities of Jigawa's poverty are not addressed by the NAPEP blueprint.

The use of poverty knowledge in the Jigawa NAPEP programme can best be explored in terms of the performance of the programme to date. Currently, NAPEP is using two skills acquisition centres in the state to carry out its programme. The co-ordinator explains that it has been difficult to start up the programme in Jigawa because of what he describes a the 'lack of seriousness' of the government. To get the government to co-operate with NAPEP the co-ordinator said that he 'bent down to gain acceptance' in order to avoid conflict with the state government. 'This is because the state government is not so much against the programme as they are lazy to give full support ... they are uninterested.'

For many actors interviewed, however, NAPEP was not, as its documents would suggest, an invited policy space. It is a space only some of them had heard of and no one knew of someone who had benefited from NAPEP or represented any other than the ruling party's interest in the space.

Conclusion: Politics, religion and poverty reduction policies

The idea of separating policy spaces into different categories is useful as an analytical tool. In reality the spaces are linked to one another, in part by the participation of actors who are engaged in more than one space. Actors in both the invited and autonomous spaces try to access official spaces, as policy from their own spaces is legitimised and strengthened by a relationship with official spaces. Thus, for example, the Zakkat is legislated as public policy although it bears more characteristics of a private effort. The more powerful the private interests, the more they are able to generalise their interests through official spaces. This is similar to what happens in corporatist policy making and in hegemonic contexts. However, autonomous spaces display more creativity, more community and grassroots orientation, greater focus and less muddling through than is the case in official spaces.

The characteristic of official spaces is that policy and programme implementation are usually far from their targets, and often far from their original objectives. Policy reversals and policy retreats in official spaces are not uncommon. The view of poverty held in most official spaces in Jigawa, the equilibrium model, leads to policy being highly politicised; if all are seen as poor, then competition for scarce resources for poverty reduction is that much broader. Thus, for example, the politics of the emirates concerning regional development and project siting become central to the poverty reduction policy process. Interventions which view poverty as vulnerability to shock and stress, on the other hand, are marked less by politics. Here, attempts are often made to find out the extent of damage or vulnerability, the numbers of people involved, particularly to try and attract aid from government and donors. This type of rational approach is often abandoned after aid has been obtained, and the politics of distribution once more predominate.

Invited spaces can be characterised as official spaces with private participation; their links with official spaces are organic and the politics of their origin ensures that they share many features of official spaces. The actors in the invited spaces are positioned all along the vertical slice which begins at the level of the community, and ends at the federal level. By contrast, the more autonomous the space, the more community actors are involved, while the more official the space, the more state actors and donors are found.

In the semi-autonomous policy spaces in Jigawa, poverty knowledge is derived from Islamic discourses, rather than from data collected in order to access external funding. This discourse identifies causes of poverty, and the solutions accorded by the tenets of Islam, including Zakkat to redistribute resources. Although there is no emphasis on unjust distribution of wealth in the political discourse of Jigawa, wealth redistribution through Zakkat is the core of the poverty reduction policy which emerges from the semi-autonomous space. The religious foundation of the Zakkat confers a high level of ownership on the process, as does its association with the emirate system rather than the state. The unique features of the Jigawa Zakkat, even among Nigeria's northern states, owe a great deal to the careful balance between officialdom and autonomy discussed above. The challenge for this rare example of success in the arena of poverty reduction is not only to maintain this careful balance over time, but also to move beyond charity towards sustainability.

Notes

1. With thanks to Alhaji Tahir Gwarzo and the team of 14 field researchers who worked on the study.
2. Hadeija, Kazaure, Dutse, Gumel and Ringim
3. This poverty reduction programme is carried out under the auspices of a project called the Millenium Village Commission, which has largely concentrated on a programme which supports industrial sugar cane production, and the retrenchment of civil servants. It also includes the Jigawa State People's Congress, established to better inform government about the needs and priorites of ordinary people.
4. Literally, purification
5. Pilgrimage to the holy sites in Saudi Arabia
6. The largest donor presence in Jigawa state
7. The Millenium Village Commission has established several farms for industrialised sugarcane production, and allocates plots to redeployed civil servants.
8. The majority of which concerned the lack of services and infrastructure, such as potable water and electricity.
9. Middle Eastern donors, however, are also not involved in the Zakkat committees.
10. This is the case in Dutse and Hadejia while there is a slight variation in the case of Kazaure where the Emir has separated from the main committee but retains the overall control.
11. Islamic scholars and teachers

13

Local Perceptions of Poverty and Governance in Benue and Kaduna States

Oga Steve Abah and Jenkeri Z. Okwori

Poverty in Nigeria is a social as well as a geographical discourse in the sense of its character, the dimensions and spread of its occurrence, and the way it is perceived by people. In social terms, understandings of poverty concern ethnicity, religion and status. Poverty is a widespread phenomenon in Nigeria, which can be severe in some cases and places; in geographical terms it is everywhere. (Sudharsan, 1997; Aluko, 1975; Sancho, 1996). It is this pervasive phenomenon, which according to the Central Bank of Nigeria (1999) is a "vicious circle, which keeps the poor in a state of destitution, disillusionment and plague," that this chapter addresses.

The chapter reports on research in Benue and Kaduna states, and examines the way that local people perceive poverty, and their views about local government as an effective agent for poverty reduction. The chapter first discusses the diversity of perceptions of poverty in these two very different states, and reflects on the implications of this diversity for the policy process. It goes on to discuss the way that local government officials see themselves as agents of poverty reduction, before finally moving to consider the way in which ordinary Nigerians see relationships of governance and representation.

While in many respects the perceptions of poverty in both states are similar, each of the states has its own peculiarities. Benue is a state in the Middle Belt of Nigeria, one of several states created in 1976 in what was the Middle Belt region of colonial Nigeria. Literally, this refers to the middle section of the country, but the term also has political meaning and significance. It is now used to describe the minority, non-Hausa speaking part of the north, which by implication means that there is a new type of relationship with the far north, which has political and linguistic advantage. Hausa, as well as being the largest single language spoken in the old north, also describes the largest ethnic group in Nigeria and the one that has occupied the ruling position longer than any other. Rather than being a geographical space, the Middle Belt has become a socio-political entity as a conglomerate of ethnic minorities spread over several states. It now sees itself as distinctly different from the Moslem north of the country and fights for its political distinctiveness and its middle position, sandwiched between the majority groups in the north, east and west.

Benue is one of the poorest states in the federation with a low level of development and high levels of income poverty. The biggest employer of formal labour is the civil service. While this may be true in many other Nigerian states, Benue stands out in two respects. It has hardly any major private industry. The only other major employer of labour other than the civil service is the Benue cement factory. However, this industry has never really operated at full capacity since it was established in the late 1970s.

The other respect in which Benue stands out is that it is a labour reserve for other states in the federation. The state is very well endowed agriculturally and has ample but unexploited human resources. Its development journey has been characterised by staccato forward leaps that are very often reversed by the different visions and agenda of various regimes, 'thus aggravating the incidence of poverty among the vulnerable groups in the society'(Obadan, 1997). The fourteen military administrators and governors it has had since it was created in 1976 have left a legacy of demands, aspirations and frustrations. Its development is a history of non-performance, backward movement and stagnation. What poverty means and how it manifests in Benue are partly accounted for and embedded in this background. This situation of poverty and non-development, for which the military rule is popularly blamed, has not changed much in present-day Benue.

Many people in Benue believe that bad leadership has been a special misfortune for them. They acknowledge that this may be a national problem but they observe that other states also created in 1976 have made much greater progress than Benue. In the final analysis Benue indigenes adjure the state as 'The food basket of the Nation' whose fruits are going to waste.

The story from Benue that this chapter tells is from Ogbadibo and Otukpo local governments. Otukpo Local Government Area is a very expansive one. It covers both urban Otukpo, the second largest town in the state, and a large number of rural communities. Otukpo, which serves as the LGA headquarters, is urban in nature, and five of Otukpo's thirteen wards are urban. Ogbadibo on the other hand is a completely rural, agriculture-based LGA, also with thirteen wards. One striking feature is the size and remoteness of this LGA. Processes of local governance are characterised by absent leaders, many of whom live in the neighbouring LGA and conduct business from a distance.

Kaduna state presents a different picture. In terms of positioning it has a claim to be part both of the Middle Belt and the North. This duality is a reflection of the ethnicity and religion of its inhabitants. The southern part of the state is made up of several ethnic groups including the Bajju, Ikulu, Kataf, and Jaba, and is therefore a zone of diverse minorities, with a predominantly Christian religious identity. The northern part on the other hand is largely Hausa, and the majority of people here are Moslems, with pockets of Christian communities among the *maguzawas*, a non-Moslem Hausa minority. Politically, this part of the state identifies with the political north and is centred on the city of Zaria, the ideological and religious centre of the emirate. The state capital Kaduna, situated further south, is both an administrative and commercial centre and a site of Christian-Moslem conflict.

The LGAs in Kaduna state where the research took place were Giwa and Sabon-Gari. Giwa, made up of 12 wards, is rural and agricultural, with commercial activities revolving around weekly markets in different parts of the LGA. In one village, Shika, there is a National Animal Production Institute (NAPRI) affiliated to Ahmadu Bello University in Zaria. The presence of the institute has a major influence on life in Giwa. Many workers in the Institute live in Shika village and bring a considerable amount of purchasing power into the economy. Another unusual feature of Giwa is the presence of a strong *maguzawa* community in Tsaunin Mayau village.

Sabon-Gari on the other hand is an area of ethnic mix and religious plurality, and is a largely urban LGA. At the time of the study it was made up of 11 wards which included Zaria town and many of its peri-urban satellite communities. At the time of our research, Samaru, the location of the largest African university south of the Sahara, was within the LGA. Basawa, with a major military establishment and a number of research centres, also belonged to Sabon Gari.[1] These establishments draw people from different parts of the country for work and training, adding to the variety of the population.

There are several factors in this background that have relevance for poverty issues, and indeed shape the policy process. One is religion, another is ethnicity. A third, which may not be contained in the background, are existing processes of governance. The factors and the nature of relationship resulting from them contribute to determine who accesses certain resources, and therefore has implications for poverty. How poverty is perceived by the ordinary people in these LGAs, the way it manifests in their lives, and the way policy addresses them as citizens are key starting points.

Perceptions of poverty in Kaduna and Benue

Poverty is viewed in different ways in different contexts. Poverty 'epresents a general condition of deprivation manifesting in social inferiority, powerlessness, isolation and degradation'(Central Bank of Nigeria, 1999). Perhaps what brings this about is the inability of people to attain the minimum standard of living (World Bank, 1990; World Bank, 1997) or the basic necessities of life (Aluko, 1975; Anyanwu, 1997). Others construct poverty as the economic failure that show in massive unemployment and the pauperisation of the working classes (Johnson, 1974). All of these suggest a multi-dimensionality of perceptions of poverty, reflected and elaborated in local examples from Benue and Kaduna states.

Poverty is prevalent in both states. It ranges from material poverty to the absence of prestige and confidence and religious persecution. In the explanations provided in many rural communities poverty also has political dimensions, represented as a poverty of political participation. This dimension of poverty concerns the ways in which government is part of or a cause of poverty, and is about how social and political structures at various levels enhance or truncate development.

Poverty is also sharply gendered in both states. While at the local level poverty affects everyone, women are more deprived in several ways. In rural communities, where they are farmers, they very often have no control over or ownership of land; where they do, they are unable to control the benefits of their labour. Although their knowledge of their own environments and poverty is highly astute, they are not very often part of the decision-making process, in either the rural or the urban setting. They are thus excluded from the ways that policy is framed at both the state and local level.

Looking at some of the views expressed by women on their poverty illuminates the central position of gendered relationships of power in the day-to-day experience of living in poverty.

> When you are in seclusion you do not own yourself. You are owned by your husband. You need his express permission to do anything. You cannot associate freely. You don't even have an economic mainstay. You depend on him for everything. And when you depend on someone for everything, you are not free.
> *Woman in Shika Village, Giwa LGA*

> Whatever we earn from our trade, contribution and meetings we have to surrender to our husbands. When we present it to them they may choose to take the whole thing. But some of the kind ones take some few notes and hand over the remaining to you. We cannot say no because they own us and if you hide the money the ancestors would deal with you. *Woman in Ukalegwu village, Ogbadibo LGA*

These two views show that in both cases the origin of the women's poverty is not lack of knowledge and enterprise, but the seizure of women's agency by men. In both cases religion is a mechanism for this seizure: in Shika it is Islam and in Ukalegwu the hybrid indigenous religion in which the wrath of ancestors is feared.[2] Nonetheless, there are differences: women in Ukalegwu have the freedom of movement and association denied to those in Shika, and indeed in the majority of Giwa LGA. In Giwa the non-Moslem women in Tsaunin Mayau are an exception as they are allowed to go out and interact with other people, to go to the farm and to engage in petty trading. But as in Benue, freedom is still relative: men exercise a tremendous influence on what women may or may not do.

Women in both contexts see their poverty as a consequence of the patriarchal design of their societies, which makes them the virtual property of their husbands. This 'ownership' takes different forms in Kaduna and Benue sites, giving rise to very context-specific understandings of poverty. So, despite being under the control of men at a general level, the women of Otukpo, Onyuwei and Ukalegwu in Benue State are very visible, owning their farms, engaging in commercial activities and seeking their own means of survival. Their perception of poverty is therefore one in which the absence of a means of livelihood is a strong element.

Discussions with the women rice millers of Otukpo provide a particularly vivid image of poverty as lacking the means of making a living. Here, women rice millers blame their poverty on the effect of government policy. They used to be very successful rice millers until things started becoming bad after the return to civil rule in 1999. The traders and bulk buyers who came from the western and eastern parts of the country to buy their rice stopped coming. They said that this was the result of government allowing the importation of foreign rice, which buyers prefer because it has no stones and is cleaner. They are therefore forced to sell their locally milled rice below profit margins. This underscores what Nettleford (2002:14) refers to as '...the huge US and European farm subsidies currently wreaking havoc on African agriculture.'

The desperate need for survival, the extent of exploitation and the women's resilience are all told in the story of the Onyonyo women at the Rice Mill in Otukpo, Benue State.

At 6 a.m. the working day of the Onyonyo women starts. They parboil rice in huge drums; spread the rice on mats laid out on cemented floor in the mill. They tend the rice till it dries. Next is to shift loads of the rice into the milling machine for de-husking. Next, they collect the husks into huge mounds and ferry them to dumps where they will eventually be burnt. Before the husks are burnt however, the women have the right to winnow through it and find escaped grains of rice – this is one of the in-kind payments they are entitled to. Another form of payment from their employer is when he gives them small measures of unhusked rice. The four women we talked to said they usually have to accumulate such measures for two weeks before it reaches any reasonable quantity to make a load into the machine for dehusking.

The quantity we saw on this day, which would be shared by four women, could not make one full meal to feed any one of the women's families. There is no other salary.

As if to make their story sink in, and perhaps sensing that we did not understand the import of what they were telling us, Esther asks us, 'Do you want to see?' Without waiting for our answer she stands up and we follow her. She shows us their bonus for the day, and follows this by tracing their chores in the mill from the point of boiling the rice through to the machine which receives the rice and the load of husks which they must take to the dump and winnow through for a living. All this while Aladi, the leader of the women, is painstakingly picking stones and the grains of rice that has escaped being dehusked in the machine from a small quantity she has scavenged from the dump.

This is the routine the women will engage in throughout the day, six days a week. Seven p.m. or 8 p.m. if it is a very busy day, is when the working day comes to an end for the Onyonyo women.

We were not sure which was more striking, the extreme poverty of these women, their exploitation or their strength. The poverty that brought them to the mill in the first instance, and their consequent exploitation, were staggering. But their strength of character even if expressed in rueful smiles and laughter, and the stoicism which makes it possible for them to survive, were their assets.

Men in Giwa LGA (Kaduna) and those in Otukpo, Onyuwei and

Ukalegwu[3] (Benue) had a rather different definition of poverty. Although most of them were in agreement that poverty can be summarised as the lack of means to make a living and to live meaningfully, there are also differences. In Giwa, poverty is seen very specifically in terms of lack of representation, expression, education and freedom. According to the members of the Shika Youth Democratic Movement, in Giwa, elected officials of the LGA are effectively linked to the traditional rulership structures in Zaria city, the seat of the Zazzau (Zaria) emirate, and the location of a highly educated political elite which exerts a great deal of control over resource allocation. It is very often on the basis of linkages to the emirate system that benefits are distributed to communities. A good example is Tsibiri, a small community on the outskirts of Shika with few natural resources, but with a tarred road, electricity, water supply, a primary school and a clinic. The Youth Movement in Shika argues that all this is because Tsibiri has a connection to the emir's palace in Zaria. This also explains why Tsaunin Mayau, an agricultural goldmine, has no such amenities: its Christian identity robs it of the benefits that the predominance of Islam and membership of the ruling house confers on Tsibiri.

This understanding of poverty as dependent on the position of a community relative to a centre of power contrasts with that put forward by men and youth in Benue. To them, poverty is located within, rather than between, communities and is really multi-dimensional. It is the lack of sense or wisdom. When you are not capable of using your head correctly you are poor; when you have children who cannot effectively look after you, or have no children at all, you are poor. These men also perceive a poverty of knowledge and realise that lack of awareness and information leaves them in so much ignorance and want.

These perceptions demonstrate how an individual's social or political position affects the way poverty is understood and experienced. Individuals, in holding these perceptions, cannot be dislocated from their families, extended social relations, or from the identity of their community in the wider world. Group rather than individual emphasis is a perception shared by both men and women.

If, as Osaghae (2001) argues, 'poverty is a shared phenomenon that inheres in communities and families rather than individuals', poverty reduction policies made with local needs in mind should have an inclusive and communal approach.

So far, however, such an approach is at odds with mainstream government models of poverty reduction, which focus largely on interventions at the level of the individual. An example of this is the series of poverty reduction programmes of both Nigeria's military and civilian governments. Ranging from the Poverty Alleviation Programme (PAP), through the programmes of the National Directorate of Employment (NDE), to the Youth Employment Scheme (YES), and now the National Poverty Eradication Programme (NAPEP), the target is the individual and the material, not the community or the non-material aspects so vividly expressed by people living in poverty.

This overview of perceptions of poverty put forward by local men and women in Kaduna and Benue states raises challenges both to the way poverty is understood and how policy is made. As we have already observed, one challenge is how policy might respond to the context-specific diversity of poverty issues. A second critical challenge rests on the dynamics of governance. The third challenge concerns the level at which effective poverty reduction should begin. If, as many have suggested, one route for responsive poverty reduction policy is via bottom-up decentralisation with roots in the autonomous, local spaces of towns and villages, it becomes particularly important to understand not only how existing agents of local government view poverty and poverty reduction activities, but how they are seen by those they are supposed to represent. This will allow an evaluation of the extent to which local actors are equipped to transmit the local diversity of poverty knowledge into the policy process, and how far they are able to implement existing government policies according to localised perceptions of poverty.

Linking governance and poverty reduction

Understandings of governance are interwoven with many of the local perceptions of poverty discussed in the previous section. In the example from Giwa LGA, a whole community becomes relatively impoverished according to their position in the configuration of political power represented by the overlapping structures of traditional and state governance.

Poverty and governance issues also overlap in the views of some local government officials, although the overlap is perceived in a different way. For example, officials of Giwa and Sabon Gari LGAs in Kaduna see poverty as not having the necessary financial and material resources to enable them live well. They also see this as being closely linked with non-literacy and a lack of connection to authority. In Giwa and Sabon Gari both these conditions are rampant and as a result the councillors and officials say they are inundated daily with personal requests for money and help. According to the Councillor representing Shika, 'All they ask me of here is money, money for personal needs. No one has ever met me requesting for development work.' For these officials, then, poverty is an influence on how citizens relate to their elected representatives, and the expectations which surround the representative relationship.

Local governance in Kaduna and Benue

As with perceptions of poverty, relations of governance vary from place to place, with significant variations between Kaduna and Benue in this regard.[4] If we define autonomous groups by their degrees of removal from official structures, then we will find more autonomous groups in Benue than in Kaduna. In Kaduna, traditional systems of governance and the state are closely connected and the resulting patterns of governance and representation are correspondingly socio-political and religious.

In both states, people's perceptions are that government has the overall responsibility to cater for its citizens. In meeting this responsibility the government is organised in the three levels of the federal, state and local. This last tier is, ostensibly, grassroots government, with administration and power devolved to it from the centre, in order to enhance development. It is supposed to deliver development directly to small geographic units in the country, through the design and implementation of its own development programmes.

Because local governments are theoretically units of development, and in reality a source of patronage, there is a constant demand for their creation by local and interest groups. Whether or not they deliver in practice, and to whom, is a different matter. Although there is a constitutional backing for the independence of local government authorities, the LGAs are meant to work hand in hand with state governments. In practice the LGAs are very much controlled by state governments. In addition, though designed to work within small areas, some LGAs are too large to deliver effectively, having to divide scarce resources over enormous areas.

There are other factors beyond size which affect the ability of LGAs to the perform their duties. One of these is the personnel charged with responsibilities at this level of government, key amongst them the elected councillors and chairpersons. The chairperson is the overall leader at the LGA level, and the closest executive officer to the people, while councillors are political leaders at the ward level and are the immediate representatives of their communities in government. However, the extent to which the localised role of the local government and its principal agents is understood, and by whom, varies from one LGA to another, and from the Middle Belt to the northern parts of the country.

Ordinary people's experience of LGAs and traditional authorities

Most people understand the roles and responsibilities of the Local Government to be to promote and/or deliver development at community level. However, in assessing whether the development agenda is usually met by the LGAs, the voices of ordinary people give indications of both success and failure.

Across the communities in Benue, the popular perceptions of government employees highlight the intertwined nature of poverty and governance. In the eyes of citizens living in poverty, part of the experience of being poor is the inability of government to live up to its expectations and responsibilities. There are tales of corrupt enrichment and embezzlement of public funds by government functionaries. People argue, understandably, that had this not been the case and if public monies were used judiciously, people would not complain of poverty. They also point to the issue of favouritism in which projects targeting poverty are made to benefit only relatives and party loyalists; the example of the NAPEP was cited. Many ordinary people believe that councillors who complain about incessant visits from their people asking for basic things like burials and school fees are insincere. This is because the people hold strong opinions that government has provided resources for development and that their demands are only necessary because the councillors are not channelling the resources properly.

In Otukpo LGA, members of the Onyonyo Group of women rice millers tell stories of poverty, destitution, exploitation and of living outside the support system (if any) of the state. This group is an independent, non-state organisation, eking out life at the margins of society. The women know local government only in theory, or by name alone. The women argue that they are in poverty because the people they queued in the rain to vote into office have abandoned them. At the rice mill in Otukpo where the buildings are falling down and the only viable industry faces the threat of total collapse, the rice millers and other women see the crisis as a sign of the failure of the LGA. The women argue that if the LGA were interested in alleviating their poverty it would ensure that the mill was viable. As Esther Okoh argues:

> The solution to poverty is to have something for people to do. Employment can reduce poverty but who gives the employment? Government can. But what if you do not have godfathers or what it takes [money] to secure employment? Sometimes the LG talks about loans for poor people. But employment as a more lasting solution is preferable to loans.

The women do not believe that to take a loan is a solution when you are poor. The chairperson of the Onyonyo group, Mrs Paulina Augustine says for example:

> I am afraid of taking loans. Supposing I take it and spend it on

feeding and taking care of my children and I am not able to pay back, what would I do? Secondly, even if I want the loan I do not know where they are giving it or what to do to get it.

The feeling of being abandoned and of not being included in the vocabulary and actions of the LGA were captured when the Onyonyo women defined their world as having only two features – the road on which they travelled every morning and evening, and the rice mill. They acknowledged that around the mill and on all sides of the road there are houses, but that they hardly saw them any more as they only focus on the mill in their everyday lives. If they were to locate the local government on their map they would put a blank space, or maybe a black one.

We see nothing from them; we hear nothing about them. They don't even know that we exist. When you talk about what the local government is doing we are like blind and deaf people!

The absence of the LGA in the lives of the ordinary people in Onyuwei, Ukalegwu, Otukpo and Ogbadibo LGAs in Benue, was exemplified in their community maps; they said that after the village there is nothing but grass. Their community maps contained no vision of the state. As both men and women in the villages said, government only makes itself known via things they hear on the radio. Government is when politicians come to campaign.

In Giwa LGA in Kaduna state, the ordinary people argued that to feel the presence and impact of the local government means that one has to be a *yan ganuwa* (from inside the wall). The majority of the ordinary people are *yan karkara*, those who may literally live outside the wall, or are outside the political realm that matters. To be a *yan ganuwa* may also mean belonging to a ruling group or to be identified with a particular ethnicity or clan group. It is the 'insiders' who very often take control of the local government structure. The story of the three hundred years of disenfranchisement of the maguzawas from Tsaunin Mayau evidences this web of relationship and its implications for poverty and exclusion.

The absence of government shown by the maps villagers draw is also a reflection of their lack of connectedness to politics and policy. The significance of the dark spaces in Otukpo, the grasses beyond the villages and the inside-outside dichotomy in Giwa is that all are signs that poverty policy is formulated without using the knowledge of the people and without their participation. This contributes to the many non-material understandings of poverty put forward in discussions with ordinary people, which relate to isolation and exclusion.

In Giwa and Sabon Gari LGAs (Kaduna), as in most parts of the North, a good number of the people know that the responsibilities of the local government include the provision of social amenities. They are also aware that the councillors are the first point of contact for making this happen, and would generally follow-up to make demands, and monitor their activities closely. This demonstrates a certain amount of political awareness on the part of the people here. It is in the urban and semi-urban areas of the LGAs where this consciousness is highest, and where people are able to distinguish between the different levels or tiers of government.

In the rural parts of the LGAs, where awareness may not be so high, they use the traditional authorities as both intermediaries and ombudsmen. For example, in Shika the youth organisation, constituted as a Community Development Association, (CDA) is known to complain, sometimes backed by physical confrontation, about lack of performance by the LGA officials when obligations are not met.

Although this kind of awareness may not be as prevalent in Otukpo and Ogbadibo local governments of Benue state, there have been cases of councillors challenging some of their chairmen's policies on the grounds that they were undemocratic. However, by and large, there is lack of united action because people fear they may be labelled trouble makers. People here are scared of being witch-hunted and even killed. And, further down the awareness ladder at the village level in Benue, residents of Ukalegwu are not even aware that councillors can be approached to hear their worries, or be challenged to perform better. The councillor did not even visit the village during the campaigns; in his place were party agents. So the people voted for someone they did not even see, simply voting for the party that they were told by the politicians to vote for.

In contrast to the majority of the people's lack of knowledge about what roles the LGA should play in their lives, the councillors and chairmen do understand their roles and responsibilities to the people. In the next section, we look at how government officials see the poverty which surrounds them, and how they perceive their role as agents of poverty reduction.

Government officials: agents for poverty reduction?

Elected local government officials, especially councillors, claimed that their knowledge of poverty comes from the nature of requests they get from their constituency members: for drugs, for school fees, for registration in senior secondary school examinations and so on. They say that they pay school fees, especially for orphans; at times, they even have to arrange for burials. Sunday Onyilokwu says:

> Our houses are 'hospitals' catering to all sorts of ailments. We are woken up first thing in the morning. They come looking for money to go to the hospital, for school fees, for registration fees, for food, name it! When they come, we do what we can. When we cannot we try to explain.

The councillors say the 'clinic' they run to meet the needs and demands of constituency members is funded from their personal resources. All these demands are made regardless of whether or not the councillors have been paid their salaries. They explained that this puts great strain on them and on their families as the LGA does not provide sufficient means to meet the demands. Although the 'clinic' is a burden, it does function to provide information on the poorest of the poor and in helping to identify those they recommend for benefiting from programmes initiated by the federal government.

Based on these experiences, the councillors characterised poverty as 'lack of something profitable to do.' The key indicator in this definition is unemployment. Councillors feel that, because they are in direct touch with the grass roots and are closely in touch with the unemployment situation, their knowledge of poverty is not theoretical but from experiencing it and seeing its symptoms in people around them.

This is how they expressed their understanding of poverty, and what they see as their roles in tackling it. In their own words:

Owoicho: Poverty is sickness of the heart due to absence of wealth. When you need to have, and you do not have it leads to sickness of heart. That is what lack of basic needs does to people.

Sunday: Poverty is complex; it has levels. You may be rich in one thing and poor in another. To really be out of poverty all the levels need to be present and balanced.

Simon: Poverty ... means lack of capacity to do things for your people. The minimum level of lack that leads to real poverty is anyone without the means to afford medication, education, food, shelter or clothing.

The primacy of personal needs over community needs in the demands made on councillors is based on people's experiences that community needs are seldom met by the LGA. It is as a result of this failure and the size of the consequent demands that some of the councillors said they were afraid of going home if they did not have enough money to spend. Whatever efforts they make, in comparison to the needs and demands, the councillors' personal actions and the poverty alleviation efforts of the federal government are terribly inadequate.

Local government as a constrained actor

None of the LGAs we studied in either state have poverty programmes of their own. And as the councillors revealed, the LGAs hardly formulate any coherent development policy. They are mostly implementing development or poverty reduction policies worked out by either the federal or the state government. This was most apparent in Otukpo and Ogbadibo LGAs in Benue state. Because the poverty alleviation programmes are not owned by the local government, the implementation process is also dictated by policy makers 'from above'. This is why under the youth employment programme in

Otukpo LGA, for example, only a total of 265 youth were recruited out of 5,200 pressing to benefit from poverty programmes. In the same way, such programmes are terminated at will by the initiating authority, leaving those benefiting stranded. This was the case when in 2000 the LGA's employment of street sweepers was brought to an end when the state government directed that the programme was over.

In no instances that we found had councillors or LGAs been consulted during the processes of formulating poverty programmes, and as the example above shows, they do not take part in planning the processes of implementation either. Worryingly, there has been no attempt to assess the poverty situation or the nature and levels of poverty in LGAs before handing down programmes, conceived at the centre in Abuja. Because of this planning abnormality, the programmes are not tailored to address the stated needs of the people. As one councillor said:

> There was no attempt to assess the poverty situation or the nature and levels of poverty in the local government area. Although there may be no accurate statistics to know the exact figures of the poor, when we take the fact that about 160,000 voted in Otukpo LGA and that about half of that are the youth, and less than half of these youths are under any form of employment, then you can see the picture of unemployment is grim here. But the plan does not reflect this situation. As a matter of truth, we are not even called to deliberate on the plans that the local government implements.

Part of the consequence of this absence of localised planning is that potentially rich LGAs are constrained to be poor as their revenue base is not developed. Benue state as a whole has raw materials that could fuel agro-based cottage industries to create both employment and income. Whatever revenue is generated, however, falls far below what could be possible, and even the revenue collected may be badly managed. In a bitter conclusion to this poor planning which has driven poverty in Idoma land, one man said, 'We can tell you that there is no sincerity of purpose at all in the Local Government here in Idoma.'

All this raises challenges about the issue of representation, and the role of local councillors as representatives. Are they representatives *of* local people's views, which would imply a role transmitting localised versions of poverty? Or are they representatives *to* local people, explaining and implementing the policies of government to its citizens? Experience in LGAs in Kaduna and Benue suggests that in fact local councillors are not able to fulfil either role, even though they might be expected to fulfil both. While councillors are seen as grassroots representatives and development agents by the people they represent, they function in a structure that limits their ability to meet the mandate for which they were elected. These constraints range from the structural, through the administrative style, to issues of perception, and mean that development activities by the LGA are inevitably seen in different and conflicting ways. That is, one perception is of the LGA as a unit of development for all, and another as a compensatory development structure for those who run it.

In the face of these constraints and failures of the LGA to fulfil the aspirations of the people, it would seem that traditional governance structures present an alternative system where the causes and nature of the people's poverty are understood and support mechanisms are oriented towards the collective rather than the individual. Across the research, people have more respect for the traditional institutions such as the emirates, chiefdoms, district and clan heads than in state institutions. They also believe in the ability of these structures to listen and give support more readily than the local government. This was definitely the case in Otukpo and Ogbadibo LGAs. And, although in Giwa and Sabon Gari LGAs of Kaduna State there may be tension in the *yan ganuwa-yan karkara* relationship, the traditional institution is still considered by most people at the grassroots to be more approachable than the LGA. On many occasions and in certain matters, the traditional structure is the route to the LGA.

Many ordinary people believe in and rely on traditional structures to solve some of their poverty problems. In Otukpo and Ogbadibo the structure of support is organised in levels from village to district. At the village level the poor are looked after by their clans. As Agboji

Ijagwuha, the Chief of Onyuwei (Otukpo LGA) revealed, 'Clans do take the burden of the poor ones among them. This is done by paying their share of community levies, donating yam seedlings to such people, etc. No clan wants to be labelled as poor or to be disrespected.' When matters are more serious than can be handled at the village level, they are taken to the district head. Along with chiefs from all the villages that make up the district, issues are discussed so that a common position is arrived at and lines of action decided. As one chief put it, 'The villages are financially poor because we do not grow as much food as we can. We have no means of transporting them out of our villages. When we are sick here we have no hospital to go to.' It is such matters as roads, hospitals and markets that the chiefs address at the district level. They also discuss and work out strategies for the maintenance of community secondary schools, deciding on levies and support for communities in crisis.

Contained in the village traditional structure, therefore, is the practice of listening to the different levels of the society in order to understand their problems and their poverty. There is also an integral system of consultation and collective decision-making in tackling village and community issues. In some senses and in some places, traditional institutions may be more democratic than the LGA, tapping community knowledge to build positive actions. This is remarkably different from the way in which the local government plans and executes its development programmes.

As discussed in previous sections, local government officials face significant constraints in acting as agents for poverty alleviation. Several factors are important here, not least the conflict of perceptions about what role local government officials play and are expected to play. For example, the perception of personal gain from being in power conflicts with the public mandate of increasing general wellbeing. The second level of tension here is that both the LGA chairperson and the councillors are in competition for resources to deliver development to their own people. Then there is the lack of coherent, locally owned policies at the lower levels of government, coupled with an undemocratic manner of administering both the projects and the LGA itself. The LGA in Nigeria therefore remains a manipulated entity, very often largely ineffective in its mandate as a unit of development, beset with structural, fiscal and governance problems.

It would appear that poverty policy formulation has been taking place in spaces unavailable to those who are meant to benefit. The voices informing those policies are therefore not necessarily the most informed, as the policy process is only open to state and federal actors. Increasing the responsiveness of policy to poverty issues at the local level would therefore necessitate a major rethink and a shift in both the structural orientation of the policy process and the boundaries of poverty knowledge.

Notes

1. The geography of the LGA has however changed since the study was undertaken. It has been split into two LGAs, Sabon Gari and Basawa.
2. In the indigenous religion, ancestors are believed to be ever present and constantly punishing the offender; while Christianity emphasises chastity, truth and honesty, the lack of which is also punishable.
3. The distinction between youth and men here like in most parts of Nigeria is very thin. Because people marry quite early here most of the youth are also automatically in the class of men.
4. Each state in Nigeria has its own LGA Law, each conferring slightly different set of roles and reponsibilities on its officers

14

From Policy to Power: Revisiting Actors, Knowledge and Spaces[1]

John Gaventa

Across the globe, concerns for poverty reduction have brought to the fore calls for policy processes which are more inclusive, transparent and accountable, while simultaneously also more evidence-based and grounded in the views and knowledges of multiple stakeholders. As a response to the perceived failures of external, expert-led poverty reduction policies, words like 'ownership', 'participation' and 'partnership' in poverty reduction policies and programmes have become a new policy mantra.

The language of the 'new' more inclusive policies for poverty reduction is widespread, found in multitudes of donor strategy documents and reflected increasingly in the discourse of government officials, international NGOs, and local civil society activists. Yet despite the rhetoric, few empirical studies exist to date of attempts towards more inclusive policy-making, especially in the poverty arena. This book has attempted to remedy that gap, by providing in-depth empirical accounts of the dynamics of poverty reduction policy in Uganda and Nigeria. Based on fresh field-based research in local communities in three districts in Uganda and five states in Nigeria, as well as in the two capital cities of Kampala and Abuja, the previous chapters have provided a rich tapestry from which to learn more about the challenges and opportunities posed in the drive for more participatory policy processes.

There is no more crucial context in which to ask questions about the dynamics of poverty policy than Africa, where poverty persists and grows deeper, despite numerous local, national and international attempts to reduce it. Within this context, Uganda and Nigeria provide contrasting experiences. In recent years, Uganda has been held up by international donor agencies as a rare 'success': policies seem to be working as poverty rates appear to be falling. Nigeria, by contrast, is cited as one of the least effective countries in terms of poverty reduction policies. There the poverty headcount continues to increase. Despite massive oil wealth, an estimated 66% of its population of 130 million live beneath the international benchmark of a dollar a day (See Chapter 3). When the peg is raised to two dollars a day, the estimate of those beneath the poverty line grows to 90%.

Despite the contrast, the poverty challenge in both countries, as across the continent, is seen by many to be linked to the need for fundamental change in the way through which the state itself makes and delivers policy. Persistent poverty, the argument goes, reflects the persistent failure of a state that was built upon structures inherited from a colonial structure, and which is often criticised for its neo-patrimonial, corrupt and rent-seeking behaviours (Chapter 2). As Mbaku and Ihonvbere point out in their book on the struggle for more democratic governance in Africa, 'Today the reconstruction of the African state to provide citizens with participatory, accountable and transparent government structures remains one of the most important issues in the continent's political adjustment in the "new" global era.' Moreover, they argue, 'to improve the continent's ability to participate effectively in the new global order...political spaces must be opened to allow for more participatory and democratic forms of governance' (2003:30).

Taking the field of poverty reduction policy as both intrinsically important and as a lens for understanding these dynamics, the research on which this book is based has used a 'vertical' slice approach, in which policy is understood as crossing international, national, district (in Uganda) or state (in Nigeria) and local levels. In general, the preceding chapters have argued that the policy process can be understood as one in which multiple actors, using different forms of knowledge about poverty, interact in a multitude of policy spaces. Rather than accepting the prescription of inclusive, participatory policy as a panacea for poverty reduction, the previous chapters suggest the need for a far more critical approach in which these policy spaces are seen as both shaped by and laden with power relations, and often disconnected from one another, as well as from the lives of the poor people they are supposed to affect. Rather than understanding policy as a linear process which can be imposed from above by a 'technical fix', the chapters reinforce the picture of a far more complex, dynamic and political process, in which important questions must be raised about who participates, with what forms of knowledge, and in whose spaces, and whether such processes lead to greater accountability and responsiveness to poor people.

More specifically, the chapters have provided further insights into the analytical categories of actors, knowledge and spaces outlined in Chapter 1, and how they interrelate one with another across different contexts. Using the same analytical lens, we turn now to weave together some cross-cutting patterns and differences that emerge from the previous chapters, and then to offer some final conclusions about the implications of the research for the challenge of building more inclusive, accountable and participatory policy processes.

From policy to power: a brief reprise

In Chapter 1 in addition to presenting the framework of 'actors-knowledge-spaces' for understanding policy processes, McGee suggests that 'the very nature of spaces, and of action within them, is fundamentally determined by power'. Throughout our fieldwork, this question of how power interacts with and affects the policy process was a recurring cross-cutting theme. Before going on, it is important to think further about the meanings of power, and how the concept of power links to the concepts of actors, knowledge and spaces.

Power is a highly contested concept, understood in policy analysis, political science, and social theory in many different and often conflicting ways. One view of power, growing largely from political science and sociology, focuses largely on key decision-makers in the policy process and asks questions about who participates, who wins and who loses in policy processes. In this tradition, power is seen to be held and wielded by key actors in clearly visible policy processes, where conflicts over key policies are debated and analysed. In much the same way as the linear view of policy has been critiqued, so this view of power in the policy process has been challenged by those who argue that power is more multidimensional.

Power not only affects who wins and who loses in visible policy processes, but also works to construct boundaries of who can enter decision making arenas in the first place. In this sense, we must also examine the more hidden ways in which power relations work to exclude certain issues or actors altogether, for instance, through back-stage manoueverings, the use of certain discourses or procedures, or the ways that unequal resources and capacities affect who participates. Extending this view further, power relations may also be more invisible, found in the internalisation of roles, norms or beliefs which may keep potential actors from engaging in policy processes at all because they do not see themselves as potential policy actors, e.g. as not having rights or agency; or because of a lack of critical awareness of the possibilities and avenues of action. (For work in this tradition, see for example Lukes 1975, Gaventa 1980; VeneKlasen and Miller 2003.)

Other views of power, drawing particularly from Foucault, place less emphasis on power as held and exercised through actors in the policy process, and more on how power shapes and bounds social relations. In this view, 'Power is at the centre of all social relations' (Foucault 1977:92) and is 'dispersed through a network of discourses of possibility that govern people's thought and action' (ibid: 32). Within this view, power is inseparable from knowledge, or using Foucault's phrase, power/knowledge: 'No body of knowledge can be formed without a system of communications, records, accumulation and displacement which is in itself a form of power and which is linked, in its existence and functioning, to the other forms of power. Conversely, no power can be exercised without the extraction, appropriation, distribution or retention of knowledge'(quoted in Sheridan 1980: 283). Within the development field, a number of studies have shown how discourses frame and bound certain potential policy issues in a way that denies potential actors their agency (Mohanty et. al. 1991) or depoliticises them in a way that makes them more easily managed by existing state power (Abrahamsen 2000). [2]

As with concepts of actors and knowledge, concepts of space are also heavily interwoven with concepts of power. Work by Cornwall

(2002a:iii), for instance, examines 'issues of power and difference in the making and shaping of spaces for participation in development', and in the micro-politics of interactions within them. She draws from the French social theorist Lefebvre, for whom 'space is a social product... it is not simply "there", a neutral container waiting to be filled, but is a dynamic, humanly constructed means of control, and hence of domination, of power' (1991:24). Inherent in the idea of spaces is also the imagery of 'boundaries', which serve to delimit spaces, what is possible within them, which actors may enter, and with what forms of knowledge. Building on the concept of boundary, Hayward (1998:2) suggests that we might understand power 'as the network of social boundaries that delimit fields of possible action.' Freedom, on the other hand, 'is the capacity to participate effectively in shaping the social limits that define what is possible.'[3]

With this more multi-dimensional view of power, then, inclusive participation is not only the right to participate effectively in a given policy space, but the right to define and to shape that space in the first place. We must go beyond the important questions of which actors act on particular policy issues, to ask which actors do not engage in potentially relevant policy processes, and indeed why certain potentially important policies are defined as out of bounds in certain spaces as well. Moreover, with changing global-local relations of power, we must examine the ways that actors, knowledge and spaces interact at different levels across a vertical slice of the policy process at the local, national and global levels – what Ferguson refers to as the 'vertical topography of power' (1998). With this in mind, we return to our framework of actors, knowledge and spaces, and the ways in which power relations are imbued within and contribute to shaping each concept and their interactions.

Actors

It is perhaps self-evident that making policy processes more inclusive will of necessity recast and broaden assumptions about who participates – or potentially participates – as key actors within them. Whereas in more state-centric understandings, policy-makers were largely considered to be government actors, the move to a broader understanding of 'governance' links government and society in new roles and opens up the process to a range of other stakeholders. As Hajer and Wagenaar (2003:3) point out 'there is a move from the familiar topography of formal institutions to the edges of organisational activity, negotiations between sovereign bodies and inter-organisational networks that challenge the established distinction between public and private ... Notions of politics itself change as new themes occupy centre stage.'

The broader 'multi-stakeholder' approach to the policy process is clearly reflected, for instance, in the World Bank's Poverty Reduction Strategy Sourcebook (2002), which argues for a participatory process 'by which stakeholders influence and share control over priority setting, policymaking, resource allocations, and/or program implementation' (quoted in Stewart and Wang 2003). In this model, the key stakeholders in poverty reduction are a broad range, including the general public, particularly the poor and vulnerable groups; the government, including parliament, local government, line and central ministries; civil society organisations, private sector actors and donors, both bilateral and multilateral. The underlying assumption is that through coming together in poverty reduction strategies, perspectives will be shared, common ownership will increase, and more informed, appropriate and sustainable policies will emerge.

When examined in practice, as in the previous chapters, the difficulties of implementing the more inclusive policy approach quickly become apparent. While in more traditional approaches to policy-making who should participate and at what stage was perhaps clear, if limited, opening up the process to include a broader range of stakeholders blurs the roles. Which stakeholders are to participate, to engage with which tasks, at what level, and with what legitimacy are not at all self-evident. As Hajer and Wagenaar again observe, 'characteristically, these new spaces of politics exist in an institutional void: there are no pre-given rules that determine who is responsible, who has authority over whom, what sort of accountability is to be expected. Yet as politics takes place between organisations, all people bring their own institutional expectations and routines with them' (9). In the absence of historical precedent or clearly accepted guidelines and procedures, the process of multi-stakeholder involvement inevitably becomes simultaneously more dynamic yet more chaotic; perhaps more inclusive yet also more 'messy' than before.

Moreover, the multi-stakeholder approach seems based on an assumption that key groupings of policy actors – be they government, donors, civil society or others – are themselves homogeneous, and that they contain lines of accountability that will allow them to interact with other groupings representatively and legitimately. The empirical reality seen in the previous chapters suggests a vastly different reality, in which each stakeholder group itself consists of heterogeneous actors, who are often themselves in conflict; in which the identities of individual actors and broader actor networks often cut across stakeholder groupings, and in which few clear structures of representation and accountability exist to link actors within and across groupings into the policy process. Within this more inchoate and messy picture, powerful actors who are long-term occupants in previous policy processes are often able to retain their predominance as apparently new policy spaces emerge.

Actors at the national level: state, civil society and donors
Who then are these actors in policies related to poverty reduction in Uganda and Nigeria? We turn first to examine actors at the national level – especially state actors, non-state actors and donors – referred to by Gould and Ojanen in their study of Tanzania as the 'iron triangle' of the policy-making process (2003:17)[4] Our work at the national level reveals how difficult it is to draw generalisations across contexts about how this triumvirate of actors enters the policy stage and what the relationships are within the triangle.

In the first instance, there are critical differences in political context, as discussed in Chapters 2 and 3. Uganda represents a unitary, single party structure of government coalescing under the National Resistance Movement, with deep historical roots in the resistance struggle against the Amin and Obote regimes. In such a context, encouraged by the presence and influence of international donors, a relatively unitary and coherent set of poverty policies have emerged, as seen in the development of the Poverty Eradication Action Plan

(PEAP) and the Uganda Participatory Poverty Assessment Process (UPPAP), considered by many to have produced some positive results (Norton et al 2001; Yates and Okello 2002). While participation of multiple stakeholders in these policy processes has not been without its conflicts and difficulties, at some level they encouraged government, civil society and donors to interact in new ways. Yet even within this context, the Movement struggles with ethnic tensions and regional disparities which still reflect the structures and attitudes of the colonial and post-independence eras. Neither is it easy to draw general lessons from this context – few countries in the contemporary continent are shaped by such a unitary structure of national governance, nor by the unifying history of the National Resistance Movement.

In Nigeria, by contrast, the notion of a unified nation-state is itself under question, as the country still searches for a common citizenship identity (Abah et al 2002) and struggles to hold together diverse socio-political regions and states in a single federation. Within this context, no single unifying or accepted 'poverty reduction policy' or plan exists that is not highly contested between the federal government and the states or even within the federal government itself, well illustrated in the wrestling match amongst the Planning Commission, the National Poverty Eradication Programme (NAPEP) and Economic Policy Co-ordinating Committee (EPCC) as to which entity would 'own' the PRSP process (Chapter 8). This single contextual comparison is an example of a significant challenge for the 'blueprint' approach underpinning the implementation of the current Poverty Reduction Strategy Papers (PRSPs). The degree of singular national 'ownership' which is possible, and the view of who is assumed to represent 'the nation', will vary enormously across political and historical contexts, rendering any policy based on a uniform set of guidelines and assumptions a very blunt instrument indeed.

While the degree of fragmentation or unity within the state itself represents a striking contrast between Uganda and Nigeria, both countries show a remarkable persistence of the same poverty policy actors over time. In Nigeria, despite the fragmentation of the state, this continuity was illustrated by the presence of powerful individuals from previous military regimes in all three of the key government committees set up by the Obasanjo government to establish a 'new' poverty programme (Chapter 8). Similarly, in Uganda, the same coalition of actors who worked together during the bush war of 1980-86 continues to exercise a great deal of power in the Movement-led government, even eighteen years after gaining control (Chapter 4). Despite the opening up of governance to new actors in both contexts, within government itself there may be a continuity of policy elites, whose very presence evokes for other actors overtones of past processes and behaviours. In Nigeria, the persistence of the same actors in the policy process suggests a continuation of a command and control style bureaucracy, riddled with patronage politics, not the new accountable, transparent and open set of actors aspired to by the more 'consultative' policy model. In Uganda as well, the NRM 'encountered difficulty in translating the inclusiveness of the resistance movement into institutions that could uphold the principles of accountable and representative policy'(Chapter 4).

Within the multi-stakeholder model of poverty reduction policy processes, the persistence of one set of policy actors in government may theoretically be offset by opening up the process to other non-state actors, who in the current policy discourse are given an increasingly important role. At the national level, the studies from Uganda and Nigeria present sharp contrasts as to what the involvement of non-state, civil society actors is likely to mean in the politics of poverty reduction. Just as the state has been shaped by somewhat different political histories in each country, so too does the relationship of the state to broader society vary across contexts. As seen in Chapter 2, in Uganda, the rhetoric and history of inclusion provides a broad umbrella under which a variety of civil society actors may engage with the state. Even within this context, however, these actors have found it a major – in many cases, insurmountable –challenge to shift from being service providers who supplement the state's delivery and implementation of pro-poor policies, to being advocates, who help 'make and shape' (Cornwall and Gaventa 2001) policy and hold the process accountable.

In Nigeria, by contrast, the role of civil society has been shaped by the 'exit'of civil society actors from the state, reflecting a history of state failure, of decades of primarily military rule, and of the failure of national formations of civil society to emerge or survive (Chapter 4 and Osaghae 1998). Given this history of state-civil society relations, the category of the 'non-state' sector encompasses such a diverse range of actors as to be virtually meaningless. The term may include national NGOs whose trajectory has been largely based on human rights advocacy rather than on poverty issues; national service delivery NGOs, which focus on poverty reduction, but in service delivery rather than policy advocacy approaches; the organised private sector and trade unions – each of which may also be in conflict with another. The vacuum created by the relative absence of poverty-oriented civil society organisations at the national level is filled by powerful actors, most obviously in this case by the organised private sector, whose agenda of privatisation has found strong alliances among certain government and donor quarters as well. Or it may be filled by self- or politically-appointed representatives, as illustrated by the fact that in Nigeria the only civil society representative on the interim-PRSP drafting team ran a very small NGO and by day was a full-time government employee.

This in itself is illustrative of another challenge to a multi-stakeholder approach: the assumption of a clear separation of actors across civil society, government, donor, private sector or other groupings. Many actors hold multiple identities. What may be a neat conceptual divide between 'state and non-state' or 'state and civil society' may in fact fall away when the multiple roles and allegiances of specific actors come into play.[5] Moreover, the assumption that many nationally based civil society actors have the capacity to 'speak for' the poor is itself defied by the position of many of these actors in society: they often come from more elite families, with few mechanisms for representation of and accountability to the poor, or they are linked to their constituencies more by ethnic identities than by a sense of allegiance to any stakeholder group of which they may be seen to be a part.

The role and influence of donors as policy actors also differs sharply between Uganda and Nigeria. In Uganda, where both state and civil society organisations are heavily dependent upon aid, donors are predominant and influential actors in national level policy processes, leading to the image of a 'parallel state', as described in Chapter 4, where the dependence of civil society organisations on donor funding creates 'donor citizens', who participate in the management of a donor-driven country. In Nigeria, by contrast, the massive foreign exchange earnings generated through oil exports diminish the dependence on external donors – yet even there the desire to gain the financial economic seal of approval from the international community offers a strong incentive to stay at the donor table. However, the relatively weaker role of the donors in Nigeria is perhaps counterbalanced by the influential presence of the oil companies, who themselves play a role as actors in poverty reduction policy – either directly in states in which they operate (e.g. Bayelsa) or indirectly as seen in the pervasive and bitter struggles in federal, state and local politics. Either way, whether through aid or oil, the influence of external actors on policy raises questions about the rhetoric and real possibilities of achieving 'national' ownership of poverty reduction processes. As we shall explore more fully later in the chapter, the power of donor discourses to shape the boundaries of legitimate policies about poverty constantly draws the attention of both state and civil society actors upwards and away from the very constituents whom the 'inclusive' discourse demands that they seek to include. The cases of Nigeria and Uganda echo the risk of 'deepening control exercised by a delocalised class of transnational functionaries over the political space where public resource allocation decisions are made' (Gould and Ojanen 2003:21). [6]

Expanding the stage: the vertical slice of actors in the policy process

The degree to which power in policy processes at the national level is skewed upwards and outwards towards external actors becomes more visible as we move from capital cities down our vertical slice through the policy process. At levels closer to the majority of the poor themselves, the important policy actors are often very different from those performing on the national stage. At both the national level and the local level one finds multiple actors who are horizontally linked by common identities, actor networks and shared discourses.

When one looks vertically, however, it is the disconnections of the policy actors at the local level from the national stage which are more profound.

Within a federal system like Nigeria, one might expect state level structures to be relevant poverty actors. Yet, only one of the states we observed, Jigawa, has a programme that might be called a state-driven poverty initiative. In Ekiti, existing programmes are largely donor-driven, by the World Bank and DFID. In Bayelsa, the state governor is clearly identified as the 'engine' of power, but 'policy' takes the form of promoting ethnic interests and those of a strong informal network of actors who surround the governor's office and protect his power. Bayelsa state itself has no separate programme or policy which could be said to focus specifically on poverty. Rather, debates on poverty policy are largely linked to tussles with the federal government over who to appoint to lead the state offices of federal programmes, how to allocate funding, and what patronage and power is offered to whom in the process. In Uganda, where districts play the key intermediary role between nation and locality, a wide disconnection is found between the narrative of 'bottom-up participatory planning processes on poverty' and the way things are actually done, as local government actors adhere to their prescribed roles of representatives of central government and technicians who 'know best' what should be done (see, for instance, the discussion of the micro politics of legislated and invited spaces in Lira District, Chapter 7).

The local unit of governance itself might be seen as a relevant poverty policy actor – but a lame one, because the policies it enacts are coming from elsewhere. In Nigeria, there are now over 700 local government units, which hold considerable resources from the federal account, for delivering local services and programmes. Yet, perhaps not surprisingly given their relatively new-found role in the context of an emerging democracy, local governments appear largely absent as key poverty actors, both figuratively and literally. In two states, key local government chairmen were found to draw pay checks and control local funds, but actually live many miles away in the state capital, leading one poor woman interviewed in a community not far from the local government offices to remark, 'it is easier to spend a week in the bush than to find the local government chairman.' Even where local councillors want to play a role as poverty actors, they are constrained: they are not consulted about poverty programmes handed down from Abuja, nor are they able to hold the local government chairmen (and it is almost always men) accountable for the huge discretion they normally have over the federal revenues given to the local level (Chapter 13). In Uganda, even though districts produce district development plans which are supposed to be informed by local realities and priorities, these lack any reference to localised perceptions or definitions of poverty, or locally determined priorities. This is the predictable outcome of a paradox: the co-existence of a rhetoric of 'bottom-up participatory planning'and a heavy financial dependence on central government, whose disbursements are conditioned to nationally defined sectoral spending priorities which may or may not coincide with local realities in any given district (Brock et. al. 2003: 6-8).

While the state at the sub-national level is seen as simply extending top-down dictates or patronage, and where the presence of local government is largely absent or weak, the case studies suggest that other non-state actors have considerable significance for poor people. In Jigawa state, the emirate system, which runs parallel to the formal government, is seen to set out to address certain needs of the poor through the traditional Zakkat system. In other states, the role of traditional chiefs and other traditional structures are significant, though in different ways. In Bayelsa, the oil companies which provide key community services and the youth organisations, such the Ijaw Youth Council, which advocate directly with them, are seen by local communities as significant poverty-related actors. In Ekiti and throughout other parts of the country, the role of community development associations is also critical in organising poverty-related projects, though not necessarily in policy advocacy.

In Uganda, with its rhetoric of unity and inclusion, at the local level the impression we gain is less of separate non-state actors than of the absence of certain key actors, especially women, within the 'inclusive' processes (Chapter 8). In either situation – whether actors in non-state spaces, or actors whose voices are suppressed in the state-sponsored processes – there is an enormous chasm between the national-level policy arena and the locality where poor peoples' realities are experienced most vividly. Theoretically, the potential bridge across the chasm would be representative structures which aggregate local interests more effectively and transmit them to the national arena. Yet these linking structures seem largely absent, ineffectual or unaccountable. On the whole, in Nigeria, political parties have not taken up clearly delineated policy positions on poverty and are felt to practise more downward patronage than upward representation. The role of the parliamentarians is also weak, as we found when one of our researchers was asked to explain to the chair of a key committee responsible for poverty what the PRSP actually was. And in both Nigeria and Uganda, while the roles and capabilities of non-state actors are expanding, few possess the representation and accountability structures that can bring local voices and interests clearly into national policy (Brock et. al. 2003:19-20).

The separation of local realities from the national stage, combined with the accentuating power of external agencies to legitimate certain actors through funding, access and other privileges, serve to reinforce the idea in both countries of policy actors operating in two distinct policy stages.[7] One is at the national level, where loose coalitions of elite actors engage in a web of state, civil society and donor structures, and another at the local level, where the actors are more strongly found in informal non-state associations, as in Nigeria; or where the local version of poverty policy is very different from what is prescribed in the national script, as in Uganda, where the word 'poverty' is scarcely heard in district council headquarters. There the mental and operational template is not 'poverty', 'poverty reduction' or the PEAP, but sectoral development – health, production, water, education, community development. The gross majority of resources transferred to the district by central government obey the logic of the PEAP and must be spent according to that template, yet the approach is still somewhat alien to the language and practice of district-level technicians and, to a great extent, of the politicians as well.

Knowledge

Equally important to the question of who acts in poverty reduction policy process is the question of what type of knowledge the actors use, and their ability to project it in a way that speaks to the audiences which they seek to influence. In the introduction to this book, we give a broad definition of what we mean by knowledge, 'ranging from official knowledge captured in national survey-based statistics, through poverty narratives woven and promoted by various actors, to popular knowledge based on people's own experience' (1:10). In policy processes which place an increasing emphasis on 'evidence'as a source of legitimacy, knowledge becomes a form of political currency which can serve to legitimate some voices over others within policy processes, but which can also be used to construct boundaries around which actors and scripts enter which policy arenas in the first place.

Paradoxically, the inclusionary rhetoric for involvement of a wider range of stakeholders in the policy process can carry with it an exclusionary bias against those stakeholders who are less able to mobilise certain kinds of evidence in the official policy arenas in accepted ways. As McGee demonstrates at the national level in Uganda (Chapter 6) , while the opening up of the policy process to more stakeholders has, to a degree, opened it to more diverse forms of knowledge, there are still significant disparities in whose knowledge counts, and who claims the potential opportunities that the new openings may offer.

When we extend this analysis outside the national level in Uganda and to the very different context of Nigeria, the pattern becomes even more clear. While there is a weak rhetorical commitment to plurality of knowledges about poverty, there are vast inequalities in the capacity of differently positioned actors to mobilise their knowledge in the policy process. In Nigeria, for instance, even the main federal government agency responsible for poverty data, the Federal Office of Statistics, is grossly underfunded and has a reputation for the political manipulation of statistics. At the state level, agencies and planning offices, as in the districts in Uganda, lack independent research or evidence-marshalling capacities. Civil society actors are even less equipped. In Nigeria, universities have been chronically underfunded for more than two decades, and are in no position to carry out poverty research or monitoring without external funding, usually tied to external donors. In both Nigeria and Uganda, civil society representatives discuss the importance of being able 'to make a good argument' during meetings, yet while civil society organisations may possess enormous knowledge arising from their work at the micro level, they have little capacity to aggregate and process it into forms that are considered relevant at the more macro level. In Uganda, processes such as UPPAP have helped to build stronger connections between micro-level understandings of poverty and the national picture, but only to a limited degree. Civil society groups still have relatively weak research and evidence mobilising skills, and without such evidence, find the legitimacy of their positions challenged.

The irony in both countries is that while the international donors promote inclusive participation, producing and mobilising knowledge in a form that will prevail in multi-stakeholder processes still depends heavily on donor funding. And where legitimacy is based on methods, messages, and the identity of the source, power resides with the donors to determine each, through their choices as to what research to fund and by whom. In the absence of independent currencies, donor-driven knowledge and discourse fills the void. Thus, in Nigeria, the chair of the PRSP drafting committee, while head of the national social science research centre, still turns to the World Bank for legitimacy and guidance, not to an independent research community. In the state of Ekiti, the research team points to the need for the 'Ekitization' of knowledge about poverty if they are to have a state-driven poverty policy. And in Uganda, despite the broadening of perspectives, McGee finds that 'the gatekeepers of orthodox poverty knowledge would appear to be the World Bank – still – and the government, whose embracing of alternative perspectives seems, in fact, to be functional to political interests and the imperative of maintaining good relationships with key creditors and donors'(6:17).

The power to mobilise evidence within the national level policy processes is enhanced greatly by the power of the dominant discourse to construct or reconstruct the questions considered relevant to poverty policy in the first place. In Jigawa, for instance, while an historic and highly sophisticated poverty measurement system is embedded in Islamic Zakkat tradition, reference to this form of knowledge does not appear among the officially funded poverty monitoring sources. While for the youth in Bayelsa, the key issues related to poverty pertain to the power of the oil companies and the perceived destruction of the environment, this is not reflected in national poverty plans. Overall in Nigeria, our partners in this research project point to the power of the poverty discourse to divert the agenda from the underlying issues of inequality or from the human rights concerns of pre-Obasanjo days, despite an increased concern at the international level to promote a 'rights-based' approach to poverty reduction. Similarly in Uganda, informants point to how a philosophy of resistance and state reform has been transformed to a discourse of poverty reduction, which – due to the international legitimacy such discourse bestows – threatens to crowd out other issues also important to the poor.[8]

The power of the discourse to frame the poverty debate does not all lie with the donors. In Nigeria, where poverty programmes are heavily funded from central government's oil-rich coffers, poverty reduction policies conjure up historical images of 'First Lady' benevolence, or of the state as 'Father Christmas', in which the poor are constructed as the beneficiaries of political patronage, not as rights-bearing citizens or as actors in policy processes. The power of this image continues, such that poverty policies continue to be associated with government handouts. Recipients demand their share of 'the democracy dividend' while other issues – such as fuel prices, around which civil society or the labour unions have mobilised through highly visible national strikes – do not enter the poverty policy discourse.

A final point about knowledge and the policy process reinforces the sense of citizen-as-beneficiary. Overwhelmingly, even in the best of consultative processes which aim at gathering more inclusive knowledge, the goal is knowledge for policy – in order to make it more informed and perhaps more effective at reaching the needs of the poor. Yet, at the same time, citizens and non-state actors are being called upon to play a new role – that of active agents who can hold accountable the official policy makers and the process in which they engage. For that role a different kind of knowledge is needed – knowledge about policy not about poverty; knowledge about the rights of citizens to express their voices, not about the needs of citizens to strengthen the policy makers' voices; knowledge which is not only an input into a somewhat opaque policy process, but which helps to make that process more transparent and which can be used to monitor its results. Yet programmes by government, donors or even civil society which emphasise this kind of knowledge on poverty reduction policy processes were scarcely found in our research, perhaps with the exception of relatively isolated work on debt and budgets done by Ugandan Debt Network (Chapter 6). Without such knowledge about the policy process, the capacity of the poor and their allies to use their knowledge about poverty to hold the policy-makers accountable, will inevitably be weak and exercised only at the invitation of the more powerful policy actors. This pattern of inclusive knowledge 'by invitation' leads us on to the discussion of the spaces in which poverty policies are formed and enacted.

Spaces

In the framework presented in Chapter 1, we visualised the policy process as a series of interlinked, overlapping spaces, traversed by different actors, ideas and practices. These policy spaces range from the more traditionally understood 'official' spaces for policy – largely found in government bureaucracies, legislatures and assemblies – to more 'autonomous' spaces, created by popular forms of action through social movements, self-help groups, and the like. Between the two, we suggested, are increasingly found new 'invited spaces', in which actors from civil society, government and donor agencies are encouraged to come together for more consultative and deliberative forms of interaction.

With this more multi-dimensional view, one gains a picture of the multiplicity of spaces which are potentially relevant for attempts to influence the poverty policy process. Even within government, there may be competing spaces for poverty policy, as we saw in the tension between the 'domestic' and 'donor-led' streams for poverty policy in Nigeria (Chapter 8). It is precisely the enormous number of different kinds of spaces which comprise any specific policy process that contributes to an appearance of incoherence in poverty reduction at the federal, state and LGA levels. The multiplicities of spaces, and their overlaps, create tensions between different actors; it is seldom clear, especially at the federal level, how the decisions taken in one space relate to, or have legitimacy over those taken in another. In Uganda, where a no-party democracy and the ruling Movement gives the image of more coherence and consensus in poverty policy processes, probing deeper has revealed that the consensus is often not borne out in reality – conflicts between donors, government departments, civil society actors, media and others often exist, visibly or invisibly, within and amongst policy spaces.

Despite the multitude of diverse spaces relevant to policies about poverty, the examples in previous chapters lend credence to the assertion that no space is simply a neutral opportunity, waiting to be filled (Brock, Chapter 7 and Cornwall 2002b). Who creates the space affects who enters it, the forms of knowledge considered appropriate there and how people participate within it. Any assessment of the potential of a policy space to become pro-poor must include an analysis of the power relations which exist within it, and which surround its construction. From the case material a number of insights emerge about power and space, and their interrelationships.

A first important lesson is that presence in a space does not in itself constitute meaningful participation within it. Rather, any space contains certain formal or informal rules of the game which enable certain actors with certain forms of knowledge to participate more effectively and more powerfully than other.[9] In Chapter 7, for instance, Brock vividly explores how the existence of an apparently 'invited' open space is riddled with practices of language, official behaviours, physical arrangements, and agenda-setting that serve to include some 'participants' in the meeting more fully than others. While effectively inhibiting the participation of the poor in general, such processes and procedures have a particular impact on women, contributing to the highly gendered nature of these policy spaces.

The lack of participation of women in the formal meeting is contrasted with their active participation outside the invited spaces, lending credence to the conclusion that women's lack of participation in spaces like council meetings is 'due to the structure of those spaces, and the dominant narratives of gender relations which they mirror' (Chapter Seven:9) rather than to the weakness of the agency of the women themselves.

While many such practices are clearly observable, other examples suggest that what occurs within policy spaces is also affected by the more hidden forms of power which surround them – that is, backstage of public spaces. In Bayelsa, as we have seen, the visible influence of the governor is shaped by the more hidden role of a network of informal actors who have the power to get his attention, shape his agenda, and even override more formal policy processes (Chapter 10). In Uganda the 'tea parties' which surrounded the consultation on the Plan for the Modernisation of Agriculture were perceived to have laid the decision-making terrain for what actually happened in the public space (Chapter 4). At the district level in Uganda 'drinking places' were key backstage sites where decisions made privately were found to conflict with public discourses by powerful actors (Chapter 5). In some instances, backstage decisions determine who receives invitations to participate on the public stage, excluding some from entering the process altogether. In other cases, more internalised forms of power, such as one's own self-expectations of what roles or which forms of knowledge are appropriate in which kind of space, shape behaviour without power holders visibly intervening at all.

If power relations work to affect who participates and who is excluded, which issues get addressed and which remain latent within certain spaces, the power to construct the boundaries which surround the space is perhaps an even greater form of power. In our earlier discussion of actors and knowledge, we saw the ways in which discourses can construct perceived boundaries around what constitutes a legitimate 'poverty issue' for discussion within that space and who the actors should be within it. However, in the case of Uganda, we saw something of a counter-example, where the ability to re-claim or re-name a set of spaces as part of the PEAP process (led by the Ugandan government) rather than part of the PRSP process (introduced by the World Bank and IMF), significantly shifted the power of the government actors to retain some element of ownership and control, and to bend the World Bank norms to Ugandan reality and preference.

Spaces in turn are shaped not only by the agency of the constructors but also by the historical and political context in which they are made. Spaces for public involvement which are constructed by similar actors with the same architecture may be filled very differently in different historical contexts. As Cornwall has written elsewhere, 'No newly-created space can be entirely cleared of traces of social relations, nor of people's previous experiences of planned intervention in other spaces' (2002:52)[10] Thus, as we found in the cases of Nigeria and in Uganda, new invited spaces may indeed be filled with actors from previous regimes, who bring with them behaviours more associated with centralised command structures than with consultation; or who associate poverty alleviation with processes of patronage and handouts, rather than as a way of empowering the poor. Newly invited actors may also be sceptical about entering a space, if their previous experiences with consultation have been perceived as negative and disempowering, as we saw in the discussion of civil society in Nigeria (Chapter 9). Similarly, in Uganda where new spaces for 'participation' are situated in an historically autocratic environment, participants may very easily defer to old cultures of deference to seniority and power (Chapter 3).

Finally, spaces exist not only in relationship to their historical context but also in relationship to each other. Just as we argued earlier that the distinctions between different sets of actors become blurred by multiple identities of single actors and actor networks, so too are the borders of spaces constantly changing. What begins as a relatively autonomous way of approaching poverty can in turn be quickly co-opted by official structures. What appears to be a new, more open, invited space may simply become a form of legitimating the power of traditional policy elites, who now benefit from the semblance of consultation. The dynamic inter-relationship of these different forms of policy spaces has led some to express concern that newly invited spaces can weaken the legitimacy and authority of existing 'representative' governments, thus undermining democracy rather than strengthening it (Gould and Ojanen 2003). Our research suggests that similar questions should be posed about a related but opposite concern. Does the capacity to define 'poverty policy' as what happens within certain invited and governmental spaces also in turn have the effect of de-legitimating and undermining more autonomous movements and structures which historically have served the poor? For instance, as the Zakkat committees in Jigawa begin to be linked to the formal government policies, will they lose the qualities derived from their 'autonomy'? By insisting that civil society actors –who often have either implemented service programmes for poverty reduction, or have been advocates for the poor against the structures of government – now participate with government in policy formation, will their other capacities be eroded? For non-state actors, when to engage or not to engage in state or donor-created spaces becomes a critical, political question. To answer that question necessitates looking at the inter-relationships of actors, knowledge and spaces.

Linking actors, knowledge and spaces

As important as a distinct understanding of actors, knowledge and spaces in policy processes is an understanding of the dynamic interrelationship of the three.[11] Looking within each circle has helped us to see how certain actors, with certain knowledge, operating in certain spaces, tend to predominate over others in the policy process. If, in looking across actors, knowledge and spaces we also find a linkage – that is, that the same actors, with similar knowledges occupy and dominate similar spaces – then we can draw further conclusions about the role of power within poverty policy processes.

Actors help to create spaces, which enables their agency within those spaces, but they may find their agency and participation bounded in other spaces. Knowledge – in the broadest sense that includes evidence, discourses and narratives – helps to construct the boundaries of spaces, and to define which actors may be seen as legitimate actors within them. Clearly some actors have more capacity to produce and wield certain knowledge currencies than others, but the value of the currency will vary across spaces – formal, quantitative knowledge has great currency with certain governmental and donor actors in formal governmental policy spaces, while informal experiential knowledge may have more sway in more localised and autonomous spaces for action. The spaces for action which are relevant to poverty policy are many, and extend from the global to the local, from the 'official' to the more 'autonomous'. Yet none of them constitutes a level playing field. Who constructs the spaces affects who enters them and which knowledge is considered relevant within them. As the political scientist E.E. Schattschneider wrote many years ago: 'It is not necessarily true that people with the greatest needs participate in politics most actively – whoever decides what the game is about also decides who gets in the game'(1960:105).

The dynamic and inter-relating quality of actors, knowledge and spaces suggests a process that is at first glance chaotic, non-linear, porous and pluralistic. This image of the policy process, as we have said, stands in sharp contrast to the more linear views of a policy process in which there is a clear beginning, middle and end, and in which the roles of various actors are clear.

But to suggest that the policy process is chaotic and non-linear is not to say that there are not patterns of power which may emerge across actors, knowledge and spaces. In a participatory and pluralistic policy process, one might expect to find multiple actors who come and go over time, a valuing of differing forms of knowledge, and a recognition of the validity of multiple spaces for poverty policy. Together these might be seen to constitute an overall poverty policy process. If on the other hand, one finds the same or similar actors, with similar knowledges, predominating in certain spaces, and if these spaces in turn are seen as more legitimate than others, one gets a picture of a more elite-dominated policy process, where power is less pluralistic than it might first appear.

In very broad terms, the picture which emerges depends very much on how widely one views the policy process. If one looks primarily at the national policy level, and primarily at the more official and newly created policy spaces, one might get an impression of an increasing dispersal of power. Policy processes appear to be broadening to include non-state as well as state actors and, especially in Uganda, attempts are made to bring different forms of knowledge into the policy process. Yet when one looks more closely, this apparent pluralism is highly bounded – certain actor networks predominate over time; some actors have far more capacity to produce knowledge for this arena than others, and the power of the dominant poverty discourse creates strong boundaries of what is considered relevant to poverty policy in the first place. If there is pluralism here, it is pluralism on a stage constructed and populated by elites – one which sits far above and removed from a series of other stages whose construction, actors and scripts are closer and more relevant to the poor themselves.

The elitism of the poverty drama on the national stage is made all the clearer when the sphere of poverty policy is widened. As we have seen in Nigeria especially, the further one moves from the formal poverty policy and from the centre, the greater the agency of local actors, with different definitions of key poverty issues, different forms of knowledge, expressed through social movements, self-help groups, ethnic and religious groups and traditional institutions. Rather than being positioned along the exit row away from the state-centric stage, as these forms of action have been widely understood (Osaghae 1998), these are perhaps better understood as taking place on a policy stage in a different theatre, parallel to but highly disconnected from the action that attracts the donors' attention at the centre. In Uganda, given the history of a movement for national unity, and given the rhetoric of inclusion rather than exit, there is perhaps less scope for parallel stages, and yet there still exists an enormous disconnection between the play which goes on at the national and donor level, and how the performance is experienced by potential poverty policy actors at the district and local levels – contributing to their participation as isolated spectators, or more metaphorically, as a Greek chorus who comment on, but do not take part in the main action. From this perspective, what might be understood as a form of 'pluralist elitism' in the policy process at the top, increasingly looks less pluralistic and more elitist when it is viewed from more local and less state-centric policy spaces. In the broader political economy of policy, it is not only in the ability to construct spaces, but in the ability by certain actors to construct certain spaces and knowledges as more legitimate than others that the greater power lies.

Implications: from inclusionary policy to pro-poor power relations

Such an understanding of the inter-relationship of actors, knowledges and spaces in the policy process poses a number of challenges for the current trend in development practice towards creating pro-poor policy processes that are more inclusive, participatory and accountable, and for the simultaneous mandate that policies become more evidence-based.

A more critical understanding of the power dynamics of spaces, and how they are constructed, calls into question prevailing assumptions found in poverty reduction processes, in particular that new 'invited' or 'consultative spaces' will inherently be more open, pluralistic or pro-poor than previous policy spaces. Rather, in creating such spaces, some assessment must be made of the politics of invitation and inclusion; of whether the newly created spaces will offer opportunities for new and previously marginalised actors to gain power or whether they will simply strengthen the power of the old. Who invites, whose knowledge is used, whether actors have the capacity to marshal the knowledge in the form required, how the invitation sits historically in relationship to prior invitations, and in relationship to other official and more autonomous spaces, will all affect the degree to which a new space has the potential to become pro-poor.

This is not a technical process, but a political one, filled with and surrounded by a history and context of complex power relations. If they are not recognised and analysed, these power relations can subvert inclusive ideas and intentions with exclusionary practices. Yet paradoxically, the very discourse of inclusion, when emanating from powerful donors or government agencies in societies shaped by prior experiences of top-down regimes, will colour how new spaces are perceived, and whether they are in fact claimed by the very marginalised actors whom the powerful are now purporting to 'include'. Moreover, even when newly empowered actors are able to marshal the evidence to support their claims, past practices raise fundamental questions about the degree to which evidence – rather than the ability to mobilise it – really informs policy choices. Nor can the creation of more inclusionary policies be done by blueprint. The examples of two African countries, Uganda and Nigeria, as well the states and districts within them, reveal very different contexts which will affect who participates, in which spaces and with what knowledge.

The lessons from this volume suggest that the creation of inclusive policy will not occur without addressing the power relations which surround the interstices of policy processes themselves, and doing so in a way that is context-specific. To address power relations in some instances may mean strengthening the capacities of less powerful actors to engage with more powerful actors. In others, it may mean democratising knowledge through strengthening the capacity of weaker actors to marshal and present their own knowledge as evidence, and broadening the rules about what kinds of knowledge counts. In yet others, rather than expanding policy spaces from the top, and inviting the weak to participate in the spaces of the powerful, it may mean finding and supporting the less visible and more autonomous spaces which are closer to and more relevant to the lives of poor people. Much is yet to be learned about which are the most appropriate entry points in different contexts for creating pro-poor power relations, and which strategies will be most effective in doing so. What is clear from this study is that without such entry points, the discourse of more inclusive poverty policy may be an appealing one, but it remains very distant from the lives of poor people.

Notes

1. This chapter has benefited greatly from the inputs of each of the chapter contributors in synthesis workshops held in Abuja, Nigeria in May 2002 and Brighton, England in March 2003, as well as from the specific comments from Karen Brock, Rosemary McGee and Paul Francis.

2. My thanks to Emma Jones and Jonathan Gaventa for their assistance in reviewing relevant power literature.

3. McGee adopts this same definition in Chapter 1 of this volume.

4. 'Historically,' Gould and Ojanen argue, 'the policy elite [in Tanzania] has been based on an exclusive dyadic link between state and donors.' However, a consequence of the 'consultative imperative' is the expansion of the policy elites to include actors from the non-state sector or civil society actors. (2003:17).

5. As observed in Chapter 5, in Uganda this pattern was found to be even more the case at the district level and below, 'with many actors in the processes of planning and politics having more than one identity, being simultaneously active in government, in civil society, as well as in their geographic and social constituencies.(5)'

6. Gould and Ojanen argue that 'the depoliticisation of governance and the transnationalisation of political space ...consolidate a hegemony of creditor interests in the development policy arena...' In the longer term – to paraphrase Callaghy's (2001:144) kindred analysis of debt relief in Uganda – the most significant consequences of the donor-imposed imperative for 'consultation' and 'civic participation' in public policy may not relate to poverty reduction at all, but to the 'new configurations of power and transboundary formations that it has helped to unleash'.

7. In this sense, the policy process is reflective of Peter Ekeh's two publics – the civic and primordial – developed further by Osaghae as reflecting in the Igbo distinction between the *olu oyibo* (white man's business) and the *olu obodo* (community business). The actors, roles, norms and behaviours are vastly different on the stages of the two publics and, in turn, are re-enforced by differences in what constitutes the relevant poverty knowledge to be narrated on each.

8. For an excellent account of similar process in the United States see Alice O'Connor(2001).

9. Schattschneider referred to such rules of the game as a 'mobilisation of bias' which works to organise some issues into politics and other issues out (1960:71).

10. Cornwall draws upon other theorists, including Lefebvre 1991 and Long and van der Ploeg 1989.

11. As McGee observed in Chapter 1, 'the interplay of actors, knowledge and policy spaces is clearly dynamic and complex, and rather than three independent circles linked by arrows is probably better portrayed as three interlocking circles with the policy process at the intersection...'

Annexe
Bibliography
Glossary
Index

Annexe

Local government structure – Uganda

Functions	Local Councils	Level
Central government • Human resources management • Rule of law and the administration of justice • Economic management, including regulation • Public financial management • Public procurement management • Revenue collection • Oversight and accountability • Public facilities and asset management		**State** composed of 56 districts
Local government • Exercise all political and executive powers • Provide services • Ensure implementation of government policy and compliance with it • Plan for the district • Enact district laws • Monitor performance of government employees • Levy, charge and collect fees and taxes • Formulate, approve and execute district budgets	LC5	**District** composed of 35 counties
Administrative unit • Advise district officers and area member of parliament • Resolve problems and disputes • Monitor delivery of services	LC4	**County** composed of 35 sub-counties
Local government • Enact by-laws • Approve sub-county budget • Monitor performance of government employees • Levy, charge and collect fees and taxes • Formulate, approve and execute sub-county budgets	LC3	**Sub-county** composed of 3-10 parishes
Administrative unit • Assist in maintaining law, order and security • Initiate, encourage, support and participate in self-help projects • Serve as communication channel • Monitor the administration and projects	LC2	**Parish** composed 3-10 villages
Administrative unit • Assist in maintaining law, order and security • Initiate, encourage, support and participate in self-help projects • Serve as communication channel with government • Monitor the administration of projects • Make by-laws • Impose service fees	LC1	**Village** composed of 5-50 households

Source: adapted from Raussen et al. 2001

Local government structure – Nigeria

Functions	Level
Federal government • Fiscal, incomes, and monetary policy • Health sector: policy development, operation of tertiary-level teaching hospitals and national programmes for disease control. • Management of tertiary education • Agricultural infrastructure • Interstate roads • Security services • Electricity and communications • Postal services	**Federation** Composed of 36 States and the Federal Capital Territory
State governments • Secondary education • Health services under Health Management Boards • Agricultural infrastructure and extension • State roads • Markets • Sanitation and refuse disposal	**State** Composed of between 6 and 44 Local Government Areas
Local Government Council • Primary education (although a National Primary Education Committee, with Federal as well as Local Government Area (LGA) representation, now administers the primary school system) • Delivery of primary health care services (including maternity centres, dispensaries, health posts) • Management of two-thirds of the road system • Domestic water supplies • Sanitation services • Markets	**Local Government Area**

Source: elaborated from information in Francis 1996 and Ali-Akpajiak and Pyke 2003

For further reference

Raussen, T., Ebong, G., and Musiime, J., 2001, 'More effective natural resource management through democratically elected, decentralised government structures in Uganda,' Development in practice, 11:4, p. 460-470

Francis, P., 1996, *State, Community and Local Development in Nigeria*, Washington, DC: World Bank

Ali-Akpajiak, S. C. A,, Pyke, T., 2003, *Measuring Poverty in Nigeria*, Oxford: Oxfam Working Papers

Bibliography

Abah, S., and Okwori, J., 2002, 'Agendas in encountering citizens in the Nigerian context', IDS Bulletin Vol.33 (2), Brighton: Institute of Development Studies

Abrahamsen, R., 2000, *Disciplining Democracy: Development Discourse and Good Governance in Africa*, London: Zed Books

Agozino, B., and Idem, U., 2001, 'Nigeria: Democratising a militarised civil society," Centre for Democracy and Development Occasional Paper No. 5, London: Centre for Development and Democracy

Ahikire, J., Madanda, A., Kwesiga, J, 2002, 'Towards effective political participation and decision-making for women councillors in decentralised local government and the role of NGOs in Uganda', Kampala: Deniva

Ake, C., 1976, 'The Congruence of Political economies and Ideologies in Africa' in Gutkind, P. and Wallerstein, I. (eds.) *The Political Economy of Contemporary Africa*, London: Sage Publications.

Ake, C., 1996, 'The Political Question', in Oyediran, O (ed). *Governance and Development in Nigeria: Essays in honour of Prof. Billy Dudley*, Ibadan: Agbo Areo Publishers.

Allen, J., 2002, *Forming Farmers' Fora: the Enmeshment of State and Civil Society and its Implications for Agricultural Modernisation in Uganda*, M. Phil thesis, mimeo, Brighton: Institute of Development Studies

Aluko, S.A., 1975, 'Poverty: Its Remedies', in *Poverty in Nigeria: Proceedings of the 1975 Annual Conference of the Nigerian Economic Society*, Ibadan: Nigerian Economic Society

Anyanwu, J.C, 1997, *Poverty in Nigeria: Concepts, Measurement and Determinants*, Selected papers for the 1997 Annual Conference on Poverty Alleviation in Nigeria, Ibadan: Nigerian Economic Society.

Appleton, S., 2001, 'Education, incomes and poverty in Uganda in the 1990s,' *Credit Research Papers* 01/22, Nottingham: Centre for Research in Develoment and International Trade

Apthorpe, R., 1986, 'Development Policy Discourse', *Public*

Administration and Development Vol. 6.

Arce, A., and Long, N.(eds), 2000, *Anthropology, Development and Modernities: Exploring discourses, counter-tendencies and violence.* London: Routledge

Awolowo, O., 1981, *The Path to Nigeria's Greatness*, Enugu: Fourth Dimensions Publishing Co. Ltd

Ayam, J., 2000, *Democratic governance, political participation and consolidation in Nigeria*, Zaria: Aḥmadu Bello University

Ayoade, J., 1998, 'States without Citizens: an emerging African phenomenon', in Rothchild, D and Chazan, N. (eds), *The Precarious Balance: State and Society in Africa*, Boulder: Westview Press

Ayoola, G., Aina, G. et al., 1999, 'Nigeria: Voices of the Poor', Washington: World Bank

Barya, J-J, 1998, 'The Domestic context for civil society in Uganda: An Analysis of the Legal, Political and Economic Aspects', Paper presented at the workshop on Foreign Political Aid, Democratisation and Civil Society in Africa, Centre for Policy Studies, Johannesburg, 11-13 March 1998

Bayart, J-F., 1986, 'Civil Society in Africa', in Chabal, P. (ed) *Political Domination in Africa: Reflections on the Limits of Power*, Cambridge: Cambridge University Press

Bayart, J-F., Ellis, S. and Hibou, B., 1999, *The Criminalization of the State in Africa*, Oxford: James Currey

Bazaara, N, 2000, 'Contemporary Civil Society and the Democratisation Process in Uganda: A Preliminary Exploration', *CBR Working Paper 54*, Kampala: Centre for Basic Research

Bazaara, N., 2001, 'When does Civil Society Make sense for Poverty Reduction and Democracy in Uganda? A Summary of the Findings', *CBR Bulletin* Vol.3 (1), Kampala: Centre for Basic Research

Bevan, P., and Ssewaya, A., 1995, 'Understanding Poverty in Uganda: adding a sociological dimension,' *Working Paper* WPS/95.10, Oxford: Centre for the Study of African Economies

Blair, H., 2000, 'Participation and accountability at the periphery: democratic local governance in six countries.' *World Development* Vol. 28 (1).

Bloomfield, D., Collins, K., Fry, C., and Munton, R., 2001, 'Deliberation and inclusion: vehicles for increasing trust in UK public governance?' *Government and Policy* Vol. 19

Booth, D. (ed), 2004, *Fighting Poverty in Africa: are PRSPs making a difference?* London: Overseas Development Institute.

Bratton, M., 1989, 'Beyond the State: Civil Society and Associational Life in Africa', *World Politics*, Vol. 41 (3)

Brett, E., 1970, 'Cooperatives and Rural Development in Uganda', in Apthorpe, R. (ed), *Rural Cooperatives and Planned Change in Africa*, Geneva: UNRISD.

Brock, K. 2002, 'Introduction' in Brock, K. and McGee, R. (eds) 2002, *Knowing Poverty: critical reflections on participatory research and policy.* London: Earthscan

Brock, K., Cornwall, A. and Gaventa, J., 2001, 'Power, knowledge and political spaces in the framing of poverty policy', *IDS Working Paper 143*, Brighton: Institute of Development Studies

Brock, K, McGee, R., and Ssewakiryanga R., 2002, 'Poverty Knowledge and Policy Processes: a case study of Ugandan national poverty reduction policy,' *IDS Research Report 53*, Brighton: Institute of Development Studies

Brock, K., McGee, R., Okech, R., and Ssuuna, J., 2003, 'Poverty Knowledge and Policy Processes in Uganda: Case Studies from Bushenyi, Lira and Tororo Districts', *IDS Research Report 54*, Brighton, Institute of Development Studies

Callaghy, T., 1987, 'The State as Lame Leviathan: The Patrimonial-Administrative State in Africa' in Zaki, E. (ed) *The African State in Transition*, London: Macmillan.

Callaghy, T., 2001 'Networks and governance in Africa: innovation in the debt regime,' in Callaghy, T., Kassimir, R., and Latham, R., (eds) 2001, *Intervention and Transnationalism in Africa: Global-Local Networks of Power*, Cambridge: Cambridge University Press

Cammack, P., 2003, What the World Bank Means by Poverty Reduction',http://idpm.man.ac.uk/cprc/Conference/conferencepapers/Cammack%20250303.pdf Access date: 21st April 2004

Cassels, A., 1997, 'A Guide to Sector Wide Approaches for Health Development: Concepts, Issues and Working Arrangements', Washington: World Health Organisation

Central Bank of Nigeria, 1999, 'Nigeria's Development Prospects: Poverty Assessment and Alleviation Study', Lagos: Central Bank of Nigeria

Chabal, P., (ed) 1986, *Political Domination in Africa: reflections on the limits of power,* Cambridge: Cambridge University Press

Chabal, P. and Daloz, J-P., 1999, *Africa Works: Disorder as Political Instrument,* Oxford: James Currey

Chazan, N., 1988, 'State and Society in Africa: Images and Challenges' in Harbeson, J., Chazan, N., and Rothchild, D (eds), *The Precarious Balance: The State and Society in Africa,* Colorado: Westview

Clay, E. and Schaffer, B., 1984, 'Room for manoeuvre: the premise of public policy' in Clay, E. and Schaffer B. (eds) *Room for Manoeuvre: an exploration of public policy planning in agricultural and rural development,* London: Heinemann

Clayton, A., 1998, 'NGOs and Decentralised Government in Africa,' *INTRAC Occasional Paper No 18,* Oxford: INTRAC

Clegg, S., 1989, *Frameworks of Power*, London:Sage Publications

Coelho, V., 2002, 'Brazilian Health Councils as Political Institutions: what is lacking?', draft paper for 'Spaces and Places of Participation' workshop, Institute of Development Studies, November 2002

Collier, P. and Pradhan, S., 1998, 'Economic Aspects of the Transition from Civil War' in Hansen, H.B.and Twaddle, M.(eds) *Developing Uganda,* Kampala: Fountain Press

Collier, P., 2000, 'Consensus building, knowledge, and conditionality,' Proceedings of the World Bank Annual Conference on Development Economics, Washington: World Bank

Communiqué from 'A workshop on Enlightenment and Empowerment for the Poverty Reduction Strategy Paper (PRSP) process' February 26th – 28th 2002, Abuja: ActionAid Nigeria and the Centre for Public-Private Co-operation.

Community Development Resource Network, 1996, 'A study of poverty in selected districts of Uganda,' Kampala: CDRN

Community Development Resource Network, 2001, 'A study of relationships between Civil Society and Local Government in Northern Uganda', Kampala: CDRN

Community Development Resource Network, 2003, 'Thoughts on Civil Society in Uganda', Kampala: CDRN

Cornwall, A. and Gaventa, J., 2000, 'From Users and Choosers to Makers and Shapers: Re-positioning participation in social policy'. *IDS Bulletin* Vol. 31 (4), Brighton: Institute of Development Studies

Cornwall, A., 2002a, 'Locating citizen participation', *IDS Bulletin* Vol. 33 (2), Brighton: Institute of Development Studies

Cornwall, A., 2002b, 'Making Spaces, Changing Places: Situating Participation in Development', IDS Working Paper 170, Brighton: Institute of Development Studies

Crewe, E. and Young, J., 2002, 'Bridging Research and Policy: Context, Evidence and Links', *ODI Working Paper* 173. London: Overseas Development Institute

Crook, R., and Manor, J., 1998, *Enhancing Participation and Institutional Performance: Democratic Decentralization in South Asia and West Africa,* Cambridge: Cambridge University Press

Crook, R. and Sverrisson, A., 2001, 'Decentralisation and Poverty Alleviation in Developing countries: a comparative analysis, or is west Bengal unique?' *IDS Working Paper* 130, Brighton: Institute of Development Studies

De Coninck, J., 1980, *Artisans and Petty Producers in Uganda,* D. Phil thesis, Brighton: University of Sussex

De Coninck, J., 1992, 'Evaluating the Impact of NGOs in rural Poverty Alleviation – Uganda Country Study', *ODI Working Paper* 51, London: Overseas Development Institute

De Vibe, M., Hovland, I., and Young, J., 2002, 'Bridging Research and Policy: An Annotated Bibliography', *ODI Working Paper* 174, London: Overseas Development Institute

De Waal, A., 1996, 'Social contract and deterring famine: first thoughts', *Disasters* Vol. 20 (3)

Department for International Development, 1997, *Eliminating World*

Poverty: A Challenge for the 21st Century – White Paper on International Development, London: The Stationery Office Limited

Department for International Development, 2000, *Nigeria Country Strategy Paper*, London: DFID

Dicklitch S., 1998, 'Indigenous NGOs and Political Participation' in Hansen, H.B. and Twaddle, M. (eds) *Developing Uganda*, Kampala: Fountain Publishers

Dicklitch, S., 1998, *The elusive promise of NGOs in Africa: lessons from Uganda*, Basingstoke, Macmillan Press.

Durotoye, A., 2000, 'The Nigerian State at a Critical Juncture: the Dilemma of a Confused Agenda', *University of Leipzig Papers on Africa* No. 38, Leipzig: University of Leipzig

Economic Policy Co-ordination Committee, 2002, *Interim Poverty Reduction Strategy Paper*, Abuja: EPCC.

Ekeh, P., 1975, 'Colonialism and the Two Publics in Africa: A Theoretical Statement', *Comparative Studies in Society and History* Vol.17 (1)

Ekeh, P. ,1983, *Colonialism and Social Structure. An Inaugural Lecture*, Ibadan: Ibadan University Press

Ekeh, P., 1986, 'Development Theory and the African Predicament', *Africa Development* Vol. 11 (4)

Englebert, P., 2000, *State Legitimacy and Development in Africa,* Boulder: Lynne Rienner

Environment Rights Action, (2002) 'The Emperor Has No Clothes,' Report of the Conference on the Peoples of the Niger Delta and the 1999 Constitution, Benin City: Environment Rights Action/ Friends of the Earth

Federal Office of Statistics, 1999, *Poverty Profile for Nigeria: A Statistical Analysis of 1996/97 National Consumer Survey,* Abuja: Federal Office of Statistics in collaboration with the World Bank.

Ferguson, J., 1998, 'Transnational Topographies of Power: beyond "the state" and "civil society" in the study of African politics', *Centre for International Development Studies Occasional*

Paper No. 19, Roskilde: Centre for International Development Studies

Foster, M., and Mijumbi, P., 2002, 'How, When and Why Does Poverty Get Budget Priority? Poverty Reduction Strategy and Public Expenditure in Uganda,' *ODI Working Paper* 163, London: Overseas Development Institute

Foucault, M., 1977, *Discipline and Punish: The Birth of the Prison,* Harmondsworth: Penguin

Francis, P., and James, R., 2003, 'Balancing Poverty Reduction and Citizen Participation: the contradictions of Uganda's decentralisation program', *World Development Vol.31 (2).*

Francis, P., and Nweze, N., 2003, 'Poverty in Enugu State, Nigeria: A review of poverty data and assessment of policies and institutions addressing poverty reduction in the state', Unpublished report for DFID Enugu State and Local Government Programme

Gass, G. and Adetumbi, O., 2000, DIFID's Civil Society Consultation Process in Nigeria: Summary Report, Unpublished report, Abuja: Department for International Development

Gaventa, J., 1980, *Power and Powerlessness: Quiescence and Rebellion in an Appalachian Valley.* Urbana: University of Illinois Press and Oxford: Clarendon Press

Gaventa, J., 1999, 'Citizen knowledge, citizen competence, and democracy building' in Elkin, S. and Soltan, K. (eds) *Citizen Competence and Democratic Institutions*, University Park PA: Pennsylvania State University Press

Gaventa, J., 2001, 'Towards Participatory Local Governance: six propositions for discussion', Paper presented at Ford Foundation Local Governance Officers' Retreat, Sussex, June 13 – 15 2001

Gaventa, J., 2002, 'The Uses of Power in Framing and Shaping the Spaces, Places and Dynamics of Participation: A discussion note for Citizenship DRC Workshop', unpublished workshop paper, Brighton: Institute of Development Studies

Gaventa, J. and Cornwall, A., 2001, 'Power and Knowledge' in Reason, P. and Bradbury, H. (eds) *Handbook of Action Research: Participative Inquiry and Practice,* London: Sage Publications

Gboyega, A., 1987, *Political Values and Local Government in Nigeria*, Lagos: Malthouse Press

Gboyega, A., 1998, 'Decentralisation and local autonomy in Nigeria's federal system: crossing the stream while searching for pebbles, *Iowa University Occasional Paper* No. 49, Iowa City: Iowa University Press

Goetz, A., 2002, 'No shortcuts to power: constraints on women's political effectiveness in Uganda', *Journal of Modern African Studies*, Vol. 40 (4)

Goetz, A., and Jenkins, R., 1999, 'Creating a Framework for Reducing Poverty: Institutional and process issues in national poverty policy – Uganda Country Report', Unpublished report, Brighton: Institute of Development Studies

Gould, J. and Ojanen, J., 2003, 'Merging in the Circle: the politics of Tanzania's poverty reduction strategy', *Institute of Development Studies Policy Paper* 2003/2, Helsinki: University of Helsinki.

Greenhill, R. and Blackmore, S., 2002, 'Relief Works: African proposals for debt cancellation, and why debt relief works,' London: Jubilee Plus

Grindle, M. and Thomas, J., 1990, 'After the Decision: Implementing Policy Reforms in Developing Countries,' *World Development* Vol.18 (8)

Grindle, M. and Thomas, J., 1991, *Public Choices and Policy Change*, Baltimore: Johns Hopkins Press

Groves, L. and Hinton, R., (eds), 2003, *Inclusive aid: power and relationshsips in international development*, London: Earthscan

Hajer, M and Wagenaar, H., (eds) 2003, *Deliberative Policy Analysis: Understanding Governance in the Network Society*, Cambridge: Cambridge University Press

Hameso, S., 2001, Development, *state and society: theories and practice in contemporary Africa*, Lincoln: Writers Choice Press

Harrison, G., 2002, I*ssues in the Contemporary Politics of sub-Saharan Africa: the Dynamics of Struggle and Resistance*, Basingstoke: Palgrave Macmillan

Hayward, C.R., 1998, 'De-Facing Power,' *Polity* Vol. 31 (2)

Healey, J., Foster, M., Norton, A., and Booth, D., 2000, 'Towards National Public Expenditure Strategies for Poverty Reduction,' *ODI Poverty Briefing* No. 7

Heron, J., 1996, *Cooperative Enquiry,* London: Sage

Hickey, S., 2003, 'The Politics of Staying Poor in Uganda', *CPRC Working Paper* 37, Manchester: Chronic Poverty Research Centre.

Hill, M., 1993, *The Policy Process: a reader,* Hemel Hempstead: Harvester Wheatsheaf

Himbara, D. and Sultan, D., 1995, 'Reconstructing the Ugandan State and Economy: the challenge of an international Bantustan.'*Review of African Political Economy* Vol. 27 (63).

Hirschman, A., 1970, *Exit, voice and loyalty: response to decline in firms, organisations and states*, Cambridge: Harvard University Press

Howell, J. and Pearce J., 2001, *Civil Society and Development: a critical exploration*, Boulder: Lynne Reiner.

Human Rights Watch, 1999, *The Price of Oil: Corporate Responsibility and Human Rights Violations in Nigeria's Oil Producing Communities,* New York: Human Rights Watch

Hunt, C., 2003, 'A Way of Wellbeing: approaching spirituality through reflective practice', in English, L.(ed) *Adult Learning*, Vol.12 (3)

Hydén, G., 1983, *No Shortcuts to Progress: African Development Management in Perspective*, London: Heinemann

Ihonvbere, J. and Shaw, T., 1998, *Illusions of Power: Nigeria in transition*, Asmara: Africa World Press

Jarvis, A and Paolini, A., 1995 'Locating the State' in Camilleri, J., Jarvis, A., and Paolini, A., (eds) *The State in Transition: Reimagining Political Space*, Boulder: Lynne Rienner

Johnson, G., 1971, 'Economic Concepts and the Social Question', in Chen, Y. (ed) *Understanding Economics: Essays in Public Policy*, Boston: Brown and Coy.

Jones, E., 2000, 'Constructing transformative spaces, transforming gendered lives,' Unpublished MPhil thesis, Brighton: Institute of Development Studies

Jones, E., 2001, 'Of Other Spaces: Situating Participatory Practices – A case study from South India,' *IDS Working Paper* 137, Brighton: Institute of Development Studies

Jones, E., 2002, 'Concepts of space and place as they relate to participation', Draft paper for 'Spaces and Places of Participation' workshop, November 2002, Brighton: Institute of Development Studies

Jones, E., 2003, 'Entangled theatres of life and citizenship: exploring the spatialities of identiy, power and performance,' Unpublished DPhil proposal, Brighton: Institute of Development Studies

Joseph, R., 1987, *Democracy and Prebendal Politics in Nigeria: The Rise and Fall of the Second Republic*, Cambridge: Cambridge University Press

Kabwegyere, T., 2000, 'Civil Society and Democratic Transition in Uganda since 1986' in Mugaju, J., and Oloka-Onyango, J., *No-Party Democracy in Uganda, Myths and Realities*, Kampala: Fountain Publishers

Karlström, M., 1999, 'Civil Society and its presuppositions: lessons from Uganda,' in Comaroff, J., et al (eds) *Civil Society and the Political Imagination in Africa,* London: University College Press

Kasfir, N., 1994, 'Strategies of Accumulation and Civil Society in Bushenyi, Uganda: How Dairy Farmers Responded to a Weakened State', in Harbeson, J. et al (eds), *Civil Society and the State in Africa*. London: Lynne Rienner

Kasfir, N., 1998, 'The Conventional Notion of Civil Society: A Critique', in Kasfir, N.(ed) *Civil Society and Democracy in Africa: Critical Perspectives*, London: Frank Cass

Keeley J. and Scoones, I., 1999, 'Understanding Environmental Policy Processes: A Review', *IDS Working Paper* 89, Brighton: Institute of Development Studies

Lasswell, H., 1956, *The Decision Process: Several Categories of Functional Analysis*, Maryland: University of Maryland

Leach M. and Mearns, R. (eds), 1996, *The Lie of the Land: Challenging Received Wisdom on the African Environment*, Oxford: James Currey

Lefebvre, H., 1991, *The Production of Space*, London:Verso

Lewis, D., 2002, 'Civil society in African contexts: reflections on the usefulness of a concept,' *Development and Change* Vol. 33 (4).

Lewis, H., 1999, 'Nigeria Country Strategy Process: Poverty Audit,' unpublished, Swansea: Centre for Development Studies

Lipsky, M., 1980, *Street-level bureaucrats: dilemmas of the individual in public services*, New York: Russel Sage Foundation

Lister, S. and Nyamugasira, W., 2003, 'Design contradictions in the "new architecture of aid"? Reflections from Uganda on the roles of civil society organisations' *Development Policy Review* Vol. 21 (1)

Livingstone, I., 1998, 'Developing industry in Uganda in the 1990s'in Hansen, H. and Twaddle, M. (eds), *Developing Uganda,* Kampala: Fountain Publishers

Long, N., 1989, *Encounters at the Interface: a perspective on social discontinuities in rural development, Wageningen Studies in Sociology* 27, Wageningen: Wageningen Agricultural University

Long, N., 1992, 'From paradigm lost to paradigm regained? The case for an actor-oriented sociology of development' in Long, N. & Long, A. (eds), *Battlefields of Knowledge: The Interlocking of Theory and Practice in Social Research and Development*, Routledge: London

Lukes, S., 1974, *Power: A Radical View*, London: Macmillan

Magbadelo, J., 2000, 'The Quest for Democratic Consolidation in Nigeria,' *Africa Quarterly*, Vol. 40 (4)

Mahmud, S., 2002, 'Citizen participation in rural Bangladesh: reality and perceptions', Draft paper for 'Spaces and Places of Participation' workshop, November 2002, Brighton: Institute of Development Studies

Mamdani, M., 1976, *Politics and Class formation in Uganda*, London: Heinemann

Mamdani, M., 1995, 'A Critique of the State and Civil Society Paradigm in Africanist Studies' in Mamdani, M. and Wambadia-Wamba, E. (eds) *African Studies in Social Movements and Democracy*, Dakar: CODESRIA Book Series

Mamdani, M., 1996, *Citizen and Subject: Contemporary Africa and the Legacy of the Late Colonialism*, New Jersey: Princeton University Press

Masaki, K., 2003, *The Politics of the Policy Process: "Participatory" River Control in Nepal*, DPhil thesis, Brighton: Institute of Development Studies

Mbaku, J. and Ihonvbere, J., 2003, *The Transition to Democratic Governance in Africa: the continuing struggle*, London: Praeger

Mbembe, A., 2001, *On the Postcolony*, Berkeley: University of California Press

McGee, R., 2000, 'Analysis of Participatory Poverty Assessment (PPA) and household survey findings on poverty trends in Uganda –Mission Report – 10-18 February 2000', unpublished report for Ministry of Finance, Planning and Economic Development.

McGee, R., 2002a, 'The self in participatory poverty research' in Brock, K. and McGee, R. (eds), *Knowing Poverty: Critical reflections on Participatory Research and Policy*, London: Earthscan: London

McGee, R., 2002b, 'Conclusion: Participatory Poverty Research – Opening spaces for change' in Brock, K. and McGee, R. (eds), *Knowing Poverty: Critical reflections on Participation Research and Policy*, Earthscan: London

McGee, R, forthcoming 2004, 'What has happened to poverty in Uganda? Contradiction, confusion and the quest for complementarity' *Development and Change*, forthcoming

McGee, R. and Brock, K., 2001, 'From Poverty Assessment to Policy Change: Processes, Actors and Data,' *IDS Working Paper* 133, Brighton: Institute of Development Studies

McGee, R. with Levene, J. and Hughes, A, 2002, 'Assessing Participation in poverty reduction strategy papers: a desk-based synthesis of experience in sub-Saharan Africa,' *IDS Research Report* 52, Brighton: Institute of Development Studies

Migdal, J., 1988, *Strong Societies and Weak States: State-Society*

Relations and State Capabilities in the Third World, New Jersey: Princeton University Press

Ministry of Finance, Planning and Economic Development, 1997a, 'Uganda Participatory Poverty Assessment', unpublished project proposal, Kampala: MoFPED

Ministry of Finance, Planning and Economic Development, 1997b, *Poverty Eradication Action Plan*, Kampala: MoFPED

Ministry of Finance, Planning and Economic Development, 2000, *Uganda Participatory Poverty Assessment Report: Learning from the Poor*, Kampala: MoFPED

Ministry of Finance, Planning and Economic Development, 2002, *Deepening the Understanding of Poverty. Second Participatory Poverty Assessment Report*, Kampala: MoFPED

Ministry of Finance, Planning and Economic Development, 2003a, 'Background to the Budget 2002/2003,' Kampala: MoFPED

Ministry of Finance, Planning and Economic Development, 2003b, *Uganda Poverty Status Report 2003*, Kampala, MoFPED

Ministry of Local Government, 2002, 'Guide for Harmonised Participatory Development Planning and Management for Lower Local Councils', Kampala: MoLG

Mohammed, A., 2000, 'A review of selected hometown associations in Katsina and Kaduna states,' Mimeo, Zaria: Centre for Democratic Development and Research Training.

Mohanty, C., Russo, A., and Torres, L. (eds), 1991 *Third World Women and the Politics of Feminism*, Bloomington: Indiana University Press

Moore, M., and Putzel, J., 1999, 'Thinking Strategically about Politics and Policy,' *IDS Working Paper* 101, Brighton: Institute of Development Studies

Narayan, D., Chambers, R., Shah, M., and Petesch, P., 2000, *Voices of the Poor: Crying Out for Change*, Oxford: Oxford University Press

National Resistance Movement, 1986, *Ten-point programme of NRM*, Kampala: NRM Publications (2nd Edition)

Nettleford, R., 2002, 'Africa, the African Diaspora and the New Millennium: Challenges for Development,' *Africa Today*, November/December.

Networks for Health, 2001, 'Report of Dialogue with Nigerian Reproductive Health and Reproductive Rights NGOs and NGO Networks,' Mimeo, Kano: Development Research and Projects Centre

NGO Forum, 2001, 'Uganda: The Economy, Poverty and Governance,' Summary Report of the Consultative Group Meeting held at Kampala International Conference Centre, May 14-17, 2001, Mimeo.

Norton A.and Bird, B., 1998, 'Social Development Issues in Sector Wide Approaches,' *Social Development Division Working Paper* 1, London: DFID

Norton A. with Bird, B., Brock, K., Kakande, M. and Turk, C., 2001, *A Rough Guide to PPAs: Participatory Poverty Assessment – An introduction to theory and practice*, London: Overseas Development Institute

Nyamugasira, W., and Rowden, R., 2002, 'New Stategies, Old Loan Conditions: do the PRSC and the PRGF support povery reduction strategies; the case of Uganda,' Kampala and Washington DC: Uganda National NGO Forum and Results Educational Fund

Obadan, M., 1997, 'Analytical Framework for Poverty Reduction: Issues of Economic Growth versus Other Strategies', Proceedings of the 1997 Annual Conference of the Nigerian Economic Society, Ibadan: Nigerian Economic Society

O'Connor, A., 2001, *Poverty Knowledge: Social Science, Social Policy and the Poor in Twentieth-Century US History*, New Jersey: Princeton University Press

OECD/DAC, 2003a, 'Nigeria: Aid at a glance,' http://www1.oecd.org/dac/images/AidRecipient/nga.gif Access date 3 September 2001

OECD/DAC, 2003b, 'Uganda. Aid at a glance,' http://www1.oecd.org/dac/images/AidRecipient/uga.gif Access date 3 September 2001

Okoko, K., and Owugah, L., 1997, 'The People's Vision Plan of Development: The Case of Bayelsa State', Research Report of the Study on Peoples Vision Plan of Development in Nigeria, Lagos: United Nations Development Programme

Okuku, J., 2002, *Ethnicity, State Power and the Decmocratisation*

Process in Uganda. Uppsala: Nordiska Afrikainstitutet

Olaa, M., 2001, 'Perspectives of Managing a National Programme and Resolving the Competing and Conflicting Interests: Experiences from the District Development Programme,' Paper presented at the 'Decentralization and Local Governance in Africa' conference, 26th-30th March 2001, Cape Town.

Oloka-Onyango, J., and Barya, J-J., 1997, 'Civil Society and the Political Economy of Foreign Aid in Uganda,' *Democratization* Vol. 4 (2)

Osaghae, E., 1989, 'The Strengthening of Local Governments and the Operation of Federalism in Nigeria,' *Journal of Commonwealth and Comparative Politics* Vol. 27 (3)

Osaghae, E., 1995, 'The Ogoni uprising: oil politics, minority agitation and the future of the Nigeria state,' *African Affairs* Vol. 94.

Osaghae, E., 1998, *Exiting from the state in Nigeria*, Ibadan: University of Ibadan.

Osaghae, E., 2001, 'Poverty Alleviation Discourses: Bridging the gap between the State and Civil Society', Unpublished background paper for IDS Poverty Knowledge and Policy Processes research

Overseas Development Institute/Oxford Policy Management (2002) 'General Budget Support Evaluability Study: Phase 1', Unpublished report to DFID

Owusu, K., 2001, *Drops of oil in a sea of poverty: the case for a new debt deal in Nigeria*, London: Jubilee Plus

Pelling, M., 2003, *The Vulnerability of Cities: Natural Disasters and Social Resilience*, London: Earthscan

Petras, J., and Veltemeyer, H., 2001, *Globalisation Unmasked*, London: Zed Books

Phillips, A., 1995, *The Politics of Presence*, Oxford: Clarendon Press

Porter D. and Onyach-Olaa, M., 1999, 'Inclusive Planning and allocation for Rural Services,' Development in Practice, Vol. 9 (1 & 2)

Robinson, M., 1998, 'Democracy, Participation and Public Policy,' in Robinson, M and White, G, (eds), *The Democratic Developmental State:political and institutional design*, Oxford: Oxford University Press.

Roe, E., 1991, 'Development Narratives, or making the best of blueprint development,' *World Development* Vol. 19 (4)

Salih, M., 2001, *African Democracies and African Politics*, London: Pluto Press

Sancho, A., 1996, *Policies and Programmes for Social and Human Development*, San Fransisco: International Centre for Economic Growth

Schattschneider, E., 1960, *The Semi-Sovereign People: a Realist's View of Democracy in America*, New York: Holt, Rinehart and Winston

Sharp, J., Philo, C., and Paddison, R. (eds) 2000, *Entanglements of Power: Geographies of domination/resistance*, London: Routledge.

Shaw, M., and Martin, I., 2000, 'Community work, citizenship and democracy: re-making the connections,' *Community Development Journal* Vol.35 (4)

Sheridan, A., 1980, Michel Foucault: *The Will to Truth*, London: Tavistock

Shore C. and Wright S., 1997, 'Policy: a new field of anthropology,' in Shore, C., and Wright, S. (eds), *Anthropology of Policy: critial perspectives on governance and power*, London: Routledge

State and Local Governance Reform Programme, 2001, 'Briefing Note', Unpublished, Abuja: DFID

State and Local Governance Reform Programme, 2003, *Governance News* No.5, Abuja: DFID

Stewart, F., and Wang, M., 2003 'Do PRSPs empower poor countries and disempower the World Bank, or is it the other way round?' *QEH Working Paper* 108, Oxford: Queen Elizabeth House

Stone, D. with Maxwell, S., and Keating, M., 2001, 'Bridging Research and Policy', Paper prepared for international workshop on Bridging Research and Policy, Centre for the Study of Globalization and Regionalization, University of Warwick.

Sudharsan, C., Ngwafor, J. and Saji, T., 1997, *The Evol.ution of Poverty and Welfare in Nigeria, 1985-1992*, Washington: World Bank

Sutton, R., 1999, 'The Policy Process: an Overview,' *ODI Working Paper* 118. London: Overseas Development Institute

Taiwo, O., 1997, 'Capacity Building for Decentralised Development: a Study of Organisations Involved in RNR Sector in South-West Nigeria'. Mimeo, Abuja: DFID

The News, 2001, 'Bayelsa State Mid Term report', June 25

The Republic of Uganda, 1995, *Constitution of the Republic of Uganda*

Transparency International, 2003, 'Global Corruption Report 2003', http://www.globalcorruptionreport.org/download.shtml, Access Date 3 September 2003

Tripp, A., 1998, 'Expanding "civil society": women and political space in contemporary Uganda', in Kasfir, N. (ed), *Civil Society and Democracy in Africa: Critical Perspectives*, London: Frank Cass

Tulya-Muhika, S., 2002, 'Preliminary Findings, Uganda NGO Sector survey', mimeo

Twaddle, M. and Hansen, H., 1998, 'The Changing State of Uganda', in Hansen, H., and Twaddle, M.(eds), *Developing Uganda*, Kampala: Fountain Press

Uganda Participatory Development Network, 2002, 'Adventure or Joint Venture? CSO participation in national government programmes: experiences and challenges,' Kampala: UPDNet

UNAIDS, 2002a, 'Nigeria. Epidemiological Fact Sheets on HIV/AIDS and Sexually Transmitted Infections. 2002 Update' http://www.who.int/emc-hiv/fact_sheets/pdfs/Nigeria_En.pdf Access Date 2 September 2003

UNAIDS, 2002b, 'Uganda. Epidemiological Fact Sheets on HIV/AIDS and Sexually Transmitted Infections. 2002 Update' http://www.who.int/emc-hiv/fact_sheets/pdfs/Uganda_En.pdf Access Date 2 September 2003

United Nations Development Programme, 1996, *Uganda Human Development Report,* Kampala: UNDP

United Nations Development Programme, 1998, *Nigeria Human Development Report*, Lagos: UNDP

United Nations Univesity, 2000, 'World Income Inequality Database,' http://www.wider.unu.edu/wiid/wiid.htm   Access Date 2 September 2003

Uganda Women's Network, 1995, 'Women and Structural Adjustment: a case study of AruaDistrict,'Kampala:UWONET

VeneKlasen, L., and Miller, V., 2002. *A New Weave of People, Power and Politics: the Action Guide for Advocacy and Citizen Participation.* World Neighbors: Oklahoma City

Walker, J., 1999, 'Civil Society, the challenge to the authoritarian state, and the consolidation of democracy in Nigeria,' *Issue* Vol. 27 (1)

Webster N. and Engberg-Pedersen, L. (eds), 2002, *In the Name of the Poor: Contesting Political Space for Poverty Reduction.* London: Zed Books

Weeks, E., 2000, 'The practice of deliberative democracy: results from four large-scale trials,'*Public Administration Review* Vol. 60 (4)

Woodroffe, J., and Ellis-Jones, M., 2000, *States of unrest: resistance to IMF policies in poor countries*, London: World Development Movement

World Bank, 1990, *World Development Report 1990: Poverty,* Oxford: Oxford University Press

World Bank, 1993, *Uganda:Growing Out of Poverty*, Washington: World Bank

World Bank, 1995, *Uganda:The Challenge of Growth and Poverty Reduction*, Washington: World Bank

World Bank, 1997, *World Development Report 1997: The State in a Changing World*, Washington: World Bank

World Bank, 1999, 'Building Poverty Reduction Strategies in Developing Countries' , September.   www.worldbank.org/poverty/strategies Access Date 11 February 2003

World Bank, 2002, *Poverty Reduction Strategy Sourcebook*, Washington: World Bank

World Bank, 2003a, Nigeria Data Profile, http://devdata.worldbank.org/external/CPProfile.asp?CCODE=NGA&PTYPE=CP Access Date 2 September 2003

World Bank, 2003b, 'Uganda Data Profile,'http://devdata.worldbank.org/ external/CPProfile.asp?CCODE=UGA&PTYPE=CP Access Date 2 September 2003

Yates, J. and Okello, L., 2002, 'Learning from Uganda's Efforts to Learn from the Poor: reflections and lessons from the Uganda Participatory Poverty Assessment Project' in Brock, K. and McGee, R. (eds), *Knowing Poverty: critical reflections on participatory research and policy*, London: Earthscan

Young, C., and Turner, T., 1985, *The Rise and Decline of the Zairian State*, Madison:University of Wisconsin Press

Glossary

Interim Poverty Reduction Strategy Paper (iPRSP): An iPRSP outlines actions the government intends to take to develop a full Poverty Reduction Strategy Paper (below). It also contains details of intended macroeconomic policy reforms and usually includes information on the country's poverty situation.

National Poverty Eradication Programme (NAPEP) (Nigeria): The target of the NAPEP is to completely wipe out poverty from Nigeria by the year 2010. An organisational structure incorporates sectoral ministries and Federal government policy actors. The National Poverty Eradication Council (NAPEC) is the apex organ for policy formulation, coordination, monitoring and review of all poverty eradication activities in the country. The NAPEP's activities take place under four programmes: the Youth Empowerment Scheme (YES), which is concerned with providing unemployed youth opportunities in skills acquisition, employment and wealth generation; the Rural Infrastructure Development Scheme (RIDS), focused on transport, energy, water and communication in rural areas; the Social Welfare Services Scheme (SOWESS), including education and health; and the Natural Resources Development and Conservation Scheme (NRDCS).

Poverty Action Fund (PAF) (Uganda): The Government of Uganda created the PAF, a ring-fenced fund, to channel savings from debt relief, obtained through the Highly Indebted Poor Countries (HIPC) initiative, into services for poor communities such as new feeder roads, health clinics, schools, bore holes and agricultural assistance. PAF-funded projects have to be in line with the priority areas of the PEAP.

Poverty Eradication Action Plan (PEAP) (Uganda) :The PEAP is Uganda's national development framework and medium term planning tool, prepared in 1997 through wide stakeholder consultations and participation. The PEAP, which is also the Country's Poverty Reduction Strategy Paper (PRSP), guides the formulation of government policy and implementation of pro-grammes through sector wide approaches and a decentralised governance system. The expenditure implications of the PEAP are translated into concrete spending decisions through the Medium Term Expenditure Framework (MTEF) and annual budgets. The PEAP 2001, during 2003 undergoing a consultative revision process, is structured around four overarching pillars: rapid and sustainable economic growth and structural transformation; good governance and security; increased ability of the poor to raise their incomes; and enhanced quality of life of the poor.

Poverty Reduction Growth Facility (PRGF): The IMF's concessional lending facility, which provides finance for Poverty Reduction Strategy Papers (PRSPs). Previously, this facility was called the Enhanced Structural Adjustment Facility (ESAF).

Poverty Reduction Strategy Paper (PRSP): PRSPs describe a country's macroeconomic, structural and social policies and programmes to promote growth and reduce poverty, as well as associated external financing needs and major sources of financing. In order for a country to qualify for multilateral debt relief, it must produce a PRSP.

Poverty Reduction Support Credit (PRSC): World Bank programme loan availabile to countries to support the implementation of a Poverty Reduction Strategy Paper (PRSP).

Index